About This Book

Why is this topic import

Teamwork is critical to almost everything we do. Whether in the workplace, a social setting, a civic duty, or a family situation, we frequently desire a more efficiently functioning team. A dynamic, finely-tuned, productive team that is generating what is required—whether a winning score or a winning product— is the sign of success. But the question for many is, "how can we build a team that achieves the ultimate goal?"

What can you achieve with this book?

In your hands is a team-building toolkit, a valuable source of knowledge for improving teamwork. This book takes the mystery out of team building by introducing ten critical aspects that must be present to ensure a successfully functioning team. The book takes you one step further and introduces a proven collection of activities, articles, and instruments to assist you to improve each of the ten aspects on the teams you work with. The collection is a rich source of ideas and approaches that have a proven track record of success. Some are new, some are classics, and all will help you take the mystery out of team-building.

How is this book organized?

The book is presented in thirteen Chapters. Chapter One discusses the concepts and importance of teamwork. Chapter Two introduces a Ten-Block Model for building a team. Chapters Three through Twelve illustrate how you can address each of the ten blocks in the model and build your team through the use of activities, concept articles, and evaluation tools. Finally, Chapter Thirteen provides you with more general team-building tools and thought-provoking articles.

About Pfeiffer

Pfeiffer serves the professional development and hands-on resource needs of training and human resource practitioners and gives them products to do their jobs better. We deliver proven ideas and solutions from experts in HR development and HR management, and we offer effective and customizable tools to improve workplace performance. From novice to seasoned professional, Pfeiffer is the source you can trust to make yourself and your organization more successful.

Essential Knowledge Pfeiffer produces insightful, practical, and comprehensive materials on topics that matter the most to training and HR professionals. Our Essential Knowledge resources translate the expertise of seasoned professionals into practical, how-to guidance on critical workplace issues and problems. These resources are supported by case studies, worksheets, and job aids and are frequently supplemented with CD-ROMs, websites, and other means of making the content easier to read, understand, and use.

Essential Tools Pfeiffer's Essential Tools resources save time and expense by offering proven, ready-to-use materials—including exercises, activities, games, instruments, and assessments—for use during a training or team-learning event. These resources are frequently offered in looseleaf or CD-ROM format to facilitate copying and customization of the material.

Pfeiffer also recognizes the remarkable power of new technologies in expanding the reach and effectiveness of training. While e-hype has often created whizbang solutions in search of a problem, we are dedicated to bringing convenience and enhancements to proven training solutions. All our e-tools comply with rigorous functionality standards. The most appropriate technology wrapped around essential content yields the perfect solution for today's on-the-go trainers and human resource professionals.

Essential resources for training and HR professionals

www.pfeiffer.com

The Pfeiffer *Book of*

Successful Team-Building Tools

Best of the Annuals

Second Edition

Elaine Biech, Editor

Pfeiffer
A Wiley Imprint
www.pfeiffer.com

Library of Congress Cataloging-in-Publication Data

CIP data has been applied for.

ISBN-13: 978-0-7879-9736-6 (pbk.)

Acquiring Editor: Martin Delahoussaye	Manufacturing Supervisor: Becky Morgan
Production Editor: Michael Kay	Composition: Leigh McLellan Design
Printed in the United States of America	

Printing   10   9   8   7   6   5   4   3   2   1

Contents

Introduction   **xi**

1   What Is Teamwork?   **1**

2   A Model for Building Teamwork   **13**

3   Clear Goals   **27**

TeamScores: Measuring and Communicating Performance   29
Peter R. Garber

High Jump: Illustrating the Impact of Expectations   35
Steven B. Hollwarth

Team Identity   43
John E. Jones

4   Defined Roles   **49**

The Hats We Wear: Understanding Team Roles   51
Kristin Arnold

No Strings Attached: Learning How Groups Organize
to Complete Tasks   55
Jeyakar Vedamanickam

Scope of Control: Taking Initiative in Problem Solving   63
Steve Sphar

Yours, Mine, and Ours: Clarifying Team Responsibilities   71
Mike M. Milstein

Symbols: Sharing Role Perceptions   77
Patrick Doyle

The Search for Balance: Team Effectiveness   87
Tom Noonan

5   Open and Clear Communication   **95**

Hit the Target Fast: Designing a Communication System
for Teams   97
Lynn A. Baker, Sr.

Rope Trick: Experiencing How Groups Function   103
Meredith Cash

Levels of Dialogue: Analyzing Communications in Conflict   111
Gary Copeland

Strengths and Needs: Using Feedback for Group
Development   121
Terri Burchett

Analyzing and Increasing Open Behavior:
The Johari Window   133
Philip G. Hanson

6 Effective Decision Making   **143**
News Room: A Group-Consensus Task   145
Heidi Ann Campbell & Heather Jean Campbell
Broken Triangles: Experimenting with Group
Problem Solving   149
Janet Mills
Lutts and Mipps: Team Problem Solving   155
Editors
Performance Unlimited: Solving Problems as a Team   161
James W. Kinneer
Lost at Sea: A Consensus-Seeking Task   165
Paul M. Nemiroff & William A. Pasmore
Making Team Decisions   173
Kristin Arnold

7 Balanced Participation   **181**
Egg Drop: Using Human Resources Effectively   183
Douglas Bryant
Comfort Zones: Establishing Team Norms   193
Chris C. Hoffman
The Car: Feedback on Group Membership Styles   203
Alfred A. Wells

8 Valued Diversity   **209**
Unearned Privilege: Understanding Dominant-Culture
Advantage   211
Julie O'Mara & Aja Oakman
The Forest vs. the Trees: Understanding Preferences for
the Big Picture or the Details   219
Bonnie Jameson
Fourteen Dimensions of Diversity: Understanding and
Appreciating Differences in the Work Place   225
Sunny Bradford
Diversity and Team Development   235
Claire B. Halverson & Guillermo Cuéllar

9 Managed Conflict   **245**
The M&M® Game: Learning to Resolve Conflict   247
Gerald V. Miller

They Said, We Said: Exploring Intergroup-Conflict
   Resolution   255
   Jason Ollander-Krane & Neil Johnson

Conflict Management: Developing a Procedure   259
   Lawrence C. Porter

Storming to Norming: Clearing the Way for Team
   Agreement   265
   Beverly J. Bitterman

Intergroup Image Exchange: Exploring the Relationship
   Between Two Teams
   Editors   271

10 Positive Atmosphere   **275**

Building Trust in Pairs: An Obstacle Course   275
   Valerie C. Nellen & Susan B. Wilkes

Trust ARCH: Building Team Support   289
   Mary B. Wacker

Work Dialogue: Building Team Relationships   297
   Judith F. Vogt & Karen L. Williams

A Note to My Teammate: Positive Feedback   313
   Deborah M. Fairbanks

Cornerstones: A Measure of Trust in Work Relationships   317
   Amy M. Birtel, Valerie C. Nellen, & Susan B. Wilkes

11 Cooperative Relationships   **329**

Enablers and Barriers: Assessing Your Team   331
   Karen Vander Linde

This and That: Improving Team Performance   337
   James W. Kinneer

Team Checkup: Monitoring and Planning for Progress   341
   Michael L. Mazzarese

Prisoners' Dilemma: An Intergroup Competition   347
   Editors

Twenty-Five Questions: A Team Development Exercise   351
   John E. Jones

12 Participative Leadership   **357**

Rope-a-Leader: Experiencing the Emergence of Leadership   359
   John W. Peterson & Sherry R. Mills

The Merry-Go-Round Project: Focusing on Leadership Style   361
   Deborah Spring Laurel

Team Interventions: Moving the Team Forward   371
   Chuck Kormanski

The Relationship Between Leader Behavior and
    Team Performance and Satisfaction   383
    Mary Ann Burress
Values-Based Leadership for the 21st Century   399
    Robert C. Preziosi

13 General Team-Building Tools   405
Take Note of Yourself: A Team-Development Activity   407
    Michael P. Bochenek
I Have an Opinion: Opening an Event   411
    Gail Rae-Davis
Thumbs Up, Thumbs Down: A Conflict-Management
    Icebreaker   415
    Roger Gaetani
That's Me: Getting to Know Your Team Members   419
    Debbie Seid
Group Savings Bank: An Introductory Experience   425
    Debera Libkind & Dennis M. Dennis
The Team Effectiveness Critique   429
    Mark Alexander
The Team Orientation and Behavior Inventory (TOBI)   437
    Leonard D. Goodstein, Phyliss Cooke, & Jeanette Goodstein
What If We Took Teamwork Seriously?   455
    W. Warner Burke
Team Building   461
    Anthony J. Reilly & John E. Jones
What to Look for in Groups: An Observation Guide   481
    Philip G. Hanson

Opportunity to Publish Your Materials   487

Reading List   489

Pfeiffer Publications Guide   491

Introduction

One can hardly pick up a magazine or a newspaper without reading a report that some company has doubled its productivity, increased efficiency five-fold, decreased error rates to Six Sigma, or increased profits by 60 percent—all due to—you've got it—*teamwork!*

Yet teamwork is one of those things that we seem to do more talking about than acting on. It seems we've moved into the 21st Century still trying to figure out how to build a highly productive team. We still ask: How can a team improve its effectiveness? and Can team building actually improve a team's performance?

The answer is yes. And this Second Edition of the *Pfeiffer Book of Successful Team-Building Tools* will help you with your team-building efforts in two ways. First, you can use the Ten-Block Model it provides to build a high performance team. Second, you will have access to the most successful team-building tools submitted to our *Annual* and *Handbook* series from 1969 through 2008.

How the Book Is Organized

Chapter One, "What Is Teamwork?," offers a definition of teamwork and presents the advantages and disadvantages of working in a team. Chapter Two, "A Model for Building Teamwork," defines the Ten-Block Model for effective teamwork. Chapters Three through Twelve are compilations of activities and articles related to each of the ten blocks of the model. Chapter Thirteen presents team-building tools of a more general nature, that is, team-building icebreakers, questionnaires, and other resources.

High performing teams are an asset that few organizations can afford to be without. Team building can be used to increase any team's performance.

> *"High performing teams are an asset that few organizations can afford to be without."*

The Pfeiffer *Annuals* have been a mainstay for many trainers, consultants, and facilitators since 1972 and the *Handbook* Series since 1969. This special compilation of material from previous Pfeiffer publications draws on the team-building expertise from authors of all the past *Annuals* and the ten *Handbooks*. It includes classic activities such as "Lost at Sea" and "Team Identity" and newer activities such as "The M&M® Game" and "No Strings Attached." Contributors include many you know, such as W. Warner Burke and Julie O'Mara, and many you will meet for the first time.

It was difficult to select from the many excellent contributions we have published over the years. We believe, however, that you have the best of the best in your hands now. All of the materials in this special book of team-building tools are yours to duplicate for educational and training purposes. You may also adapt and modify the materials to meet your audience's needs. Please ensure that the credit statement found on the copyright page is included on all copies you make. If the materials are to be reproduced in publications for sale or are intended for large-scale distribution (more than one hundred copies in twelve months), prior written permission is required. Reproduction of material that is copyrighted by another source (as indicated in a footnote) requires written permission from the designated copyright holder. Please call us if you have questions. We believe our liberal copyright policy makes it easier for you to do your job.

Most importantly, this special publication will load your toolbox with activities, surveys, and information you can readily use to build high performing teams.

Elaine Biech
Editor

The Pfeiffer *Book of*

Successful Team-Building Tools

1

What Is Teamwork?

What comes to mind when you hear the word "teamwork"? Most likely an assortment of thoughts comes to mind, including positive ones such as working together, achieving common goals, and having fun. On the other hand, negative thoughts may come to mind, too, such as personality conflicts, difficult communication, and time-consuming meetings.

Throughout your life you have been a member of many teams: athletic teams such as baseball or tennis; volunteer teams such as fund raising or fire fighting; school teams such as debate or chorus; social teams such as card clubs; or civic teams such as city-wide support groups. You are a member of a family—and that is a team also. Plus, you are on a variety of teams at work. Some of these groups of people are true teams. But are they all?

What Is a Team?

A team is a group of people who are mutually dependent on one another to achieve a common goal. Some definitions of a team require that the group must also be functioning well together. Although "functioning well" is not a part of our definition, it is definitely a part of our purpose as trainers and consultants. This book of team-building tools will assist you to improve how well any team functions.

> "A team is a group of people who are mutually dependent on one another to achieve a common goal."

1

Exhibit 1.   Twelve Advantages of Working in Teams

1. More input leads to better ideas and decisions.
2. Higher quality output.
3. Involvement of everyone in the process.
4. Increased ownership and buy-in by members.
5. Higher likelihood of implementation of new ideas.
6. Widens the circle of communication.
7. Shared information means increased learning.
8. Increased understanding of other people's perspectives.
9. Increased opportunity to draw on individual strengths.
10. Ability to compensate for individual weaknesses.
11. Provides a sense of security.
12. Develops personal relationships.

ADVANTAGES OF WORKING IN TEAMS

Exhibit 1 provides a dozen advantages of working in teams. These are described in more detail below.

The Results

Probably the key advantage of teamwork is a better end result. Organizations find that teams can be more responsive to the changing needs of the marketplace. Teams can be closer to the customer's needs, more informed about advanced technology, and faster to respond than traditional hierarchies.

A team working together has more and better input than individuals working alone. If everyone who works in the process is involved, it is less likely that steps will be missed. This results in *better ideas and decisions* and *higher quality output*.

How the Job Gets Done

Ever had a great idea that just didn't fly? Often the reason is a lack of buy-in from others in the organization. Teamwork requires the *involvement of everyone*, which means *increased ownership* and a *higher likelihood of implementation of new ideas*.

Improved Communication

The basis for almost any problem in any organization is usually communication. Good teamwork can *widen the circle of communication*. Teamwork goes a step beyond, however, and helps people understand each other's jobs and roles in the organization. This leads to an appreciation for colleagues and a desire to help make their jobs easier.

More Learning

The simple fact that people talk to one another in teams means that their *shared information means increased learning*. This sharing also *increases understanding of other people's perspectives* and provides the team with the *opportunity to draw on individual strengths* and to *compensate for individual weaknesses* in a positive way. Team members learn from each other.

Personal Satisfaction

Team members generally report a sense of personal satisfaction. A team may *provide a sense of security* that allows individuals to take risks and make decisions that they would not make if they were working alone. This generally leads to growth for the organization as well as the individual.

Because most of us spend about 25 percent of our lives at work, it should be a pleasant experience. Teamwork can lead the way to making work pleasurable by helping to *develop personal relationships*. In fact, you should not feel as if you are getting up to go to work, but instead that you are getting up to go to play each day!

"... you should not feel as if you are getting up to go to work, but instead that you are getting up to go to play each day!"

DISADVANTAGES OF WORKING IN TEAMS

Exhibit 2 provides a dozen disadvantages of working in teams. These are described in some detail in the following text.

Time

The biggest disadvantage of teamwork is that it *requires more time*. This is especially true when a team is in the start-up mode, which *can lead to many*

Exhibit 2. Twelve Disadvantages of Working in Teams

1. Requires more time.
2. Can lead to many meetings.
3. Often difficult to schedule mutual time.
4. Requires individuals to give more of themselves.
5. May take longer to make a decision.
6. May be used as an excuse for a lack of individual performance.
7. Personality conflicts are magnified.
8. Disagreements can cause strained relationships.
9. Potential for subgroups to form.
10. Teams can become exclusive rather than inclusive.
11. May lead to unclear roles.
12. "Group think" can limit innovation.

meetings. There will always be a concern about "too many meetings," but the team can be aware of this and ensure that all meetings they do hold are necessary for productivity and efficiency.

It will also always be *difficult to schedule mutual time* for meetings or collaborative work time and people may feel they are required to *give more of themselves.* And during these meetings, it will *take longer to make decisions* than if one person had made the decision.

The positive side is that this will get better over time. The team will eventually see a payoff. Problems that once took huge chunks of time will disappear. Communication gaps that required additional time to fill in will be gone. Processes that required much rework will be done right the first time.

Individual Performance

Individual performance may suffer initially. As we said above, teamwork requires that individuals give more of themselves to the team. This is difficult to do for anyone who has been a loner in the organization or who has not been dependent on others to get the job done. It requires new and different interpersonal skills.

Individuals may use the team as *an excuse for a lack of performance.* This will eventually be recognized. If your team is just forming, it may take some time before you discover the non-performance, and the problem may turn out to be due to a need for role clarification.

Conflict

When individuals are required to work together, *personality conflicts are magnified*. This will lead to *disagreements*, which *can cause strained relationships*. Expect that some of your team members will be very disturbed by this.

Inherent Disadvantages

As positive as working together may seem, groups bring with them their own unique set of drawbacks. There is always the *potential for subgroups to form* and split the team. Teams can become too strong and *become exclusive, rather than inclusive*—forgetting to include new members, to ask for temporary support, or to communicate with customers or suppliers. People may have *unclear roles* to play and not be as productive as they could be.

And finally, a phenomenon called *"group think" can limit innovation*. Group think generally occurs when a team has been very successful and begins to believe that it will never fail. The team begins to do things on the suggestion of a single member, without question. Unfortunately, you won't know that group think is occurring until a disaster occurs. The best-known historical situation was the Bay of Pigs.

With all these drawbacks, should we forget about teamwork? Of course not! Teamwork is still worth it. Teamwork is important. However, teams must be made aware of the potential drawbacks, and team building can help a team move forward. What can you do about the disadvantages identified above? The following quick thoughts give some ways that will help you to prevent and remedy potential team issues.

- If *time* is an issue, discuss it. Sometimes being aware of a problem will keep everyone focused on making it better. Sometimes reminding team members of time that was saved by solving a problem is necessary.

- If *individual performance* suffers initially, the team will often take care of the issue as a team. If not, the team leader may need to discuss the issue with the individual.

- If *conflict* is the issue, it needs to be addressed head on. Members must see that conflict can be an important and positive part of teamwork. The team will have to develop a plan to manage conflict. If it is too serious, a team-building intervention may be necessary.

- If *group dynamics* is an issue, training may often be the solution.

You can see that there is much to learn about being a good team player and that there is much you can do to improve teamwork.

Exhibit 3. Teamwork: What Do You Think?

Instructions: Read each statement once. Check whether you think the statement is true or false.

True False

1. A team needs a strong leader, even if the leader intimidates some team members.

2. The team should meet only if all members are able to attend.

3. There are often times when individual team members must do what they think is right, even if it conflicts with a team decision.

4. Consensus decisions generally take too much time and result in a watered-down decision.

5. It is healthy for several team members to talk at the same time; it shows team energy and enthusiasm.

6. Teams should take time up front to establish clear roles for each member.

7. It is difficult for a team to succeed when it does not have clear goals.

8. Teams are more successful when they are able to avoid conflict.

9. A team should set aside meeting time to explore member feelings and relationships.

10. The team should not actively try to get quiet members to participate. They will participate when they have something to contribute.

11. In truly effective teams, members have a personal liking for one another.

12. Once a team gets an established way of working, it is unproductive to spend time changing it.

EXPLORE YOUR TEAMWORK ASSUMPTIONS

We all make assumptions about almost everything. Are you aware of the assumptions that form the basis of your teamwork philosophy? Complete the quiz in Exhibit 3 to identify the assumptions you hold and to see some other ways to view the issues that surround teamwork.

One of the greatest difficulties about trying to improve teamwork is that there are few black-and-white answers, but many shades of gray.

What are the answers to the true/false statements in Exhibit 3? The answer to all of those questions is "It depends!" So if you were absolutely certain about your own answer, you might want to step back and think about other possibilities. That nebulous "It depends" makes teamwork difficult, but it also tests the members' ability to see things from another vantage point. As we said, there are few pat answers in teamwork.

Let's take a look at those "It depends" answers.

Question 1. Of course team leaders should not intimidate team members! Yet, as wrong as that may sound, there is another side. Have you ever met someone who was intimidated by everyone—especially if he or she had the title "leader"? Easily intimidated people need to learn to become more comfortable with speaking up.

The second word in this statement that can be interpreted in many ways is "strong." The definition of "strong" depends on one's background and experience. Some people see "strong" as a very positive attribute for a leader, for example, someone who seems to be able to handle any problem with ease or who shares the recognition but accepts most of the responsibility when things go wrong. Some people see "strong" as a negative quality, for example, someone who takes over when the team should do something themselves. A team needs the first "strong" leader, not the second.

Question 2. This is a tricky one. Lots of questions come to mind. How often does the team meet? What is the purpose of the meeting? Will the team make a critical decision? Why is someone missing? If the purpose of the meeting is to make an important decision, the team must consider whether the decision needs to be made now, whether they know the missing member's opinion, and whether the decision will affect the missing member.

No, you can't wait until everyone is there to have every meeting. You may never meet! However, you must think ahead to what will occur at the meeting and how it will affect missing team members before deciding whether to meet or not. You must also think about how to communicate what happened to team members who were missing. One excellent communication method is for someone who is present to relay the information to the missing person. The team should ask for a volunteer to do this as the meeting starts. That way the individual will know to take more detailed notes and to give full attention to discussions of particular interest to the missing person.

Question 3.   At first glance, you would probably say "False!" Of course team members can't do what they want when it is in conflict with a team decision. If team members can do that, you don't have a team at all!

But, what about the times when the individual team member is correct, but just unable to convince the rest of the team? What if the team is making a decision that is unethical, illegal, or unsafe? Should the single team member sacrifice personal values? These are difficult questions, and they are a great example of how difficult teamwork can be.

Question 4.   Consensus decisions are always the best. Right? Wrong! Reaching a decision by consensus can lead to a watered-down decision. But even a watered-down decision with 100 percent support is better than a perfect decision (if there is such a thing) with no support.

"But even a watered down decision with 100 percent support is better than a perfect decision . . . with no support."

Reaching a consensus does take time; therefore, any team should choose with care which decisions require a consensus. By the way, reaching consensus does become easier with time and practice.

Question 5.   Wow! Isn't that a loaded statement? Of course, lots of people talking at the same time can show energy and enthusiasm. But what about the times when five people on the team feel enthusiastic and the sixth person feels trampled? Is that the makeup of a healthy team?

The one-person-speaking-at-a-time rule has a lot of practical, common sense behind it. How can you hear information being shared by one person if you are listening to another? Can good decisions be made if everyone hasn't heard the same thing? And what does this mean for communication outside the team?

Once again, it depends. Everyone talking does show excitement in the team, but there are drawbacks. Timing is crucial. Is everyone listening when they should be? Are the right people talking when they should be? Are the right people listening when they should be? The answers to these questions will guide what should be happening.

Question 6.   Establishing clear roles for all team members may take a lot of time. Aren't there other more important things to do up front? Aren't there problems to solve? The team has real work to do, and establishing roles doesn't seem that important. Besides, don't all people know what their jobs are? All of this is true, yet there is another side.

Establishing roles up front guarantees that everyone has a clearly identified job. It prevents the same task from being done twice, some tasks not being done at all, and other tasks being redone because they weren't done right the first time.

Establishing roles early in a team's existence is well-invested time. It keeps things organized. And although the team should spend time in discussion early, roles evolve over time. Team members, as well as the leader, must pay attention to this.

By the way, most teams assign roles such as recorder, time keeper, facilitator, advisor, or process coach. All of these are important functional roles for the team, and most team members will know their "job-related" roles. A team should also consider the natural roles people bring to the team. Some are good organizers, some are creative, and some are good conflict managers. The team should be aware of these natural attributes and utilize them to contribute to the effort.

Question 7. Generally, it is true that a team must have clear goals. But what about the team that is still figuring out what it is supposed to be doing? What about the team whose goal is continually changing? What about the troubleshooting team? Each of these is a special case and, although their goals change quickly—monthly, daily, or perhaps even hourly—they will most likely have goals for a shorter time period.

It may also be that establishing a goal defines the limitations of a team and may inhibit the team members from accomplishing as much as they can because the team quits when it reaches the stated goal. Also, some unique individuals feel constrained by goals.

A team will most often succeed more easily if everyone on the team knows the goal and is working toward it. In most teams, people are heading in the same *general* direction, but may not be heading in the same *specific* direction. That is, they are all heading west, but are taking a different routes. This might cause some to end up in San Diego, some in Seattle, and others in Denver.

Teams should try to clarify their goals as specifically as possible to prevent rework, different outcomes, falling short of potential, and inefficient use of time. By the way, goals are most efficient if the organization's goals, the team's goals, and the individual's goals are all aligned.

Question 8. Avoiding conflict would be great! It keeps things clean and neat. No frustration! No messy communication. No arguments. All of this is great—if there truly are no disagreements on the team. This is rarely true.

Even on the team on which everyone gets along, there are differences of opinion. If a team claims not to have any conflict, they have probably learned to manage it well. And instead of calling it "conflict," they consider it "good discussion." This may be seen as "avoiding conflict."

In the statement, however, if we consider the word "avoid," defined in the dictionary as "steering away from," the team could be missing many opportunities. Avoiding conflict may mean sweeping issues under the rug and not dealing with them head on. This could lead to a major explosion at a later time. It could also lead to mediocre outcomes.

Conflict, when managed well, opens the team to many possibilities. Conflict often leads to a great solution, a new idea, and satisfaction for everyone on the team.

"Conflict, when managed well, opens the team to many possibilities."

In conclusion, conflict usually leads to a team that has more successes. Often, a team that believes it has no conflict is probably doing a great job of managing its conflict.

Question 9. Teams have lots to do and meetings generally take too long anyway, so it would seem inefficient to take valuable meeting time to explore member feelings and relationships. Besides, shouldn't all this touchy-feely stuff take place outside of meeting time? All of this is true, and you can make a very strong case for it.

On the other hand, value is added by discussing relationships within the team. First, the individuals involved usually build a stronger relationship. Second, others around usually learn something from the discussion. Third, the team benefits, because smoothing out the relationship will smooth out the teamwork. If a difficult relationship has been improved, less inappropriate time will be dedicated to it. In addition, the improved relationship will lead to better communication and support. This increases the effectiveness of the entire team.

Question 10. There is, of course, something to be said for allowing quiet members to speak up when they feel comfortable. If pushed for comments, some individuals may be intimidated or feel "put on the spot." We could also assume that most people's responses will be best when they feel ready to offer a suggestion. In fact, sometimes they may have a problem that is no one's business.

Yet, there is another way to think about it. It is every team member's responsibility to help balance discussion and ensure that everyone is contributing. That means individuals should monitor themselves and speak up when it is important to voice their opinions.

At times, team members may need to force themselves out of their comfort zones in order to be good team players. And at other times, team members may need a push to contribute. All team members must do their part and participate as needed—even if it is uncomfortable at times.

"At times, team members may need to force themselves out of their comfort zones in order to be good team players."

Question 11. Wouldn't it be great if every member of a team liked every other member? In this case, it depends on how you define the word "like." Does "like" mean that you would want to invite the person to dinner or take a vacation with him or her? Or does "like" mean that you get along well with the person at work and you respect his or her expertise?

People do not need to have a relationship outside of the workplace to be members of a good team. They do, however, need to respect one another. They also need to appreciate the diversity that each person brings to the team. They need to recognize that just because someone is different, it isn't wrong. The team needs those differences.

Question 12. It makes a lot of sense to get something up and running smoothly and to try to maintain it. It is simply more efficient when you don't continue to change things. Fewer changes means fewer communication mishaps.

Today there is another way to look at the topic of change. Some even say, "If it isn't broken, break it!" That just means that no matter how well things are working presently, there is always a better way. This is known as continuous process improvement.

Note: The activity in Exhibit 3 is useful to conduct with a team. Have everyone on the team complete the statements and then try to reach a unanimous decision as to whether each statement is true or false. A great deal of learning will occur through the discussion.

The team will need to make a call on this one. It can do that by exploring several questions, such as: What effect will change have? Do the benefits outweigh the problems? How much time will it take to make the change? Will we be more productive if we change? Does this productivity outweigh the time spent in making the change? Even if we know the change would cause more problems and decrease productivity a bit, is it necessary to ensure a competitive edge?

So there it is. Any of the statements could be true, or they could be false. It depends. Many things in teamwork are the same. It depends.

I hope this exercise was a thought-provoking one and that it has set you up for more learning throughout this book.

Teamwork is not natural for most of us. Why is that? Most of us were brought up to do the best we could as individuals. Even now, you are most likely rewarded according to how much you accomplish as an individual, not as a good team member. Have you ever been rewarded for helping someone else, even though it meant that you didn't accomplish your goals? It takes some new thinking. And it takes some new skills—or at least some concentration on skills that you may have but don't always use.

"Teamwork is not natural for most of us."

---

2 A Model for Building Teamwork

Have you ever been a member of a high performing, smoothly running team? If you have been, it's an experience that you are not likely to forget. Probably people trusted one another, worked cooperatively, enjoyed the task, and achieved goals higher than anyone may have imagined. Experts agree that effective, successful, high performance teams have several similar characteristics. What are they? The ten main characteristics are described below.

Ten Characteristics of Successful Teams

Figure 1 provides a visual model of the characteristics that exist within most successful teams. We hope this information will provide a starting point for you to begin to build a stronger team.

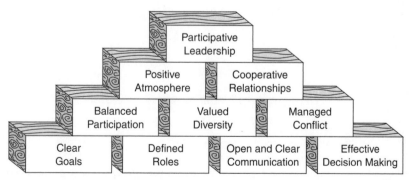

Copyright © 1999 ebb associates inc

Figure 1.   Ten Characteristics of a High Performance Team

13

The blocks shown in the model were not assigned random positions. Each has been placed in its respective spot for a reason. The blocks at the bottom (*clear goals, defined roles, open and clear communication,* and *effective decision making*) are the *foundation*. They must be strong and be in place early. The items in the second row (*balanced participation, valued diversity,* and *managed conflict*) are a step above the base and also required early in the team's formation. The third row contains characteristics that make working on a team personally satisfying and rewarding, but these are not imperative to completing the task. However, most team members will tell you that a *positive atmosphere* and *cooperative relationships* are the ultimate goals of teamwork.

The *participative leadership* block is the only one that can be removed without disturbing any of the other blocks. What does this tell you? Perhaps that one single leader is not always necessary. The position of the block, however, also suggests that participative leadership will generally emerge later in a team's formation. Let's examine each of these blocks required to build a team.

The bottom row of blocks serves as the foundation: clear goals, defined roles, open and clear communication, and effective decision making. What makes these so valuable to a team?

Clear Goals

Clearly defined goals are essential so that everyone understands the purpose and vision of the team. You might be surprised at how many people do not know the reason they are doing the tasks that make up their jobs, much less what their team is doing. Everyone must be pulling in the same direction and be aware of the end goals.

Clear goals help team members understand where the team is going. Clear goals help a team know when it has been successful by defining exactly what the team is doing and what it wants to accomplish. This makes it easier for members to work together—and more likely to be successful.

"Clear goals help team members understand where the team is going."

Clear goals create ownership. Team members are more likely to "own" goals and work toward them if they have been involved in establishing them as a team. In addition, the ownership is longer lasting if members perceive that other team members support the same efforts.

Clear goals foster team unity, whereas unclear goals foster confusion—or sometimes individualism. If team members don't agree on the meaning of the team goals, they will work alone to accomplish their individual interpretations of the goals. They may also protect their own goals, even at the expense of the team.

How can a team ensure that its goals are clear and understood by everyone? A good test is to have each team member list the team's goals, then compare differences and similarities and agree on the final goals. Final goals should be written and distributed to each team member, then reviewed periodically.

Defined Roles

If a team's roles are clearly defined, all team members know what their jobs are, but defining roles goes beyond that. It means that we recognize individuals' talent and tap into the expertise of each member—both job-related and innate skills each person brings to the team, such as organization, creative, or team-building skills.

Clearly defined roles help team members understand why they are on a team. When the members experience conflict, it may be related to their roles. Team members often can manage this conflict by identifying, clarifying, and agreeing on their individual responsibilities so that they all gain a clear understanding of how they will accomplish the team's goals.

Once team members are comfortable with their primary roles on the team, they can identify the roles they play during team meetings. There are two kinds of roles that are essential in team meetings.

Task Roles. Task roles contribute to getting the work of the team done. People in these roles supply the information, ideas, and energy necessary for the group to accomplish its goals. Task roles generate, organize, and complete the work and include roles such as the proposer, the coordinator, and the procedurer.

Maintenance Roles. Maintenance roles contribute to group cohesion and effectiveness. People in these roles establish and maintain interpersonal relationships and a group-centered atmosphere. Maintenance roles address people and atmosphere issues and include specific roles such as the reconciler, the motivator, and the relaxer.

All team members have responsibility for both task and maintenance roles. These roles are flexible, with members pitching in as needed to fill any void that occurs. Recognize that team members have different strengths in carrying out these roles. Accept these differences. Encourage team members to use their strengths, but also encourage them to "try on" new roles as part of their development.

Open and Clear Communication

The importance of *open and clear communication* cannot be stressed enough. This is probably the most important characteristic for high performance teams. Most problems of all kinds can be traced back to poor communication or lack of communication skills, such as listening well or providing constructive feedback.

"Most problems of all kinds can usually be traced back to poor communication or lack of communication skills . . ."

Enough books have been written about communication to fill a library. That makes it difficult to identify only a few key points in this area. Excellent communication is the key to keeping a team informed, focused, and moving forward. Team members must feel free to express their thoughts and opinions at any time. Yet, even as they are expressing themselves, they must make certain they are doing so in a clear and concise manner.

Unfortunately, most of us are not very good listeners. Most of us could improve our communication if we just started to listen better—to listen with an open mind, to hear the entire message before forming conclusions, and to work toward mutual understanding with the speaker. We allow distractions to prevent us from giving our full attention to the speaker. We allow our minds to wander instead of focusing on the speaker. We allow our biases and prejudices to form the basis for our understanding. Instead, we should allow the new information we are hearing to form the basis for our understanding.

Many benefits exist for working toward improving communication for your team. Consider those listed in Exhibit 1.

If team members attend to no other high performing team characteristic, working to improve their communication with other team members will increase trust, decrease problems and rework, and build healthy interpersonal relationships. Invest in improved communication; it will pay off!

The Pfeiffer Book of Successful Team-Building Tools

Exhibit 1.   Benefits of Good Team Communication

There are many benefits for improving communication on your team:

- Open communication encourages team members to express their points of view and to offer all the information they can to make the team more effective.

- Clear communication ensures that team messages are understood by speakers and listeners.

- Two-way communication increases the likelihood that all team members hear the same message.

- Good listening skills ensure that both the speaker's content (words) and the intent are heard.

- Attention to nonverbal communication helps further identify feelings and hidden messages that may get in the way of teamwork.

Effective Decision Making

Decision making is *effective* when the team is aware of and uses many methods to arrive at decisions. Consensus is often touted as the best way to make decisions—and it is an excellent method and probably not used often enough. But the team should also use majority rule, expert decision, authority rule with discussion, and other methods.

The team members should discuss the method they want to use and should use tools to assist them, such as force-field analysis, pair-wise ranking matrices, or some of the multi-voting techniques.

Effective decision making is essential to a team's progress; ideally, teams that are asked to solve problems should also have the power and authority to implement solutions. They must have a grasp of various decision-making methods, their advantages and disadvantages, and when and how to use each. Teams that choose the right decision-making methods at the right time will not only save time, but they will also most often make the best decisions.

This completes the four basic foundation characteristics: clear goals, defined roles, open and clear communication, and effective decision making. The next three blocks in the model build on their foundation.

Balanced Participation

If communication is the most important team characteristic, participation is the second most important. Without participation, you don't have a team; you have a group of bodies.

"Without participation, you don't have a team; you have a group of bodies."

Balanced participation ensures that everyone on the team is fully involved. It does *not* mean that if you have five people each is speaking 20 percent of the time. Talking is not necessarily a measure of participation. We all know people who talk a lot and say nothing. It does mean that each individual is contributing when it's appropriate. The more a team involves *all* of its members in its activities, the more likely that team is to experience a high level of commitment and synergy.

Balanced participation means that each team member joins the discussion when his or her contribution is pertinent to the team assignment. It also means that everyone's opinions are sought and valued by others on the team.

Participation is everyone's responsibility. As a team moves from a forming stage to more mature stages of group development, team members must make certain that everyone is an active participant. If you have team members who did not participate early in the formation of the team, they will withdraw even more as the going becomes more difficult. To achieve the best participation, a team might start by asking some of the questions found in Exhibit 2.

Two important things influence team participation: the leader's behavior and the participants' expectations.

Leader's Behavior

A *leader's behavior* comes as much from attitude as from anything. Leaders who are effective in obtaining participation see their role as being a coach

Exhibit 2. Questions to Ask for Increased Participation

- Did everyone on the team give his or her point of view when we established the ground rules?
- Did everyone have input into our goals?
- When we solve problems, do we make sure everyone has spoken before we decide?
- Do we consistently ask the shy members of our team what they think?
- Do we seek opposing points of view?
- Do we ask all team members what they want?

The Pfeiffer Book of Successful Team-Building Tools

and mentor, not the expert in the situation. Leaders will get more participation from team members if they can admit to needing help, not power. Leaders should also specify the kind of participation they want right from the start. Will everyone share their own ideas and then decide what to do or will the group discuss the pros and cons of the leader's idea? If everyone knows the answer, then there are no lingering questions.

"Leaders who are effective in obtaining participation see their role as being a coach and mentor, not the expert in the situation."

Leaders need to create a participative climate. They must make it a practice to speak last to avoid influencing others. Often a leader may put an idea on the table "just to get things started." But what happens? Everyone jumps on the idea and stops thinking. People may feel, "Well, if that's what she wants, that's it."

Leaders need to reward risk taking. Those "half-baked" partial ideas that people bring up may be just what gets the team moving toward a solution, idea, or new opportunity. Leaders must always protect the minority views. Anyone can think like everyone else. It takes courage to think and speak differently.

---

*"Anyone can think like everyone else.
It takes courage to think and speak differently."*

Leaders need input from everyone, but usually some team members have been selected for their expertise and experience. To ask for input, the leader must recognize those people for their expertise and/or experience, direct questions to them, and lead the discussion that results so that everyone is included. That's what participation is all about.

Participants' Expectations

Participants must volunteer information willingly rather than force someone to drag it out of them. They should encourage others' participation as well by asking question of others, especially those who have been quiet for a while.

Participants can assist the leader by suggesting techniques that encourage everyone to speak, for example, a round robin. To conduct a round robin, someone directs all members to state their opinions or ideas about the topic under discussion. Members go around the group, in order, and one person at a time says what's on his or her mind. During this time, no one else in the group can disagree, ask questions, or discuss how the idea might work or not work, be good or not good.

Only after everyone has had an opportunity to hear others and to be heard him- or herself, a discussion occurs. This discussion may focus on pros and cons, on clarifying, on similarities and differences, or on trying to reach consensus.

Participants can also encourage participation by establishing relationships with other team members between meetings. Another thing they can do is to call people by name. We all like to hear our names used by others—especially in positive ways!

Remember that each and every member of a team has responsibility not only to participate, but also to ensure that everyone else is given the opportunity to participate.

Valued Diversity

Valued diversity is at the heart of building a team. Thus, the box is at the center of the model. It means, put simply, that team members are valued for the unique contributions that they bring to the team.

"Valued diversity is at the heart of building a team."

Diversity goes far beyond gender and race. It also includes how people think, what experience they bring, and their styles. A diversity of thinking, ideas, methods, experiences, and opinions helps to create a high performing team.

Sometimes team members may realize that they do not have the kind of variety they need. They will note this, discuss it, and then do what is necessary to become more diverse. In the short term, the team may tap into expertise from another department for a specific project. In the long term, the team may identify the specific requirements it is missing so that the next person they bring in can fill the gaps.

Whether individuals are creative or logical, fast or methodical, the effective team recognizes the strengths each person brings to the team.

The Pfeiffer Book of Successful Team-Building Tools

Sometimes these differences are perceived by individuals as *wrong*. The high performing team member sees these differences as imperative for the success of the team and respects the diverse points of view brought by others.

Yes, it is more difficult to manage a highly diverse team, but the benefits will show up in the end. It takes work and a very special group of people to encourage the differences that each brings to the team. Flexibility and sensitivity are key.

Managed Conflict

Conflict is essential to a team's creativity and productivity. Because most people dislike conflict, they often assume that effective teams do not have it. In fact, both effective and ineffective teams experience conflict. The difference is that effective teams manage it constructively. In fact, effective teams see conflict as positive.

Managed conflict ensures that problems are not swept under the rug. It means that the team has discussed members' points of view about an issue and has come to see well-managed conflict as a healthy way to bring out new ideas and to solve whatever seems to be unsolvable. Here are some benefits of healthy conflict.

- Conflict forces a team to find productive ways to communicate differences, seek common goals, and gain consensus.
- Conflict encourages a team to look at all points of view, then adopt the best ideas from each.
- Conflict increases creativity by forcing the team to look beyond current assumptions and parameters.
- Conflict increases the quality of team decisions. If team members are allowed to disagree, they are more likely to look for solutions that meet everyone's objectives. Thus, the final solution will most likely be better than any of the original solutions that were offered.
- Conflict allows team members to express their emotions, preventing feelings about unresolved issues from becoming obstacles to the team's progress.
- Managed conflict encourages participation. When team members feel they can openly and constructively disagree, they are more likely to participate in the discussion. On the other hand, if conflict is discouraged, they withdraw.

Teams can benefit tremendously from the conflict they experience. Make it a point to maintain an environment in which conflict is not only managed, but encouraged.

"Teams can benefit tremendously from the conflict they experience."

Positive Atmosphere

To truly be successful, a team must have a climate of trust and openness, that is, a *positive atmosphere*. A positive atmosphere indicates that members of the team are committed and involved. It means that people are comfortable enough with one another to be creative, take risks, and make mistakes. It also means that you may hear plenty of laughter, and research shows that people who are enjoying themselves are more productive than those who dislike what they are doing.

Trust is by far the most important ingredient of a positive atmosphere. How do team members reach a point where they can trust one another? What are the characteristics that make some people seem more trustworthy than others? Trust and credibility can be described behaviorally. They can be seen in a more logical way than you might think. Consider for a minute. What do people need to do to build trust with you?

Did you think about honesty? Dependability? Sincerity? Open-mindedness? You've just identified some of the characteristics and behaviors that build trust. It's important to keep in mind that what one person sees as trustworthy is not necessarily what another sees. We each have different values. So when you want to build trust and credibility with others, it's as important to know what those individuals value as it is to know what is already your "strong suit."

Let's examine some characteristics and behaviors that build trust:

- To build trust with some people, you will need to be *honest* and *candid*. The messages this sends are: "I say what I mean." "You will always know where I stand." "You can be straight with me."

- To build trust with some people, you will need to be *accessible* and *open*. The messages this sends are: "I'll tell you what works best for me." "Tell me what works for you." "Let's not work with hidden agendas."

- To build trust with some people, you will need to be *approving* and *accepting*. The messages this sends are: "I value people and diverse perspectives." "You can count on being heard without judgment or criticism."

■ To build trust with some people, you will need to be *dependable* and *trustworthy*. The messages this sends are: "I do what I say I will do." "I keep my promises." "You can count on me."

Interestingly, these seem to be very strong, positive messages. But some people may perceive them differently. Like everything that involves human beings, there is not one clear way. Generally, to build trusting relationships with others, people must also provide credible evidence. There are two types of evidence: objective and subjective.

Objective evidence includes facts and figures or other measured and quantified data. *Subjective* evidence includes the opinions of others who are highly regarded (friends, family, or competent colleagues) and perceived as relevant resources and knowledgeable about the subject.

Of course, trust is not built overnight. Individuals have their own requirements for how long it takes to build trust with them, including these four:

1. *One time or until you prove otherwise.* "I guess you might call me optimistic. I tend to start with a clean slate."

2. *A number of times.* "I need some history. I tend to 'let my guard down' after a few positive interactions with people or after people have demonstrated their trustworthiness."

3. *A period of time.* "I need some history, too, but I tend to prefer a period of time to a specific number of times before I am comfortable placing trust in people."

4. *Each time.* "I value consistency. Call me pessimistic if you like, but I think I'm just being realistic. I guess I can be hard to convince."

Building trust on a team will be one of your greatest challenges. If a team you work with has done a good job of building trust, the other aspects of a positive atmosphere will come more easily. Those aspects include: individuals who are committed to the team's goals; an atmosphere that encourages creativity and risk taking; people who are not devastated if they make mistakes; and team members who genuinely enjoy being on the team. A positive atmosphere is one of the characteristics of a mature team.

> ## *"Building trust on a team will be one of your greatest challenges."*

Cooperative Relationships

Directly related to having a positive atmosphere are *cooperative relationships*. Team members know that they need one another's skills, knowledge, and expertise to produce something together that they could not do as well alone. There is a sense of belonging and a willingness to make things work for the good of the whole team. The atmosphere is informal, comfortable, and relaxed. Team members are allowed to be themselves. They are involved and interested.

Cooperative relationships are the hallmark of top performing teams. These top teams demonstrate not only cooperative relationships between team members, but also cooperative working relationships elsewhere in the organization.

Although it takes more than a list of ideas to build positive, cooperative relationships, there are several actions you can take. Teams can be made aware of the following areas:

- Recognize and value the different strengths that each member brings to the team. Focus on each person and on why he or she is on the team. The team should be certain to utilize each person's unique strengths.

- Provide a forum in which team members can give and receive constructive feedback. One of the best measures of a positive, cooperative relationship is whether people are honestly providing feedback to one another.

- Conduct self-evaluations as a part of normal business. Individuals can evaluate themselves as well as the team. Remember that it is everyone's responsibility to encourage growth and learning.

- Build an environment of trust and cooperation. Trust is the linch-pin between a positive atmosphere and cooperative relationships. It's like the chicken and the egg. It's difficult to tell which came first. The team members should demonstrate a team spirit that values cooperative relationships outside the team as well.

- Celebrate the team's successes. Most teams are very task-oriented and forget to celebrate their successes. Don't forget to reward yourself as a team. Some ways could include going out to lunch together, having a picnic, or publicly announcing an achievement to the rest of the organization.

Completing assignments brings closure to the task aspect of teamwork. Celebrating team accomplishments brings closure to the interpersonal aspect of teamwork. To maintain the highest possible performance on a team, all team members should be responsible for relationship building.

Participative Leadership

The *participative leadership* block is not at the top of the model because it is the most important. It is at the top because it is the only block that can be removed without disturbing the rest. *Participative leadership* means that leaders share the responsibility and the glory, are supportive and fair, create a climate of trust and openness, and are good coaches and teachers.

In general, it means that leaders are good role models and that the leadership shifts at various times. In the most productive teams, it is difficult to identify a leader during a casual observation.

In conclusion, a high performing team can accomplish more together than all the individuals can apart.

"A high performing team can accomplish more together than all the individuals can apart."

LEARNING TO BE A TEAM

Remember, too, that there is often learning that must occur for everyone on the team. But learning isn't enough. People's behaviors must change as well. Behavioral change can be the most difficult part of teamwork, and it may be quite uncomfortable at first.

Try this experiment. Cross your arms. Now look at how your arms are crossed. Which one is on top? Now cross them the other way—with the other arm on top. Keep them crossed and read on. Keep them crossed as long as you can. How does it feel? Uncomfortable? Awkward? Strange? Keep them crossed! Keep reading! Having a hard time concentrating? Wish you could uncross them? Well go ahead, uncross your arms.

It was uncomfortable to cross your arms the other way (not the *wrong* way). Crossing your arms is a very simple task, yet when you tried to do it differently, it felt uncomfortable. In fact, for some of you, it may have been so uncomfortable that you couldn't even concentrate as you continued to read.

Yet, if you wanted (for whatever reason) to change the way you cross your arms and you continued to cross your arms the new way for six months, what do you think would happen? Eventually, it would become comfortable and the natural way to cross your arms.

Would you ever slip back to crossing your arms the other way? Yes. Especially when you were under the stresses of short timelines or were facing problems.

Will the team members you work with ever slip back to working more as individuals than as team members? Yes. Especially when time is short, problems pop up, or the discussion or task becomes difficult. Let's think about that. When do team members need teamwork the most? When time is short, problems pop up, or something becomes difficult. Think about the implications. When teamwork is needed the most, teams are most likely to slip back to working as individuals.

Recognize that dedicating yourself to building high performance teams requires you to encourage team members to do *many* things differently. It is not nearly so easy as learning to cross your arms differently. It takes practice and patience on the part of every team member. Teams don't start off great. They *learn* to be great.

"Teams don't start off great. They learn to be great."

This book provides you with a collection of successful tools to build high performance teams and to help teams learn to be great. The next ten chapters feature these tools, addressing each of the ten building blocks of high performance teams described in this chapter.

Clear Goals

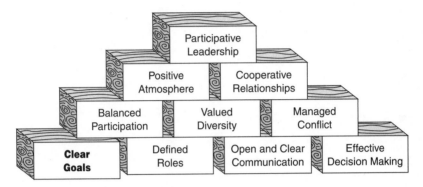

Copyright © 1999 ebb associates inc

Activities

- TeamScores: Measuring and Communicating Performance
- High Jump: Illustrating the Impact of Expectations
- Team Identify

Clear Goals, the first block in the foundation of the team-building model, are critical to ensure that everyone on the team is heading in the same direction. Much time, money, and energy—to say nothing of motivation and enthusiasm—are lost when everyone on the team is not aiming for the same outcome.

The three activities in this chapter focus on three aspects of goal setting: identifying goal measures, demonstrating how expectations affect performance, and exploring the dynamics associated with goal accomplishment. You will find "TeamScores" helpful for clarifying team goals as well as for understanding what's important in communicating these goals to the rest of the organization. "High Jump" is an out-of-your-seat activity that will literally have your participants jumping and that proves the importance of actual measures for achieving goals. "Team Identify" is a classic activity with a new twist. The activity asks the group to assess various dynamics at work while they are accomplishing the activity, such as level of involvement, conflict management, and closure. As a team-building facilitator, you will want to help the group relate these activities to how they accomplish the team goals and what they may wish to improve.

TeamScores: Measuring and Communicating Performance

Peter R. Garber

Goals

- To help team members identify measures of team effectiveness that are important to their team and the organization.

- To encourage team members to develop a means for assessing and reporting measures of the team's effectiveness.

- To provide a means for team members to keep track of the team's effectiveness.

Group Size

All members of an ongoing team.

Time Required

One and one-half to three hours, depending on the size and complexity of the team.

Materials

- A copy of the TeamScores Work Sheet for each team member.
- A pencil for each team member.
- A newsprint poster of Figure 1, prepared ahead of time by the facilitator. *Note:* More than one poster may be required.
- A newsprint poster of Figure 2, prepared ahead of time by the facilitator.
- A newsprint flip chart and several felt-tipped markers.
- Masking tape for posting newsprint.

Performance Measures	Important to Team	Important to Organization

Figure 1. Columns for Identifying and Categorizing Performance Measures

Physical Setting

A quiet room in which the team members can work without being interrupted. A table and chairs should be provided.

Process

1. The facilitator introduces the activity as a way for the team members to assess the strengths of their team as well as the areas in which it

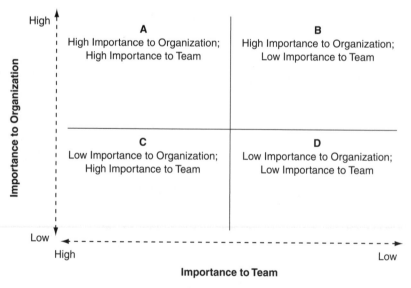

Figure 2. Matrix for Identifying Importance of Performance Measures

The Pfeiffer Book of Successful Team-Building Tools

can improve. The facilitator stresses that this kind of assessment is essential; without the feedback it provides, the members cannot know exactly what progress they have made, what they have done well, and where they need to exert more effort. The facilitator also states that such feedback on performance is largely responsible for the team members' motivation. (Five minutes.)

2. The facilitator states that the appropriate measures of a team's performance depend on the nature of the team, its functions, and its contribution to the organization. After displaying the newsprint poster of Figure 1, the facilitator asks the members to contribute ideas about performance measures (elements of team functioning or effectiveness) that are important to their team and/or their organization. The facilitator cites examples, saying that they may or may not apply: cost reduction, reduced downtime, yield, speed, accuracy, productivity, and safety. As the members suggest measures, the facilitator records them, asks whether they are important to the team and/or to the organization, and puts check marks in the appropriate columns. If the members contest a measure, the facilitator asks them to defer that discussion until later. (Ten minutes.)

3. When the measures have been listed, the facilitator displays the newsprint poster of Figure 2 next to the poster(s) of Figure 1. The team members are asked to rate each measure as either *high* or *low* in importance to the team and to the organization. (Consensus is not necessary, as long as general agreement is reached. If there is a lot of contention about a measure, however, the facilitator may want to suggest assigning it to quadrant D.) As the team members make their decisions, the facilitator records each measure in the appropriate box on the matrix. (Ten minutes.)

4. The facilitator clarifies the implications of the completed matrix:

   "The measures in quadrant A are the most important to both your organization and your team and should receive the most attention from you. The measures in quadrant D are the opposite: They are the least important to the organization and the team and should receive the least of your attention. You will need to do further analysis of quadrants B and C to determine just how much attention they warrant."

5. Each member receives a copy of the TeamScores Work Sheet and a pencil. In addition, the facilitator gives the team a newsprint flip chart and several felt-tipped markers. The members are asked to discuss the work-sheet questions and to record their answers on newsprint. As they work, the facilitator serves as a process advisor. (One-half hour

to two hours, depending on the needs of the team. Although the timing is somewhat flexible, the activity works best if the facilitator and the team members agree on approximately how much time will be spent on this step.)

6. At the end of the allotted time, the facilitator asks the team members to report their responses to the questions. If the team members desire more time to refine and finalize their responses, the facilitator assists them in making arrangements to do so. (Ten to fifteen minutes.)

7. The facilitator leads a concluding discussion with questions such as the following:

   ■ What have you learned about the value of identifying and developing measures to assess team performance? About the value of tracking team performance?

   ■ How do you feel about the plans you have made and the responsibilities you have assumed?

   ■ What do you think might be the outcomes of this work? What might be some side benefits of this process?

   ■ How can you continue and reinforce what you have started here?

   (Ten to fifteen minutes.)

Variations

■ Depending on the maturity of the team members, the team's stage of development, and time constraints, more than one session may be planned to address all of the questions on the work sheet.

■ The activity may be used with more than one team from the same organization as a means of developing intergroup communication and information sharing.

TeamScores Work Sheet

Instructions: As you and the other team members discuss the following questions, make notes on this work sheet. Once you have agreed on a response for an item, one of you should write that response on newsprint.

1. Are there additional "A" measures that should be included in the assessment of your team's performance? Any additional "B" or "C" measures that should be included?

2. Are any measures in quadrant D of so little importance that you should discuss them with others in the organization to determine whether they can be eliminated?

3. How will you use the measures you identified to assess your team's performance? What performance standards or criteria will you use?

4. What can serve as your team's "scoreboard"—a visual reminder of how the team is performing in relation to these measures?

5. What information related to the measures will be included on the team's scoreboard? (For example, how will you acknowledge exceptional performance, feedback from top management, and so on?)

6. How will the information on the scoreboard be generated or obtained? Who will have responsibility for what?

7. How will the scoreboard information be communicated to others outside the team?

Performance Measure   **How It May Be Communicated**

8. How will the team designate responsibility for updating the scoreboard? Will this responsibility be rotating or fixed? Who will be responsible for what time period?

9. How can the material on the scoreboard be kept current, accurate, and most useful to you? How often will it be updated?

HIGH JUMP:
ILLUSTRATING THE IMPACT OF EXPECTATIONS

Steven B. Hollwarth

Goals

- To demonstrate the impact of both negative and positive expectations on performance.
- To encourage participants to consider how expectations affect the extent to which they reach their goals.

Group Size

Two to five subgroups of three to six members each.

Time Required

One hour to one hour and fifteen minutes.

Materials

- A copy of the High Jump Instruction Sheet A-1 for each participant.
- A copy of the High Jump Instruction Sheet A-2 for each participant.
- A copy of the High Jump Instruction Sheet B-1 for each participant.
- A copy of the High Jump Calculation Sheet for each participant.
- Two sheets of newsprint for each subgroup, posted to the wall prior to the arrival of the participants. (See Step 1.)
- A set of ankle weights for each subgroup. All sets must be identical, and each set should weigh no more than five pounds (two and one-half pounds per ankle). *Note:* Depending on the general physical condition of the participant group, the facilitator may opt for lighter ankle weights.
- A yardstick for each subgroup.
- A felt-tipped marker for each participant. No two members of a subgroup should have markers of the same color.

- A newsprint flip chart and a felt-tipped marker for the facilitator's use.
- Masking tape for posting newsprint.

Physical Setting

A room large enough for the subgroups to work without discovering that one subgroup has different instructions. The room must have a ceiling of at least eleven feet. Movable chairs should be provided for the participants.

Process

1. Prior to the arrival of the participants, the facilitator tapes two sheets of newsprint to the wall in each area where a subgroup will work: The top of the first sheet should be at least eleven feet from the floor (see the High Jump Instruction Sheet A-1, second paragraph), and the top of the second sheet should be taped to the bottom of the first. The facilitator should identify each subgroup's area by writing a number (1, 2, and so on) at the bottom of the second sheet.

2. After the participants have arrived, the facilitator introduces the activity by explaining that they will be asked to take part in two exercises but that they will not be competing against one another. The facilitator also stresses the importance of following the written instructions that will be distributed.

3. The facilitator divides the participants into subgroups, with approximately the same number of members in each. Each subgroup is asked to select an area and to congregate in that area. Each participant is given a felt-tipped marker. No two members of the same subgroup are given a marker of the same color. (Five minutes.)

4. A copy of the High Jump Instruction Sheet A-1 is given to each participant. After the participants have reviewed the instructions, the facilitator states that *any participant who is unable to do the exercise because of physical reasons need not participate.* Then the participants are told to start jumping. When all jumps have been marked, the facilitator instructs the participants to exchange markers with other members of their subgroups so that no one ends up with the color that he or she used for the first jump. (Ten minutes.)

5. Each member of *one subgroup only* receives a copy of the High Jump Instruction Sheet A-2. All other participants receive copies of the High Jump Instruction Sheet B-1. Each subgroup is given a pair of ankle weights. As the participants are reviewing their instructions, the facil-

itator circulates and speaks to the groups. To the group with the High Jump Instruction Sheet A-2, the facilitator makes comments such as the following:

> "Now that you have warmed up with the first jump, you'll be able to jump higher this time. You are asked to jump only two inches higher, so that will be easy. Even with the weights on your ankles, you'll be surprised at how high you can jump. Some of you may even jump three inches higher."

To the other groups, the facilitator makes comments such as the following:

> "Don't be disappointed if you don't jump as high this time. After all, you'll be jumping with five more pounds than you did last time, and you can't imagine how heavy those five pounds will feel. Just see how close you come to your first mark."

(Ten minutes.)

6. After the facilitator has spoken to each group and after each participant has reviewed his or her instructions, the facilitator announces that it is time to put on the ankle weights and start the second round of jumping. (Five to ten minutes.)

7. After the second round of jumps, a copy of the High Jump Calculation Sheet is given to each participant. A yardstick is given to each subgroup. The facilitator asks the participants to follow the instructions on the handout and to ask questions if they have trouble calculating their scores. (Five to ten minutes.)

8. When all scores have been calculated, the facilitator reconvenes the total group and asks the members of each subgroup to call out their scores. The facilitator records these on the flip chart, saving the special subgroup's scores until last. *Note:* Ordinarily, the scores of the members of the special subgroup are significantly higher than those of the other participants. (Five minutes.)

9. The facilitator elicits observations regarding the scores and asks for speculations about why one subgroup had higher scores. (Five minutes.)

10. A copy of the High Jump Instruction Sheet B-1 is given to each member of the special subgroup, and a copy of the High Jump Instruction Sheet A-2 is given to all other participants. The participants are instructed to read their sheets. (Five minutes.)

11. The facilitator leads a discussion, asking questions such as the following:

- How would your second jump have been different if you had read the instruction sheet that you just received? Why?

- If you believe that you *cannot* do a task, what effect does that belief have on your performance? What is the impact of setting and visualizing a low goal?

- If you believe that you *can* do a task, how does that belief affect your performance? What is the impact of setting and visualizing a high goal?

- What are some examples of how your expectations of yourself affected the extent to which you reached your goals?

- How can you apply what you have learned in your personal life? In your current job? In your career?

(Fifteen minutes.)

Variation

- Activities other than jumping may be used. However, trials would be necessary to confirm that the activity was responsive to positive and negative expectations.

HIGH JUMP
INSTRUCTION SHEET A-1

Each member of your subgroup will take a turn jumping as high as possible. You are not competing with anyone else.

Each member will be responsible for tracking his or her own jump. As you jump from a standing position, hold your writing hand as high as possible and use your felt-tipped marker to mark the height of your jump. You may hold the marker any way you wish, and you may bend your knees before making the jump.

The first person who jumps should stand near the left side of the paper; make a mark on that part of the paper; and then initial the bottom of the paper, under the mark. The next person should move slightly to the right of that mark, so that the second mark will not be directly above or below the first person's mark. The second person should also initial the bottom of the paper, parallel with his or her mark. The third person should stand and jump slightly to the right of the second mark, and so on.

Your goal is to jump as high as you can. Use any energy, knowledge, or experience that will help you to accomplish this task.

High Jump
Instruction Sheet A-2

Your task is to jump even higher than before. Use a marker of a different color to mark the height of this jump (switch markers with someone in your subgroup). You are to follow the sequence and procedure you used for the first jump, so the first member will mark this jump directly (or almost directly) above or below his or her first mark. It is not necessary to sign the paper again.

Remember that you are not competing with anyone else. Your goal is to *jump two inches higher* than you jumped the first time.

The difference in this jump will be the weight that you attach to each ankle. The ankle weight is symbolic of the challenges that you must meet to be successful. If you formulate a clear vision of what you want to accomplish, you will find that your subconscious will tap inner strength to overcome obstacles. Your muscles will be more responsive, your coordination will be better, and your performance will be more effective.

Before jumping, look at your first mark. Visualize two inches higher on the paper. Your goal is to make a mark two inches above the one you are looking at. Remember that you are capable and you can do it.

When the facilitator gives you the signal, the first jumper should attach the ankle weights and go for the high jump!

High Jump
Instruction Sheet B-1

Your task this time is to jump with weights attached to your ankles. Use a marker of a different color to mark the height of this jump (switch markers with someone in your subgroup). You are to follow the sequence and procedure you used for the first jump, so the first member will mark this jump directly (or almost directly) above or below his or her first mark. It is not necessary to sign the paper again.

Remember that you are not competing with anyone else. Your goal is to see how high you can jump when you are encumbered with weights.

The ankle weights can have the same effect as emotional baggage (stress, anger, fear, frustration, and so on). You will be amazed at how heavy the weights feel as you try to lift your feet off the floor. Also, anything that upsets the natural movements of your body introduces inefficiency in physical activities. You may recall instances in which you started wearing a new type of shoe and kept tripping. Your body "knew" how high to lift your foot in your old shoes, but the new shoes required a different lift.

When the facilitator gives you the signal, the first jumper should attach the ankle weights and jump. Please try not to laugh at the other jumpers! Show them the same courtesy that you want them to show you.

High Jump
Calculation Sheet

Using the yardstick, calculate the difference in the height of your two jumps, to the nearest inch.

If your first jump was higher, your score will be the negative difference in the two jumps. For example, if your first jump was two inches higher than your second jump, your score is –2.

If your second jump was higher, your score will be the positive difference multiplied by two. For example, if your second jump was two inches higher than your first jump, your score is +4.

If your jumps were equal (or less than one-half inch apart), your score is zero. If your first jump was slightly higher, list your score as –0; if your second jump was slightly higher, list your score as +0.

Record your score on the bottom of this sheet. Calculate only your individual score, not your subgroup's score.

Team Identity

John E. Jones

> ### Goals
>
> - To develop cohesion within work groups established as part of a larger training group.
> - To explore the dynamics of group task accomplishment.

Group Size

Unlimited. Subgroups are best established to have five to seven members each. Any number of such teams can be directed simultaneously in the same room.

Time Required

Approximately one and one-half hours.

Materials Utilized

- Newsprint and felt-tipped pens (various colors), and masking tape.
- Team Identity Poster Formats.
- Team Identity Processing Guides.
- Pencils or pens.

Physical Setting

There should be room enough for groups to work independently. Wall space should be adequate for hanging a poster for each group in different locations around the room.

Process

1. The facilitator introduces the structured experience by explaining the goals of the activity and by giving a brief overview of the design.

Participants should be given the expectation that this activity will be both fun and productive.

2. Groups are formed by any convenient method (numbering off, choosing each other, forming homogeneous groups, etc.).

3. The facilitator explains that these groups will function as task teams from time to time throughout the training. He indicates that there can be a large difference between a *group* and a *team* and that this activity is intended to promote a sense of identification with one's task team.

4. The facilitator distributes a copy of the Team Identity Poster Format to each participant. He instructs the teams to create a name for themselves, a symbol (logo), and a motto. They have thirty minutes to complete the planning and production of this task. As soon as they have completed their planning, they should send a representative to the facilitator to get newsprint and colored pens.

5. At the end of the task phase the facilitator distributes a copy of the Team Identity Processing Guide to each participant and reads aloud the instructions printed on the form. The facilitator gives the participants five minutes to make notes privately.

6. Teams are instructed to discuss each of the items on the Team Identity Processing Guide and to select a different member to prepare to summarize each of the five items. (Twenty minutes.)

7. The facilitator calls for summary statements to each item from all teams. The large group is instructed to listen for common themes in these reports. (Fifteen minutes.)

8. The facilitator instructs the teams to put their posters on the walls, considerably apart from each other. Each team designates one member to stay with the poster to answer questions that members of other teams might have about the poster.

9. Team members are instructed to break up their groups and to go individually to the posters of all the other teams. They may ask questions and give reactions. The team members assigned to stay at these "stations" (one at each poster) are instructed to answer the other participants' questions and to note their reactions. (Twenty minutes.)

10. As soon as everyone has seen all the posters, the teams are instructed to reassemble. They then hear and discuss a summary of reactions noted by their representatives who stayed with the posters. (Five minutes.)

11. The facilitator invites each team to make a statement about itself to the larger group.

12. The facilitator brings closure to the activity with these questions:

- What did you learn about completing tasks as a team?

- What would you do differently as a team in the future?

- How can you apply what you learned in your day-to-day teamwork?

TEAM IDENTITY POSTER FORMAT

TEAM NAME

(acronym or other memorable designation)

TEAM LOGO

(diagram, picture, words, colors)

TEAM MOTTO

(a saying or slogan related to the team's
purpose, values, composition, or preferred
way of working)

TEAM MEMBERS

(may include titles)

TEAM IDENTITY PROCESSING GUIDE

Now that you have completed the development of your team's identity, take a few minutes to look back at the interaction that occurred. Each of you should write notes on this form before you discuss how your group worked on the task of making your poster. Then look for patterns in the perceptions of the members of your team. The facilitator will call for a report from your team on each of the following items. You will be instructed to designate a different member to give the summary for each item. Again, work *independently* first, then discuss each of these questions as a group.

1. *Organization*

    a. How did your group organize itself to accomplish the task?

    b. How did you feel during this getting-started phase?

2. *Involvement*

    a. How involved were all of the members during the problem solving?

    b. How did you feel about your own involvement?

3. *Creativity*

    a. What creative processes were used or occurred spontaneously?

    b. What was happening with you during the creative activity?

4. *Conflict*

    a. If there were disagreements, how were these handled by the team?

    b. How did you feel when there was group tension?

5. *Closure*

    a. How did the group decide that its task was done?

    b. How did you feel at the end of the team's production phase?

4 Defined Roles

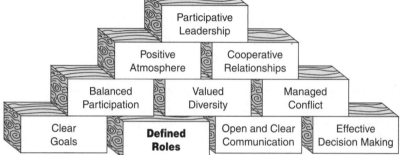

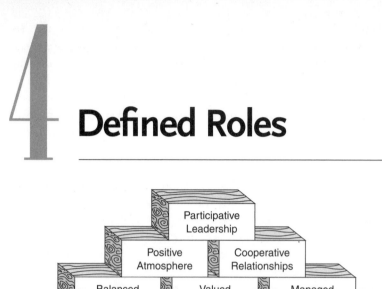

Activities

- The Hats We Wear: Understanding Team Roles

- No Strings Attached: Learning How Groups Organize to Complete Tasks

- Scope of Control: Taking Initiative in Problem Solving

- Yours, Mine, and Ours: Clarifying Team Responsibilities

- Symbols: Sharing Role Perceptions

Article

- The Search for Balance: Team Effectiveness

Defined Roles is the second critical block in the foundation of the team-building model presented here. Usually, members of a team have a fairly clear idea of what their roles are and it is only during times of crisis when role clarification poses a problem. But role issues may also come up during problem solving, when new roles may be required. They may also occur when the crisis is thought to be too daunting to manage or outside the team's scope or when there is a lack of clarity about who does what. This usually occurs during a transition from one team member to another. Much like the game of football, most work teams "drop the ball" during the hand-off.

This chapter offers you four activities that address team issues around defining roles. "The Hats We Wear" make exploring difficult issues fun, "No Strings Attached" will have the team actively solving a dilemma and later exploring what roles, organization, and communication could ensure increased success in the future. "Scope of Control" and "Yours, Mine, and Ours" are thought-provoking activities that further define role expectations.

The chapter also provides you with an activity, "Symbols," and an article, "The Search for Balance," that focus on the task and maintenance roles that contribute to successful team meetings and the assignment of tasks.

THE HATS WE WEAR: UNDERSTANDING TEAM ROLES

Kristin J. Arnold

Goal

■ To demonstrate the concept of informal roles and how they affect team dynamics and the decision-making process.

Group Size

Six or more participants from the same team or organization.

Time Required

Approximately fifty minutes.

Materials

■ Six baseball caps (hidden in a bag until used) with the following labels on five of the caps and a sixth cap with nothing written on it.

  ■ Obey me.

  ■ Ask my opinion.

  ■ Ask my opinion, but ignore it.

  ■ Ignore me.

  ■ Laugh at me.

  You can print these instructions on index cards and tape the cards to the front of the hats or print the caps with liquid paint.

■ One copy of a list of ten items that must be prioritized (of pertinence to the group) for each participant.

■ Pens or pencils for participants.

Physical Setting

A room that can be arranged with six chairs in a circle in the center with space for observers around the perimeter.

Process

1. Begin with a list of ten (or so) items that the group needs to prioritize. (*Note:* you may have to put together a list based on previous team discussions, but make sure that the list is meaningful and relevant to the group.) Hand out copies of the list and pens or pencils to all participants. Ask the participants to individually rank the importance of each item from 1 to 10 (or so) with 1 being the most important. (Ten minutes.)

2. When the participants have completed their individual rankings, ask for six volunteers. Ask them to bring their chairs and sit in the middle of the group in a circle. Ask those who remain to be process observers and watch how this team of six individuals accomplishes the task. (Five minutes.)

3. Tell the team of six:

    "Your task will be to reach consensus on the priority of items on the list within ten minutes. However, before you start, you must follow a few ground rules. I have several hats, which I will place on your heads. Please do not take them off until I tell you that you may. For those of you who are looking at these hats, follow the instructions on them to whatever extent you choose. Process Observers, please watch how the team achieves its objective. You have ten minutes."

    The team may be uncomfortable and will probably ask you for clarification. Simply repeat the ground rules. After ten minutes, if the team has not finished, allow them thirty additional seconds. (Ten minutes.)

4. Then debrief the team: (*Note:* Do not let them look at their hats yet.) Ask the team these questions:

    - Who has the final list that the team agrees to?
    - Do you like the result? What do you like/not like about it?
    - What did you like about the activity? What did you not like about it?

5. Begin to debrief each of the six participants in turn. Ask: "Can you guess what is written on your hat?"

6. Have each participant look at his or her hat. Ask, "Are you surprised?"

    (*Note:* Save the participant wearing the hat with nothing printed on it for last. This participant will think that there is something on it—reemphasizing the point that we all come together with "hats" on.)

The Pfeiffer Book of Successful Team-Building Tools

7. Facilitate the debriefing of the entire team:

   - What did you think about this activity?

   - How do the roles we play affect our teams' goals?

   - What do you think about the hats we wear when we come together on a team?

   - How do our hats affect our decision-making process?

   - What can we incorporate from this activity into our future work as a team?

   (Fifteen minutes.)

Variation

- Print other roles on the caps that are more pertinent to your team.

No Strings Attached: Learning How Groups Organize To Complete Tasks

Jeyakar Vedamanickam

Goals

■ To give participants an opportunity to experience how group members organize themselves to accomplish a task.

Group Size

Three or four subgroups of five to eight members each.

Time Required

One hour and five to fifteen minutes.

Materials

■ A copy of the No Strings Attached Prework Sheet for each subgroup.

■ A copy of the No Strings Attached Answer Sheet for each subgroup.

■ A copy of the No Strings Attached Observer Sheet for each subgroup's observer.

■ Two pieces of string, each sixty inches long, for each subgroup.

■ A pencil for each subgroup's observer.

■ A clipboard or other portable writing surface for each subgroup's observer.

Physical Setting

A large room with plenty of space to separate the subgroups so that they do not disturb one another. If possible, furniture should be moved against the walls and out of the participants' way.

Process

1. The facilitator assembles subgroups of five to eight members each and asks each subgroup to select one member to serve as an observer. Each subgroup is given a copy of the prework sheet and two strings. Each observer is given a copy of the observer sheet, a pencil, and a clipboard or other portable writing surface. (Five minutes.)

2. Each subgroup is instructed to connect two persons with the strings, as indicated in step 1 on the prework sheet. The facilitator monitors this step, ensuring that people are connected with strings as intended. (Five minutes.)

3. The facilitator announces the task for each subgroup:

   "Without breaking the strings or tampering with any knot, untangle the two people from each other. This is a group task, so anyone in your group except the observer is free to help in any way."

   If the participants ask questions, the facilitator repeats the task and recommends soliciting help from the other subgroup members. After stating that the subgroups have twenty minutes, the facilitator asks them to begin. (Five minutes.)

4. After twenty minutes, the facilitator asks the subgroups to stop working on the task. Each subgroup is given a copy of the answer sheet. (To save time and to ensure that the participants do not become fixated on the task, the facilitator may demonstrate the solution with two participants.) (Twenty-five minutes.)

5. The facilitator reconvenes the total group and asks the observers to report: First the observers take turns reporting their answers to item 1 on the observer sheet, then item 2, and so on. (Ten to fifteen minutes.)

6. The facilitator leads a concluding discussion based on the following questions:

   - How do you feel about what your group achieved or did not achieve? What helped or hindered?

   - How do you feel about how your group organized itself to accomplish the task?

   - If you were to try a similar task again, what would you do differently?

   - What parallels do you see between what happened in your group and what happens in other groups that you belong to?

- What have you learned about how groups organize that you can use in the future to help accomplish group tasks?

(Fifteen to twenty minutes.)

Variations

- The task may be completed in pairs, with one observer per pair.
- The subgroups may be asked to compete to finish first. The facilitator would then process what the effect was of the competition.

No Strings Attached Prework Sheet

Instructions: Tie the two strings to connect two volunteers of your group as shown in the figure below. *Be careful not to tie the strings too tightly around the hands.*

Volunteer 1

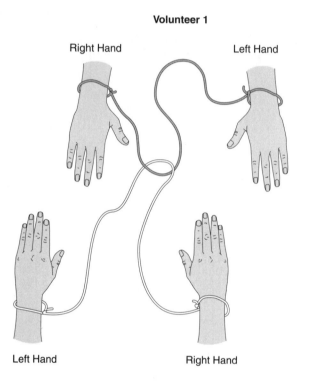

Right Hand   Left Hand

Left Hand   Right Hand

Volunteer 2

No Strings Attached Answer Sheet

Step 1

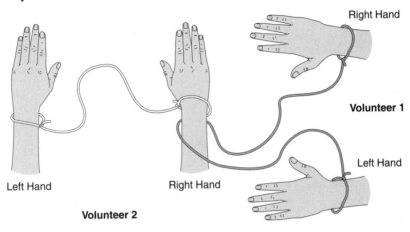

Right Hand

Volunteer 1

Left Hand

Left Hand

Right Hand

Volunteer 2

Step 2

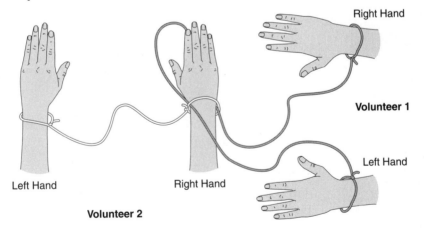

Right Hand

Volunteer 1

Left Hand

Left Hand

Right Hand

Volunteer 2

Step 3

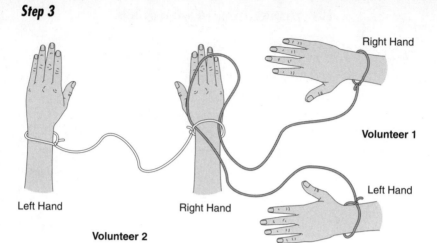

Right Hand

Volunteer 1

Left Hand

Left Hand

Right Hand

Volunteer 2

Step 4

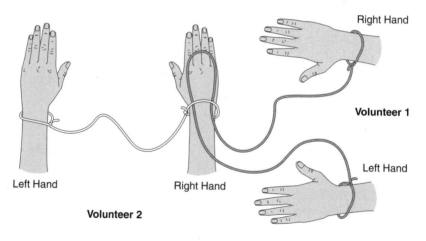

Right Hand

Volunteer 1

Left Hand

Left Hand

Right Hand

Volunteer 2

The Pfeiffer Book of Successful Team-Building Tools

No Strings Attached Observer Sheet

Instructions: Observe the members of your group as they strive to untangle the two people attached by strings and write answers to the following questions:

1. How are the group members organizing themselves to accomplish the task?

2. What kind of leadership is evolving? How does it evolve? How does the leadership affect task accomplishment? How does it change as the members keep working on the task?

3. How would you describe the communication between group members? What helps their communication? What hinders it?

4. What difficulties arise? How do the members deal with those difficulties?

SCOPE OF CONTROL: TAKING INITIATIVE IN PROBLEM SOLVING

Steve Sphar

Goals

- To encourage participants to take initiative in solving problems.

- To raise participants' awareness of two common barriers to taking initiative: (1) our self-limiting beliefs that we cannot influence events outside our scope of control and (2) our resistance to doing things that we find difficult, unpleasant, or uncomfortable, even if they would help bring about the desired outcome.

Group Size

All members of an ongoing team, divided into subgroups of three or four members each. If the team has fewer than six members, subgroups need not be formed. However, the facilitator may still want to form two small subgroups so that each participant can participate fully.

Time Required

One to one and a half hours.

Materials

- A copy of the Scope of Control Theory Sheet for each participant.
- A copy of the Scope of Control Task Sheet for each participant.
- A pencil for each participant.
- A flip chart and a felt-tipped marker for each subgroup.
- Masking tape for posting.

Physical Setting

A room large enough so that the subgroups do not disturb one another. A table and chairs should be provided for each subgroup, and there should be wall space for posting flip-chart paper.

Process

1. The facilitator distributes copies of the theory sheet and reads the content aloud while the participants follow along. Afterward the facilitator answers any participant questions. (Ten minutes.)

2. The facilitator asks the participants to assemble into subgroups of three or four members each and distributes copies of the instruction sheet, pencils, flip charts, and felt-tipped markers. The facilitator asks the participants to read the task sheet. As they are reading, the facilitator draws a reproduction of the Scope of Control Diagram on the flip chart. Afterward, the facilitator briefly reviews the instructions, listing action items on the flip-chart diagram. For example, the facilitator may use a desired result such as "to reduce delays in shipping to no more than forty-eight hours" and then fill in some action items in appropriate places on the diagram. (Twenty minutes.)

3. The facilitator helps the participants choose a problem that their team currently faces. (This problem should be one that the participants can agree to work on during this activity.) The facilitator then asks for the participants' help in formulating a problem statement and a desired result. (Five to ten minutes.)

4. Each subgroup is asked to complete a Scope of Control Diagram, using the desired result as the basis. The facilitator stipulates that the subgroups have thirty minutes to complete this task, asks each subgroup to select one member to fill in the diagram and present it later to the total group, and then asks the subgroups to begin. While the subgroups are working, the facilitator monitors their work and answers questions as necessary. When the remaining time is down to ten minutes, the facilitator lets the subgroups know so that they can complete their work on time. (Thirty minutes.)

5. After thirty minutes the facilitator calls time, reconvenes the total group, and asks the subgroup spokespersons to take turns presenting their diagrams. After each presentation, the facilitator asks for comments, reactions, and questions. (Twenty to thirty minutes, depending on the number of subgroups.)

6. The facilitator gives all newsprint to a volunteer to create a handout and distribute it to all participants. The participants are urged to follow through by creating a specific action plan (designating who will do what and by when) for achieving the desired result.

7. The facilitator leads a concluding discussion by asking the following questions:

   ■ How do you feel about the quality of work done in your group? How do you feel about the quality of your group's diagram?

   ■ What did you learn about generating actions to reach a goal?

   ■ What did you learn about ways to influence actions that are outside your scope of control?

   ■ What did you learn about your own resistance to actions that are outside your comfort zone?

   ■ What would you say are the advantages of using this technique? What might be the disadvantages?

   ■ In what other situations could you use this technique?

   (Twenty minutes.)

Variations

■ This activity may be used with newly hired people or new managers. In this case, the participants create individual rather than subgroup diagrams. The facilitator should assign a desired result that is relatively simple, such as "where I plan to be in my job or career one year from today."

■ The activity may be used for life/career-planning purposes.

SCOPE OF CONTROL THEORY SHEET

We have all been faced with a problem that we at first thought was too big or too far beyond our control to solve. Such problems appear daunting and stifle creativity. But the truth is that there is almost always something you can do to influence the outcome or help arrive at a solution.

When you feel "stuck" on a problem, that response is generally due to one or both of two common barriers:

1. *The belief that you cannot do anything about the problem.* This belief can stem from the nature of your position in the organization, which may not afford you the power or authority to bring about the desired outcome. This belief is self-limiting. If you focus on what you *cannot* do, that is all you will see. A perspective that looks to what you *can* do opens up your creative-thought process and can lead to solutions that you never would have seen otherwise. If the actions necessary to the success of a project lie outside your direct control or authority, the key is to search for the things that you can do to *influence* those actions.

2. *Internal resistance to doings things that you find difficult, uncomfortable, or unpleasant.* Like everyone else, you have your "comfort zone" or the areas in which you feel strong and competent. And, like everyone else, you probably rely on these strengths when you are trying to solve problems. But there are usually other activities—ones that lie outside your comfort zone—that would be extremely helpful to the success of a project. Most of us block out such activities, either consciously or unconsciously, because we do not feel as competent or comfortable in executing them.

You can get past these barriers by first identifying activities that are outside your control and outside your comfort zone, prioritizing these activities, and then forming an action plan for completing them and achieving the goal.

SCOPE OF CONTROL TASK SHEET

Scope of Control Diagram

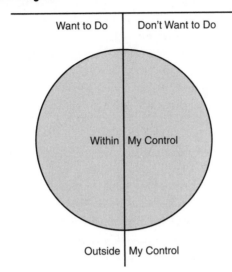

Instructions: The Scope of Control Diagram consists of two elements: a circle and a vertical line. The circle represents the scope of your authority or control. Inside the circle are actions within your ability to carry out, delegate, or otherwise control; outside the circle are actions you cannot control.

The vertical line divides the diagram in two. It runs through the areas you control and the areas you do not. The area to the left of the line represents actions you are willing to carry out, and the area to the right represents actions you are not willing to carry out. The vertical line is important, because it forces you to acknowledge the areas you choose to avoid.

You will be working with the other members of your group to complete the diagram. Here is an explanation of what you will do:

1. *Reproduce the diagram.* Draw the basic structure on a piece of flip-chart paper so that you will have plenty of blank space to fill in.

2. *List the action items.* At the top of the diagram, state your problem or goal in terms of the *desired result.* (This focus will help keep you thinking of the problem or goal in positive terms.) Be specific in describing the desired result (for example, "to reduce delays in shipping to no more than forty-eight hours" rather than "to fix shipping problems").

Then think of as many action items as possible that would help bring about the desired result. "Action item" simply means any activity or action, whether taken by you or someone else. Write each action item in the appropriate area of the diagram.

For example, outside the circle might be items such as "Build a new plant," "Hire new staff members," or "Move operations to a new location." Depending on your authority in the organization, items inside the circle might include "Provide computer training for the staff" or "Develop sales plan for new region." Each item would be listed to the left or right of the vertical line depending on your preference for doing that activity.

3. *Rate the items inside the circle.* After you have listed as many action items as you can think of, rate all items inside the circle, on both sides of the vertical line, in terms of importance. "Importance" refers to how critical the item is to achieving the desired result. Write the appropriate number on a scale of 1 to 10 (1 = low importance, 10 = high importance) beside each item. This step yields a list of actions that are under your control—ones that you can undertake now to begin solving the problem or meeting the goal.

4. *Rate items outside the circle.* Give the items outside the circle, on both sides of the vertical line, two ratings. The first is an importance rating on a scale of 1 to 10 (1 = low importance, 10 = high importance). The second, also based on a scale from 1 to 10, represents the degree to which you can influence the action (1 = very little influence, 10 = very great influence). Write both numbers next to each item.

Add both numbers for each item. The totals serve as the basis for prioritizing items that are outside your direct control but over which you can exert varying degrees of influence. Note that you do not have to prioritize items exclusively on this numerical basis. You should feel free to adjust priorities based on your own judgment.

5. *Expand the list of items outside your scope of control.* For each item, write down things you can do to influence the action. These new action items should be things that are currently within your control—things that you can do now. For example, you may not have the authority to "hire new staff members," but you can prepare a presentation for your manager on why new staff members are needed. In your list, try to include both those things that you have the will to do and those things that you feel resistance to doing.

When you complete this task, you will have two lists of action items. One consists of items over which you have direct control. The other consists of items that you cannot control but you can influence, and it includes action items for ways to exert your influence. By combining these two lists, you can develop an action plan (describing exactly what you will do and by when) for achieving the desired result.

Yours, Mine, and Ours: Clarifying Team Responsibilities

Mike M. Milstein

Goal

- To assist the team members in clarifying and establishing agreements about which activities are their team's responsibility and which are the responsibilities of individual members (including the formal leader).

Team Size

All members of an ongoing team. The process works best with a minimum of three members and a maximum of eight members.

Time Required

Approximately three to three and one-half hours for a team with five or six members. The facilitator should add or subtract ten minutes for each member above or below that number.

Materials

- A set of colored 3" × 5" index cards for each team member. There should be as many colors of index cards as there are members, plus one; for example, if there are four team members, there should be five different colors of index cards. The set of cards that each member receives should include six cards of each color. *Note:* If there are more members than there are colors of index cards available, the facilitator may use white cards and code them with different colors of felt-tipped markers, making a colored stripe along the top edge of each card.

- A pencil for each team member.

- Two sheets of newsprint and a felt-tipped marker for each team member.

- A newsprint flip chart and a felt-tipped marker for the facilitator's use.
- Masking tape for posting newsprint.

Physical Setting

A room with tables and movable chairs for the team members. Each member must have enough tabletop surface so that he or she can create stacks of index cards and prepare two newsprint posters.

Process

1. The facilitator describes the goal of the activity, emphasizing that when team members establish agreements about which activities are the team's responsibility and which are the responsibilities of individual members, they can enhance not only the effectiveness of their team but also their individual security and motivation as members of that team.

2. Each team member is assigned a color of 3" × 5" index cards, and one color is reserved for the team; these color assignments are announced and written on newsprint. Each member is given a set of index cards and a pencil.

3. The facilitator gives instructions as follows:

   - Using the cards of the color assigned to him or her, each member (a) writes brief descriptions of *six work activities* (one activity per card) that are his or her *most important* responsibilities and prerogatives; and (b) rank orders the activities, writing the rank of each on its card.

   - Using the cards of the color assigned to another team member, each member (a) writes brief descriptions of *six work activities* (one activity description per card) that are the *most important* responsibilities and prerogatives of that member; and (b) rank orders the activities, writing the rank of each on the card. This procedure is completed for every other member of the team.

   - Using the cards of the color assigned to the team, each member (a) writes brief descriptions of *six work activities* (one activity description per card) that are the *most important* responsibilities and prerogatives of the team as a whole; and (b) rank orders the activities, writing the rank of each on its card.

   The facilitator elicits and answers questions about the task and then asks the members to begin. (Approximately forty minutes.)

4. After the members have completed the task, they are instructed to distribute their completed cards to the appropriate team members and to give the cards identifying team activities to the facilitator.

5. The facilitator gives each team member two sheets of newsprint and a felt-tipped marker and then explains the process for reviewing and analyzing the content of the cards:

   ■ Each member reviews the cards received and compares them with the ones that he or she wrote.

   ■ Each member sorts the cards into stacks that reflect the same basic intent.

   ■ Each member summarizes his or her conclusions on two newsprint sheets: one listing *activities and rankings* about which there is widespread agreement and the other listing *activities and rankings* about which there is not widespread agreement. On the latter sheet, the member writes "S" (for "self") beside activities that he or she identified and others did not and writes "O" (for "others") beside activities that others identified and he or she did not; discrepancies in rankings are similarly identified.

   (Thirty minutes.)

6. The members are instructed to take turns posting their newsprint sheets and sharing their conclusions with the team. The facilitator explains that the purpose of each presentation and the ensuing discussion is to try to reach agreement on each member's six most important activities and their rankings. The members are told that each presentation should follow this pattern:

   ■ The member who is making the presentation summarizes activities and rankings on which he or she and fellow team members generally agreed and then asks the team members if they concur with this analysis. If there is disagreement, the facilitator assists in a discussion intended to help the team to move toward clarity and agreement regarding activities and their rankings. If the team members are unable to reach clarity and/or agreement, the activities and rankings under dispute are listed on a separate sheet of newsprint.

   ■ The member summarizes activities and rankings on which he or she and fellow team members disagreed. Again, the facilitator assists in a discussion intended to move the team toward clarity and agreement. Where disagreements persist, the activities and rankings in question are added to the separate sheet of newsprint, which is then set aside.

After all team members have taken a turn, the team is asked whether it might be useful to set up another time to meet and address the activities and rankings that require further clarification and/or agreement. If the members want a follow-up session, the details of that session are determined, including the process to be followed. The separate sheets of newsprint listing activities and rankings in dispute are given to one of the members to retain or transcribe into handout form for use at the follow-up session. (Approximately fifteen minutes per team member.)

7. The team members are asked to be seated around one of the tables. The facilitator gives them the team cards, and they separate the cards into two stacks: (a) activities and rankings representing general agreement, either according to the cards or as a result of discussion, and (b) activities and rankings that represent disagreement. The two sets of activities are listed on separate newsprint sheets and are posted. The facilitator leads a discussion about the activities and rankings that represent disagreement, helping the team members to move toward clarity and agreement regarding the team's six most important activities and their rankings. If disagreement persists, the facilitator encourages the members to set up another follow-up session and to determine a process to follow during that session. The newsprint list of activities and rankings in dispute is given to one of the members to keep for use at the follow-up session. (Forty-five minutes.)

8. The facilitator leads a concluding discussion based on the following questions:

   ■ How are you feeling about your team at this moment? How do you feel about being a member of this team?

   ■ In what ways has this experience been helpful to you and to the team as a whole? What have you learned? What surprised you?

   ■ When are activities best completed by the team? When are they best completed by individual members?

   ■ In your day-to-day work with your team, how will you use what you have learned as a result of this experience?

Variations

■ If this activity is being conducted as a result of prior diagnosis and team-member agreement regarding the need to distinguish team activities from individual-member activities, in step 1 the facilitator should review information about the diagnosis and agreement.

■ The facilitator may request in advance that the team members bring with them to the activity any existing documentation that could be useful, such as written job descriptions.

■ If extra time is available, the individual and team activities and rankings that remain in dispute may be addressed in the same session.

■ This activity may be used to identify the kinds of decisions that should be made by individual members or by the team.

Symbols: Sharing Role Perceptions

Patrick Doyle

> ## Goals
>
> - To familiarize the team members with the various roles that exist in a team.
>
> - To provide the team members with an opportunity to share perceptions of their roles in their team.
>
> - To provide the team members with the opportunity to practice giving and receiving feedback.

Group Size

All members of an ongoing team.

Time Required

Approximately one hour and fifteen minutes.

Materials

- A copy of the Symbols Role Sheet for each team member.
- A copy of the Symbols Individual Role Tabulation Sheet for each team member.
- A pencil for each team member.
- Several pairs of scissors.
- A clipboard or other portable writing surface for each team member.
- A copy of the Symbols Team Role Tabulation Sheet, prepared in advance on newsprint.
- A newsprint flip chart and a felt-tipped marker.
- Masking tape for posting newsprint.

Physical Setting

A room large enough so that the team members can work comfortably.

Process

1. The facilitator introduces the goals of the activity by saying:

   "Every team requires that certain roles be filled. In this activity we are going to take a look at fifteen specific roles. As a result of this activity, you will have the opportunity to see how you view your own roles, how others see you, and how your team fulfills these functions."

   (Five minutes.)

2. Each team member is given a copy of the Symbols Role Sheet, a pencil, and a clipboard or other portable writing surface. The facilitator leads a discussion of the roles listed to ensure that the team members understand them before starting work on the activity. (Ten minutes.)

3. The team members are instructed to work independently to assign the roles on the Symbols Role Sheet. (Ten minutes.)

4. After distributing a copy of the Symbols Individual Role Tabulation Sheet to each team member, the facilitator directs the team members to complete the first column, "How I See Myself," by checking off the roles to which they assigned themselves. (Five minutes.)

5. The facilitator instructs the team members to cut apart the role sheet along the dashed lines and to distribute the resultant slips of paper to the people whose names are listed on them. The role sheets that have not been assigned to a particular individual are collected by the facilitator. The team members are then instructed to complete the second column of the Symbols Individual Role Tabulation Sheet, "How Others See Me," and to spend some time reflecting on the implications. (Fifteen minutes.)

6. The facilitator tallies the team roles on the prepared newsprint poster (see Materials) by having the team members read the results of their second columns aloud. Each team member has the opportunity to ask clarification questions, such as "What do I do that leads others to put me in this role or that leads others not to see me in a role in which I see myself?" (Fifteen minutes.)

7. The facilitator leads a concluding discussion based on these questions:

- What were your feelings and thoughts as you assigned your fellow team members to roles? What were your feelings as you assigned yourself to roles?

- How did you feel about the roles you were assigned by others? What similarities and differences did you find between how you see yourself and how others see you? What roles would you like to fulfill?

- Under what circumstances do the members of your team compete for roles? Under what circumstances do you leave roles unfilled?

- How do these roles help the team accomplish its goals? What particular strengths or areas for team improvement do you see?

- What is one role each of you could fulfill right now to improve the team effort?

Variations

- After step 7 each team member may be asked to choose a particular role that he or she currently fills or would like to fill within the team. Other team members then provide feedback about the choice, its feasibility if not currently filled, what action steps might be needed, areas of improvement, and so on.

- Additional discussion might focus on the roles not perceived as filled within the team and ways in which those functions could be (or are being) covered.

Symbols Role Sheet[1]

Instructions: These roles are to be assigned to members of your team, including yourself. Base your decisions on your own perceptions of how your team functions, considering factors such as a person's leadership ability, tasks, personality, and so on. A person may be assigned to more than one role, and certain roles may be left unfilled.

Clarifier: Interprets ideas or suggestions; defines terms; clarifies issues before the team; clears up confusion.

_____

Compromiser: Offers compromises that yield status when his or her ideas are involved in conflicts; modifies in the interest of team cohesion or growth.

_____

Consensus taker: Asks to see whether the team is nearing a decision; "sends up trial balloons" (asks questions and makes comments) to test possible solutions.

_____

_____

[1]From *Process Politics: A Guide for Group Leaders,* by Eileen Guthrie and Warren Sam Miller, 1981, San Francisco, CA: Pfeiffer. Originally adapted from NTL Institute, "What to Observe in a Group," by Edgar H. Schein, 28-30, *Reading Book for Human Relations Training,* edited by Cyril R. Mill and Lawrence C. Porter, Copyright 1976. Used with special permission from NTL Institute for Applied Behavorial Science, 300 N. Lee, Ste. 300, Alexandria, VA 22314.

Encourager: Is friendly, warm, and responsive to others; indicates by facial expressions or remarks the acceptance of others' contributions.

Follower: Goes along with the movement of the team; passively accepts the ideas of others; serves as an audience in team discussion and decision making.

Gatekeeper: Helps to keep communication channels open; facilitates the participation of others; suggests procedures that permit sharing remarks.

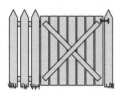

Harmonizer: Attempts to reconcile disagreements; reduces tension; gets people to explore differences.

Information seeker: Asks for factual clarification; requests facts pertinent to the discussion.

? ? Facts
Facts ? ?
? Facts
? Facts ?

Informer: Offers facts; gives expression of feelings; gives opinions.

Initiator: Proposes tasks, goals, or actions; defines the team problems; suggests procedures.

Opinion seeker: Asks for clarification of the values pertinent to the topic under discussion; questions values involved in the alternative suggestions.

? Values
? ?
Values ? ?
? Values
? Values ?

Orienter: Defines the position of the team with respect to its goals; points to departures from agreed-on directions or goals; raises questions about the directions pursued in team discussions.

_____

Reality tester: Makes critical analyses of ideas; tests ideas against data to see if the ideas would work.

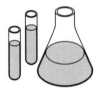

_____

Standard setter: Expresses standards for the team to attempt to achieve; applies standards in evaluating the quality of team processes.

_____

Summarizer: Pulls together related ideas; restates suggestions; offers decisions or conclusions for the team to consider.

$$\frac{X + Y}{Z} =$$ _____

SYMBOLS INDIVIDUAL ROLE TABULATION SHEET

Instructions: Begin by completing the first column. Put a check mark next to each role that you assigned yourself. After the facilitator distributes the role assignments made by your fellow team members, complete the second column by writing the number of times you were assigned a certain role by members of your team. When you have completed the second column, note the similarities and differences in the roles you assigned yourself and those assigned to you by your fellow team members.

	How I See Myself	**How Others See Me**
Clarifier	_____	_____
Compromiser	_____	_____
Consensus taker	_____	_____
Encourager	_____	_____
Follower	_____	_____
Gatekeeper	_____	_____
Harmonizer	_____	_____
Information seeker	_____	_____
Informer	_____	_____
Initiator	_____	_____
Opinion seeker	_____	_____
Orienter	_____	_____
Reality tester	_____	_____
Standard setter	_____	_____
Summarizer	_____	_____

SYMBOLS TEAM ROLE TABULATION SHEET

Instructions to facilitator: Prepare newsprint in advance using the format provided. Adjust the number of columns so that all team members' names can be listed.

	Name 1	Name 2	Name 3	Name 4	Total
Clarifier	_____	_____	_____	_____	_____
Compromiser	_____	_____	_____	_____	_____
Consensus taker	_____	_____	_____	_____	_____
Encourager	_____	_____	_____	_____	_____
Follower	_____	_____	_____	_____	_____
Gatekeeper	_____	_____	_____	_____	_____
Harmonizer	_____	_____	_____	_____	_____
Information seeker	_____	_____	_____	_____	_____
Informer	_____	_____	_____	_____	_____
Initiator	_____	_____	_____	_____	_____
Opinion seeker	_____	_____	_____	_____	_____
Orienter	_____	_____	_____	_____	_____
Reality tester	_____	_____	_____	_____	_____
Standard setter	_____	_____	_____	_____	_____
Summarizer	_____	_____	_____	_____	_____
Total Number of Roles	_____	_____	_____	_____	_____

THE SEARCH FOR BALANCE: TEAM EFFECTIVENESS

Tom Noonan

Abstract: A major challenge for organizations today is to match the right person to the right job so that every team consists of the most effective members possible. Unfortunately, when the wrong candidate is chosen for a job, often the choice is attributable to insufficient, inaccurate, or ignored data.

Dr. Meredith Belbin of the Industrial Training Research Unit of Cambridge University in England has conducted extensive research and has developed a system that can help in placing the right person in the right job. Belbin's research has led to the identification of nine roles that are critical to team success. The team that possess all nine roles—without an imbalance of too many people in too few roles—is well on its way to being a high-performance team.

Belbin's system is the subject of this article. The nine roles—Plant, Coordinator, Resource Investigator, Monitor Evaluator, Implementer, Team Worker, Complete-Finisher, Specialist, and Shaper—are defined, and the uses and benefits of team-role theory are thoroughly discussed.

Business today is not business as usual. New values, new technologies, new geographical relationships, new lifestyles, and new modes of communication have combined to create a much different business environment from that of yesterday. As has often been said, change is the only constant.

In addition, global market competition demands that businesses learn to respond quicker with less cost and higher quality. Those organizations that are able to adapt to rapid and unpredictable levels of change will be more likely to survive in the next century.

It is obvious to many in the field of human resource development that the decision-making processes and structures of the past cannot meet the challenge of the future. Many believe that teams are the answer and that the members of those teams should be the best-qualified people available to solve problems and implement solutions.

TEAM ROLES: A SYSTEM FOR DEVELOPING HIGH-PERFORMANCE TEAMS

The Difference Between Functional Roles and Team Roles

Dr. Meredith Belbin of the Industrial Training Research Unit of Cambridge University in England has studied management teams for more than twenty years (Belbin, 1994). His research has resulted in a system for understanding the roles that people play in teams and for enhancing the effectiveness of teams. Belbin has found that every team member plays dual roles: a functional role and a team role. An individual's *functional role* contributes to his or her team's performance in the form of specific expertise (for example, a person's functional role may be as an engineer, an accountant, a copywriter, or a salesperson).

An individual's *team role* is less obvious but is equally critical to a team's performance. Indeed, the members' ability to play their team roles effectively may mean the difference between success and failure for a team.

The concept of team roles is apparent every day in the predictable behaviors of team members. For example, one member may be the one who always comes up with bright ideas, another may typically press for decisions, and yet another may tend to challenge new ideas. This natural pattern of behaviors is observable in any team. The enduring behavioral characteristics of team members lead to their assuming particular roles within the team.

The Nine Team Roles

Over a seven-year period, Dr. Belbin and the members of his research team studied more than 120 management teams during competitive business simulations. Great volumes of data were collected during every team session, including a variety of recorded contributions from different team members.

Psychometric tests were used to generate a profile of psychological traits for each participant. From these test results and the observations of Belbin's researchers, team-role patterns began to emerge. It became obvious that each team member had a preferred or natural role, a secondary role (one that he or she was able to assume when necessary), and least-preferred/best-avoided roles.

Belbin's initial research produced eight team roles, and later a ninth role was identified. All nine, which are briefly described in Figure 1, are important to team performance.[1]

In reality, any team member can play—and probably has played— each role while contributing to the objectives of a work team. The important issue is the extent to which each member contributes from his or her natural team-role strength(s).

Allowable Weaknesses

Although each team role contributes a valuable strength to the composition of a team, it also carries the weight of what Dr. Belbin refers to as an "allowable weakness." For example, the Plant has the strength of being able to generate original ideas but also has the allowable weakness of being disinterested in details.

Attempting to overcome an allowable weakness may dilute a person's strength, though. Consequently, team members should be encouraged to tolerate one another's weaknesses and to focus instead on one another's strengths.

Plant: Devises creative solutions to problems.

 Coordinator: Interprets objectives; encourages decisions; facilitates appropriate resources.

 Resource Investigator: Finds useful contacts and resources outside the team.

 Monitor Evaluator: Discerns options; makes insightful judgments.

 Implementer: Translates ideas into action and organizes the process.

 Team Worker: Resolves disagreements; concentrates on diplomacy.

 Completer-Finisher: Fixes errors; ensures work is complete; meets deadlines.

 Specialist: Offers knowledge or skills that others may not have.

 Shaper: Challenges others to overcome difficulties.

Figure 1.   Belbin's Nine Team Roles

The Pfeiffer Book of Successful Team-Building Tools

DESIGNING TEAMS FOR HIGH PERFORMANCE

High performance seems to happen in one of two ways. In a crisis, a team often rises to the occasion. Whether the team members are saving lives in a hospital's emergency room or coming together and pooling resources after a devastating earthquake in a community, their performance level tends to be sustained for a short period, the length of the crisis.

The second way in which a team rises to the occasion is by mastering the phases of team development. Although few teams consciously follow the process of their own development, certain characteristics have been found to be common to long-term high performance. For example, in such a team there is a "chemistry" formed in which the members contribute on the basis of their individual strengths. Also, activities are well coordinated and focused on team goals. Finally, the roles are balanced so that there is adequate coverage of all nine without a concentration on only one or a few roles (Drexler, Sibbet, & Forrester, 1988).

A balance of roles within a team increases the likelihood of positive contributions from individual members, decreases the likelihood of destructive conflict among members, and enhances the team's ability to adapt to changing and unpredictable circumstances.

THE USES OF TEAM-ROLE THEORY

Assessing roles in an existing team helps the members to recognize, acknowledge, and take advantage of the different contributions from individuals. When the team members share information about natural roles (those that they naturally assume without effort) and least-preferred roles, they are able to identify any areas of imbalance as well as any roles that are not covered within the team.

The process of learning about, identifying, and employing team roles offers other advantages:

- Tasks can be assigned to members on the basis of the roles for which they are best suited.

- The team leader or mentors within the team can coach other team members on developing secondary roles that represent avenues of growth for them and for the team.

- New team members can be selected for team-role balance, thereby ensuring the right mix of natural role composition.

- Team members can be redeployed after a merger or an acquisition on the basis of roles needed within new teams. Thus, unfavorable situations can provide a unique opportunity to create balanced teams that are designed for success.

No one individual is so well-rounded that he or she can assume all of the roles necessary for effective team performance. But by assembling the right mix of individuals, an organization can create the most effective team possible.

THE BENEFITS OF TEAM-ROLE THEORY

As a management consultant, I am always wary of claims that one product, one system, one profile, or one management tool can meet many different client needs. However, during the 1994 Belbin Users Conference in Cambridge, England, I became convinced that the Belbin system of measuring team-role contributions, composition, and suitability (using self-perception inventories, observer assessments, and job analyses) can and does live up to the claims of its proponents. Human resource and organization development professionals who need accurate and useful information to encourage, influence, and facilitate change can benefit greatly from examining and using Belbin's approach.

At the conference were company representatives (from British Nuclear Fuels, IBM, British Airways, the Rover Group, and others), industrial psychologists, and independent consultants who made presentations about the utility and wide applicability of Dr. Belbin's system. My personal experiences with this system—in companies like Exxon Chemicals, GE Aircraft Engines, GE Appliances, AT&T Global Information (formerly NCR), Motorola, Pulte Home, and many others—reinforce the presenters' claims.

Following is a sampling of the benefits experienced and shared by the presenters:

- Increased involvement of team members, based on employing natural team roles to help meet team objectives;

- An ability to identify areas in which conflict is most likely to occur within a team;

- The provision of a framework (using Belbin's terminology) for openly and safely discussing sensitive team-viability issues;

- The identification of the most appropriate tasks for individual team members;

- The provision of a context within which team members can set/voice their expectations of one another;

- The realization that the functional leader does not have to "do it all";

- Higher-quality decisions and teams that are more highly motivated to carry out those decisions;

- An enhanced understanding and more effective management of one's own contribution to team effectiveness;

- An increased understanding of people's reactions to stress and outside pressures;

- An enhanced ability to diagnose people's readiness for change;

- Facilitation of an open dialogue about the organization's cultural norms and expectations;

- Facilitation of discussions about job design for current and future business operations; and

- The development of greater insight into the match or mismatch of candidates for new roles or jobs.

Conclusion

Currently Dr. Belbin's observations and conclusions are underutilized as a system for human resource management. I strongly urge practitioners to take a look at this approach and to discover what I have—that it is an excellent way to help organizations meet the challenges of the Twenty-First Century.

References

Belbin, R.M. (1994). *The Belbin team-roles package.* San Francisco, CA: Pfeiffer.

Drexler, A., Sibbet, D., & Forrester, R. (1988). *Team building: Blueprints for productivity and satisfaction. Alexandria,* VA: National Training Laboratories/San Francisco, CA: Pfeiffer.

Open and Clear Communication

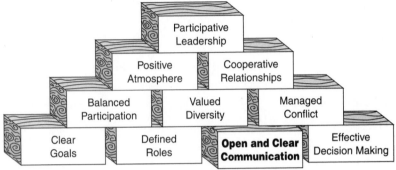

Copyright © 1999 ebb associates inc

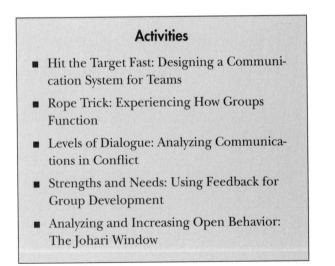

Activities

- Hit the Target Fast: Designing a Communication System for Teams

- Rope Trick: Experiencing How Groups Function

- Levels of Dialogue: Analyzing Communications in Conflict

- Strengths and Needs: Using Feedback for Group Development

- Analyzing and Increasing Open Behavior: The Johari Window

Open and Clear Communication is the most important building block in the team-building model. It is so important that you will probably include communication in some form in any team-building session you conduct. If a team can improve its communication, many other issues will be eliminated—or at least reduced. Exhibit 1 in Chapter Two listed the benefits of improving communication for a team. Look back and review them now.

We could fill an entire book with communication activities, but we have chosen the five presented in this chapter. With a world that is moving faster and faster, time pressure is the norm rather than the exception. "Hit the Target Fast" explores the importance of establishing a team communication system when under time pressure. "Rope Trick" gives teams a chance to examine subgroup communication. "Levels of Dialogue," based on work by Will Schutz, gives team members an opportunity to experiment with levels of openness and experience different levels of listening. Be sure to read the variations on this one. "Strengths and Needs" is a feedback exercise. However, the title doesn't hint at the powerful action-planning tool encompassed in the activity. This is a long activity, but it covers many aspects of communication as well as giant steps toward developing a team. The final activity uses the Johari Window. If you've never experienced the power of this old favorite, try it soon.

Hit the Target Fast: Designing a Communication System for Teams

Lynn A. Baker, Sr.

Goals

- To help team members gain awareness of the elements that constitute a team-communication system that is effective in situations involving time pressure.

- To offer team members an opportunity to design such a system.

- To offer team members an opportunity to become more aware of how they communicate when under time pressure.

Group Size

Three to five ongoing work teams (as many as thirty participants). The activity works best with teams of four to six members each; if a team has eight or more members, it should be split into two subgroups.

Time Required

One hour and twenty to thirty-five minutes.

Materials

- A copy of the Hit the Target Fast Task Sheet for each team member.
- Blank paper and a pencil for each team member.
- A clipboard or other portable writing surface for each team member.
- A newsprint flip chart and several colors of felt-tipped markers for each team.
- Masking tape for posting newsprint.

Physical Setting

A room large enough so that the teams can work separately without disturbing one another. Movable chairs must be provided. Tables are useful but not essential; if tables are available, the clipboards or portable writing surfaces are not necessary.

Process

1. The facilitator introduces the activity by stating its goals.

2. The teams are assigned to separate areas. The facilitator distributes copies of the Hit the Target Fast Task Sheet, blank paper, pencils, and clipboards or other portable writing surfaces. In addition, each team is given a newsprint flip chart and several markers in different colors. The team members are instructed to read the handout. After everyone has read it, the facilitator elicits and answers questions about the task. The facilitator also states that at the conclusion of the task, one or more representatives from each team will be asked to give a three-minute presentation describing that team's communication system and why/how it will work effectively in the situation. The teams are encouraged to create newsprint posters to illustrate their communication systems. (Ten minutes.)

3. The facilitator informs the teams that they have twenty-five minutes to complete the task and asks them to begin. As they work, the facilitator circulates from team to team to answer questions and to keep the teams informed of the remaining time. (Twenty-five minutes.)

4. After twenty-five minutes the facilitator calls time, reassembles the total group, and asks the teams to take turns presenting their communication systems. After each presentation the facilitator encourages feedback by asking (1) whether and to what extent the system meets the criteria on the task sheet and (2) how the system might be improved. (Twenty to thirty-five minutes, depending on the number of teams.)

5. The facilitator leads a discussion based on these questions:

   ■ What was your experience as you worked under time pressure with your team?

   ■ How would you describe the way your team generally communicates under time pressure? How is your approach similar to the one you designed for the gunnery team? How is it different?

- How is your team's communication under time pressure different from its usual pattern of communication?

- What have you learned about effective communication under time pressure?

- How can your team communicate more effectively under time pressure? What obstacles might you face in implementing a new system? How could you overcome those obstacles?

(Twenty minutes.)

Variations

- After Step 5 the individual teams may reassemble to design communication systems for their own use when they are under time pressure.

- This activity may be used with a single team as part of a team-building session.

- To include an element of competition, the facilitator may tell the team members that the first team to complete the task wins.

Hit the Target Fast Task Sheet

The Situation

A four-member gunnery team wants to practice in preparation for combat. Their weapon is a mortar, designed for lobbing shots to out-of-sight targets. Their practice target is one-half mile from the mortar and cannot be moved closer. A hill fifty feet high is between the mortar and the target, blocking direct view. The diameter of the target is thirty yards.

The following resources—and only these—are available to the members of the gunnery team. The members need not use all of them.

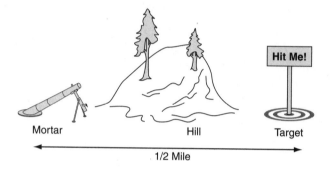

- A battery-powered *buzzer* with extra *wire* (assume any length);

- A *flagpole* (not implanted; assume any length);

- A bag of triangular-shaped *flags* (assume any number and colors) plus *cord* (any length);

- A *shovel;*

- A *ladder* (assume any length);

- A pair of *binoculars;* and

- *Ammunition* (plenty is available, but the fewer the number of rounds required to hit the target, the better).

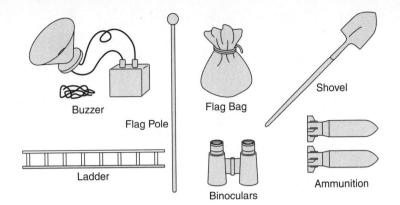

Buzzer

Flag Pole

Flag Bag

Shovel

Ladder

Binoculars

Ammunition

The Task

The members of the gunnery team know how to fire and adjust the mortar, but they do not know how to hit the target accurately and quickly. Your team's task is to *design a communication system* for them, addressing (1) how they can deploy or position themselves, (2) how they can use the available resources, and (3) how they can communicate effectively.

The system you design must work for the team members not only during practice, but also in an actual combat situation—when they must act quickly and efficiently to hit the target and still protect themselves. That system should:

- Be clear and easy to understand;
- Be quick to implement;
- Account for things that could go wrong; and
- Incorporate safety measures to protect the members of the gunnery team.

ROPE TRICK:
EXPERIENCING HOW GROUPS FUNCTION

Meredith Cash

Goals

- To offer participants an opportunity to experience how group members organize themselves to accomplish a task.

- To offer participants a chance to experience how group members communicate in planning and completing a task.

- To develop participants' awareness of the leadership styles that arise in groups as the members complete tasks.

Group Size

Three subgroups of ten to twelve members each. *Note:* Two of the members of each subgroup are observers.

Time Required

One hour and thirty to forty-five minutes.

Materials

- A copy of the Rope Trick Observer Sheet for each of the six observers.

- A pencil for each observer.

- A clipboard or other portable writing surface for each observer.

- For each participant except the observers, a kerchief (or other suitable material) to be used as a blindfold.

- A fifty-foot length of clothesline rope (available at supermarkets or hardware stores), cut into three pieces: (1) a piece twenty feet long to make a square, (2) a piece eighteen feet long to make a triangle that will fit on top of the square, and (3) a piece twelve feet long to make a circle that will fit inside the square. See Figure 1 for an illustration of the "house" structure that the participants ultimately create with these pieces of rope.

■ A newsprint reproduction of Figure 1, prepared by the facilitator prior to conducting the activity.

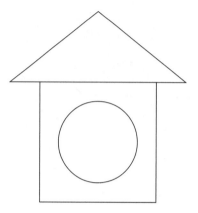

Figure 1.   The Rope House

■ A newsprint flip chart and felt-tipped markers.

■ Masking tape for posting newsprint.

Physical Setting

An unobstructed indoor or outdoor area that is at least 40' × 50'. There must be enough room for the members of all three subgroups to move around while constructing shapes from the rope.

Process

1. The facilitator introduces the activity, divides the participants into subgroups of ten to twelve members each, and designates the subgroups as A, B, and C. Two members of each subgroup are asked to be observers. (Ten minutes.)

2. The subgroups are positioned in separate circles, and the facilitator places one of the three pieces of rope inside each circle. The participants are advised not to touch the rope prior to beginning the activity. The facilitator distributes blindfolds to all participants except the observers and instructs the participants to put on their blindfolds so that they cannot see. (Ten minutes.)

The Pfeiffer Book of Successful Team-Building Tools

3. The participants are told that first they will be completing a practice round. The facilitator explains the process:

- Each subgroup forms a geometric shape with its rope, *using the full extension of that rope:* Group A forms a square, Group B forms a circle, and Group C forms a triangle.

- The members of each subgroup are to spend some time planning how they will construct the shape before they begin. The planning time ends when one of the members touches the rope.

- Once a member has touched the subgroup's rope, all members must pick up the rope.

- Every member must adhere to certain restrictions about handling the rope: Once the rope is picked up, the hand that picks it up must remain on the rope throughout the activity. Each member may slide his or her hand along the rope (for example, by holding his or her thumb and forefinger together and creating a "hole" for the rope to slip through), but may not release the rope with that hand.

- There are no restrictions on the use of the other hand.

- The observers' job is to monitor the activity; to announce the remaining time at five-minute intervals; and to help people get over or under ropes and away from obstacles. The facilitator will help with these responsibilities.

(Five minutes.)

4. The facilitator announces that fifteen minutes are allotted for the practice round, including both planning and forming the geometric shapes, and then tells the subgroups to begin.

5. While the subgroups are working, the facilitator and the observers monitor for adherence to the rules and restrictions and for safety concerns. Also, if a subgroup's rope becomes knotted and/or the members are hopelessly entangled, the facilitator or an observer instructs one member to remove his or her blindfold for one minute to rectify the situation. (Fifteen minutes.)

6. At the end of the fifteen-minute period, the facilitator calls time, asks the participants to remove their blindfolds, and posts the newsprint reproduction of Figure 1. The facilitator explains that now that the participants have completed the practice round, they are ready for the second round: They will again be blindfolded, create the same geometric shapes, and adhere to the same rules and restrictions. However, this time the subgroups need to combine their efforts so that

they can ultimately create the outline of a primitive house," using the square for the basic structure, the triangle for the roof, and the circle for the window. The facilitator announces that the time allotted for this task is ten minutes.

7. The facilitator gives each observer a copy of the Rope Trick Observer Sheet, a clipboard or other portable writing surface, and a pencil. The facilitator explains that during the upcoming round the observers are to write answers to the questions on their observer sheets, again monitor for the participants' safety, and again help people get over or under ropes and away from obstacles. This time, however, the facilitator will assume the responsibilities of ensuring adherence to the rules and restrictions and announcing the remaining time at intervals.

8. The facilitator asks the participants to put on their blindfolds and begin the second round of the activity. (Ten minutes.)

9. When all subgroups have placed their ropes, the facilitator instructs the members to remove their blindfolds and to view their creation. (Five minutes.)

10. The total group is reassembled. The facilitator asks the observers to give brief reports on the contents of their observer sheets. (Approximately fifteen minutes.)

11. The facilitator leads a concluding discussion about the second round. The following questions may be useful:

   ■ How do you feel about the final product? How would you assess the quality of your functioning as you and the other subgroups worked together?

   ■ What would you do differently if you were to do this task again?

   ■ How did this activity represent the ways in which work teams organize, communicate, and accomplish tasks?

   ■ What have you learned from this activity that you will use in the future?

   (Ten to fifteen minutes.)

Variations

■ If the subgroups are composed of ongoing teams, the final processing may focus on how the teams actually work and how the members' interaction can be improved, based on the learnings from this activity.

- Processing may also occur after the practice round.
- Within each subgroup, half of the members may be required to wear blindfolds. The other members participate without blindfolds but are required not to speak. The subsequent dynamics are discussed during the processing.

ROPE TRICK OBSERVER SHEET

Instructions: During the upcoming round, jot down answers to the following questions. In addition, monitor for the participants' safety and help them get over or under ropes and away from obstacles. Do not answer any questions about how to complete the task. When the second round has been completed, you will be asked to report your observations to the total group.

1. How do the members organize themselves to accomplish the task?

2. What kind of leadership evolves? How does it occur? How does it change as the members work? How would you describe the effectiveness of leadership communication?

3. How do the subgroup members communicate with one another? How effective is their communication?

4. How does the group deal with problems?

5. What else do you notice about the group's process? What do you notice before they pick up the rope? After they pick up the rope?

6. How efficiently and effectively does the subgroup complete its task?

7. What do you see being applied from the practice session?

LEVELS OF DIALOGUE: ANALYZING COMMUNICATIONS IN CONFLICT

Gary Copeland

<table>
<tr><td>

Goals

- To increase personal effectiveness in resolving conflict through increased awareness and open dialogue.

- To demonstrate one method of becoming aware of the unconscious emotions that can block open and direct communication.

- To enable the participants to receive feedback about their levels of verbal communication, both in sending and receiving messages, and about the congruence of their nonverbal communication.

</td></tr>
</table>

Group Size

Up to ten trios.

Time Required

One hour and thirty minutes to one hour and forty minutes.

Materials

- One copy of the Levels of Dialogue Theory Sheet for each participant.
- One copy of the Levels of Dialogue Awareness Log for each participant.
- One copy of the Levels of Dialogue Observer Sheet for each participant.
- A pencil for each participant.
- A clipboard or other portable writing surface for each participant.

- A newsprint poster prepared in advance with the following information:

	Speaker	Listener	Observer
Round 1	A	B	C
Round 2	B	C	A
Round 3	C	A	B

- A newsprint flip chart and a felt-tipped marker.
- Masking tape for posting newsprint.

Physical Setting

A room large enough for pairs to work without disturbing one another. Movable chairs are desirable; tables, desks, or other barriers should be avoided.

Process

1. The facilitator distributes pencils and clipboards, along with copies of the Levels of Dialogue Theory Sheet, the Levels of Dialogue Awareness Log, and the Levels of Dialogue Observer Sheet. He or she presents a lecturette on the Levels of Openness, the Levels of Listening, and the Awareness Log. (Twenty minutes.)

2. Participants are asked to complete the following information on the Levels of Dialogue Awareness Log:

   "Recall several recent conflict situations in which you withheld your feelings, did not tell the whole truth, or were otherwise less than fully open. Write down the reason that you gave yourself for doing this (what you feared would happen). Then identify what you believe is the fear you have about yourself that influenced your decision to withhold in that situation. The distinction between these two different fears is important. For instance, 'I'm afraid I would get fired' is what I feared would happen; 'I'm afraid I couldn't tell my family I lost my job' or 'I'm afraid I couldn't cope with the stress of finding another job' is my fear about myself."

   (Five minutes.)

3. The facilitator assembles the participants in trios and asks each trio to designate one member as "A," another member as "B," and the third member as "C." The facilitator announces that the activity will be con-

ducted in three rounds so that each person will have a turn as speaker, listener, and observer. *(Note to facilitator: If the group does not divide evenly into trios, one or two pairs may be formed; in this case, the role of the observer will be omitted.)* The facilitator posts the prepared newsprint poster of assignments and indicates that in the first round, the "A" participants will be speakers, the "B" participants will be listeners, and the "C" participants will be observers. (Five to ten minutes.)

4. Each speaker is instructed to choose an incident from the Awareness Log that he or she would be willing to discuss within the trio. The speakers are asked to experiment with levels of openness, especially in terms of their fears about what might have happened and their fears about themselves. Similarly, the listeners should focus on Levels 4 and 5 of listening by inviting further explanation and paraphrasing. The observers are asked to identify which levels of openness and listening they notice, at which level the speaker and listener spent the most time, and how nonverbal communication was used. Participants are told that each round of the activity will last for fifteen minutes, including the discussion between the speaker and the listener and the debrief with the observer. The facilitator gives the instruction to begin. (Five minutes.)

5. After ten minutes, the facilitator reminds participants of the time and indicates that they should be concluding their discussions and moving on to the debrief with the observers. Observers are asked to summarize their observations and reactions within their trios, using their notes from the Levels of Dialogue Observer Sheet. *(Note to the facilitator: If the participants are working in pairs, they can share how the experience felt and what they noticed.)* (Fifteen minutes.)

6. The facilitator instructs the members of each trio to switch roles and to repeat the activity two more times, until each member has held the roles of speaker, listener, and observer. The facilitator calls time after each discussion and instructs the participants to debrief as directed in Step 5. (Thirty minutes.)

7. After the final round of the activity, the facilitator reconvenes the total group. The facilitator leads a concluding discussion based on the following questions:

   - How did you react to the experience in the speaker role? The listener role? The observer role?

   - How did the quality of the conversation change over the course of the activity?

- What did you learn about yourself or your communication patterns?
- What did you learn about levels of dialogue?
- How might you use this learning to improve communications in your daily life?

(Ten to fifteen minutes.)

Variations

- With intact work groups, depending on their sophistication and willingness, each participant may be asked to identify issues or conflicts he or she may have with another team member and then discuss the issue directly with that person using this process. This does increase risk and may require more skill and intervention on the part of the facilitator. Additional time for each discussion is generally needed.
- The role of observer can be eliminated, and the activity can be done in pairs.

The Pfeiffer Book of Successful Team-Building Tools

LEVELS OF DIALOGUE THEORY SHEET

Levels of Openness

When "sending" messages, people need to be clear, concise, and direct; they need to describe behaviors or events rather than attribute motives to the actions of others or make character judgments. In *The Truth Option* (Schutz, 1984), Schutz describes "levels of openness" that are dependent on our awareness of our feelings about what is happening (consciousness) and our willingness to express those feelings (courage).

Level –1: Unaware. Sometimes it takes time to become aware of how you feel. Until you become aware of how you feel, you cannot tell others.

Level 0: Withholding. Withholding is the level at which you become aware of how you feel but you are unwilling to express it, at least directly, to the person involved.

Level 1: "You are . . . ." Level 1 openness is the realm of judgments, accusations, and name calling.

Level 2: "About you I feel . . . ." A person who makes a statement of this sort is revealing something about himself or herself rather than making judgments about the character of another person. This invites dialogue and increases understanding.

Level 3: "Because . . . ." At Level 3, you describe the circumstances, events, or behaviors that gave rise to the feelings revealed at Level 2.

Level 4: "Which means . . . ." Everything that happens in our lives has meaning for us. "Meaning," however, is whatever we choose it to be; it therefore is different for each person. This level of openness allows true dialogue to occur and creates an opportunity to clear up the current misunderstanding and to build a stronger relationship for the future.

Level 5: "My fear about myself is . . . ." Level 5 is the deepest level of openness and requires a great deal of self-awareness to achieve. Admittedly, few people reach this level of openness in conversations; however, when they do, the results are often astonishing. As in Level 4, communicating at this level creates a real opportunity for understanding.

Levels of Listening

When receiving messages, people need to listen carefully, make eye contact, and occasionally paraphrase what the other person is saying, as in "What I hear you saying is . . . ." These "levels of listening" (Copeland, 1991) parallel the "levels of openness."

Level –1: Unaware. The unaware listener is someone more preoccupied with his or her own thoughts or activities than with what you have to say.

Level 0: Avoiding. In contrast, the avoiding listener is acutely aware of the messenger, but does not want to hear what he or she has to say.

Level 1: "No! You are . . . ." When confronted, the Level 1 listener deflects the focus back to the speaker. Immediately deflecting the focus in this manner only serves to escalate emotions and limit the possibility of genuine dialogue, understanding, or resolution.

Level 2: "You shouldn't feel that way." At Level 2 the listener is quick to correct any "inappropriate" feelings being expressed (meaning any feelings that make him or her uncomfortable). This level of "listening" tends to stop communication so that neither party understands the other very well.

Level 3: "Let me tell you . . . ." Level 3 listening is listening for an opportunity to tell your own story; it is characterized by interruptions. The "competitor" tops your story with his or her own successes or calamities, the "debater" corrects your facts, and the "problem solver" waits for an opportunity to solve your problems.

Level 4: "Tell me more." This level is a significant departure from the ones preceding it. At Level 4, the speaker is invited to explain the point, give examples, and discuss how he or she feels and why. Only at this level does a speaker begin to feel that the listener genuinely cares and wants to understand.

Level 5: "What I hear you saying is . . . ." When you paraphrase and reflect back the speaker's concerns, especially when you include the quality and quantity of his or her feelings, that person knows that he or she has been understood. This does not mean that you necessarily agree, but you understand his or her point of view.

Conclusion

Communication is a lively two-way process in which people alternate speaking and listening. Ideally, a person who listens attentively at Level 5 also responds at an appropriate level. The benefits of improving our communications are enormous, and those benefits are attainable. We are most believable when all aspects of our communications are congruent, that is, when our tone, volume, inflection, and body language are in harmony. Not only does this increase effectiveness and productivity, but when we become conscious of the fears that limit us and have the courage to communicate at deeper levels, we can build trusting interpersonal relationships that enrich our lives.

References

Copeland, G. (1991). *Levels of dialogue.* Muir Beach, CA: Will Schutz Associates.

Schutz, W. (1984). *The truth option: A practical technology for human affairs.* Berkeley, CA: Ten Speed Press.

Levels of Dialogue Awareness Log

Instructions: Complete this log by recalling several recent conflict situations in which you withheld your feelings, did not tell the whole truth, or were otherwise less than fully open. Write down the reason that you gave yourself for doing this (what you feared would happen). Then identify what you believe is the fear you have about yourself that influenced your decision to withhold in that situation.

Incident (Withhold or Lie)	Fear of What Might Happen (Level 4)	Fear About Myself (Level 5)
1. *I pretended I was not upset by what Terry said.*	*We would get into an argument.*	*I handle conflict poorly. I say things I don't mean to hurt people's feelings*
2.		
3.		
4.		

Source: *The Awareness Log* by Thompson Barton, 1989, Muir Beach, CA: Will Schutz Associates Update.

LEVELS OF DIALOGUE OBSERVER SHEET

Instructions: Use Table 1 to indicate the level at which the speaker and the listener are operating by placing a checkmark next to that level each time you observe it. Note examples of both verbal and nonverbal behavior whenever possible.

Table 1. Levels of Openness and Listening[1]

Specific Examples	Speaker Using This Level	Levels of Openness	Specific Examples	Speaker Using This Level	Levels of Openness
		−1. Unaware			−1. Unaware
		0. Avoiding			0. Withholding
		1. "No! You are…"			1. "You are…"
		2. "You shouldn't feel that way…"			2. "About you I feel…"
		3. "Let me tell" you…"			3. "Because…"
		4. "Tell me more…"			4. "Which means…"
		5. "What I hear you saying is:"			5. "My fear about myself is…"

---

[1]Levels of Openness are reprinted with permission from *The Truth Option* by Will Schutz. Copyright © 1984 by Will Schutz, Ten Speed Press, Berkeley, CA. Levels of Listening are based on *Levels of Dialogue* (Copeland, 1991). Used with permission.

Address the following questions as you debrief the discussion with your partners:

Which levels were used most? How do you account for that?

Which levels were used least? How do you account for that?

What feelings were communicated verbally? Nonverbally?

STRENGTHS AND NEEDS: USING FEEDBACK FOR GROUP DEVELOPMENT

Terri Burchett

Goals

- To provide an opportunity for the team members to give one another feedback about the strengths they bring to their team.

- To offer the team members a chance to identify what they like on the job and what they would like to change and then to share this information with one another.

- To provide a structure through which the team members can express what they need from one another.

- To provide an opportunity for the team members to do action planning based on their strengths, likes, items they would like to change, and needs.

Team Size

All members of an ongoing team.

Time Required

This activity is conducted in two sessions. Session 1, sharing feedback, requires two to three and one-half hours, depending on the size of the team. Session 2, action planning based on the information shared in the first session, requires approximately three hours.

Materials

Session 1

- For each team member, enough copies of Strengths and Needs Work Sheet A to equal the number of other members. (For example, if there are six members, each member receives five copies of the work sheet.)

- One copy of Strengths and Needs Work Sheet B for each team member.

- For each team member, enough copies of Strengths and Needs Work Sheet C to equal the number of other members.

- One copy of the Strengths and Needs Sample Planning Chart for each team member.

- A pencil for each team member.

- A clipboard or other portable writing surface for each team member.

- A newsprint poster prepared in advance with the following content:

  Guidelines for Receiving Feedback

  - Listen to feedback; do not discount, debate, analyze it.

  - If you don't understand, ask for clarification/examples.

  - Paraphrase feedback. Verify that you heard correctly.

  - If you wish, thank the person who gave feedback.

- Masking tape for posting newsprint.

Session 2

- Each team member's poster-sized planning chart (prepared in advance and brought to the session by each member).

- Each team member's notes about (a) how he or she can capitalize more on personal strengths and likes and (b) what he or she might be able to do about desired changes and about meeting others' expressed needs (prepared in advance and brought to the session by each member).

- A copy of the Strengths and Needs Action-Planning Guide for each team member plus a supply of extra copies in case the members want them.

- A large supply of blank paper (enough so that each team member can have at least ten sheets if desired).

- A pencil for each team member.

- A clipboard or other portable writing surface for each team member.

- The newsprint poster on guidelines for receiving feedback (prepared for the first session).

- A newsprint flip chart and several colors of felt-tipped markers.

- Masking tape for posting newsprint.

Physical Setting

For Session 1, a room with movable chairs placed in a circle. The circle should be close to the wall on which the facilitator plans to display the newsprint poster (see Materials, Session 1).

For Session 2, a room with movable chairs and plenty of wall space for posting newsprint. It is preferable, but not essential, to have a table on which the team members can work to complete their strengths poster (see Process, Session 2, step 10).

Process

Session 1

1. The facilitator explains that the activity will be conducted in two sessions: In the first session the members will give one another feedback about their strengths as team members, educate one another about what they like and what they would like to change on the job, and state what they need from one another; in the second session the members will do action planning based on information shared during the previous session. The facilitator explains that by sharing this information and acting on it, the members can strengthen their team and further its development. (Five minutes.)

2. Each team member is given the appropriate number of copies of Strengths and Needs Work Sheet A, a pencil, and a clipboard or other portable writing surface and is asked to read the instructions on the work sheet. Subsequently, the facilitator reviews the instructions and elicits and answers questions about them. (Five minutes.)

3. Each team member is instructed to complete one copy of the work sheet for every member of the team except himself or herself. (Ten to fifteen minutes.)

4. After all members have completed their copies of work sheet A, the facilitator explains that each team member will take a turn at receiving feedback and that the maximum time each person has for giving feedback is one minute. The facilitator posts the prepared newsprint sheet of guidelines for receiving feedback, reviews these guidelines with the team members, and elicits and answers questions. These guidelines remain posted throughout the session. (Five minutes.)

5. The facilitator asks for a volunteer to receive feedback. (If no team member volunteers, the facilitator selects one and explains that the remaining members will take turns in clockwise order.) After all feedback statements have been read aloud and clarified to the feedback

recipient's satisfaction, the facilitator instructs those who read statements to give their sheets to the feedback recipient. Then the facilitator either asks for another volunteer or selects the person who is next in clockwise order. The feedback procedure is repeated until all members have received feedback.

6. The facilitator distributes copies of Strengths and Needs Work Sheet B and asks the team members to complete this sheet according to the instructions. (Ten minutes.)

7. After the members have completed work sheet B, they are told that they are to take turns reading their work sheets aloud to the team. The facilitator emphasizes that while one member is reading, the others are to listen carefully; afterward the listeners may ask questions for clarification. Then the facilitator asks for a volunteer or selects a team member to begin, and the procedure continues until all members have taken a turn.

8. Each team member is given the appropriate number of copies of Strengths and Needs Work Sheet C and is asked to read the instructions. Then the facilitator reviews the instructions and elicits and answers questions about them. (Five minutes.)

9. The facilitator instructs each team member to complete one copy of the work sheet for every member of the team except himself or herself. (Fifteen to twenty minutes.)

10. After all members have completed their copies of work sheet C, the facilitator explains that each team member will take a turn at receiving feedback about what the other members need from him or her and that the maximum time each person has for giving feedback is one minute. The facilitator then reminds the team members of the posted guidelines for receiving feedback. (Five minutes.)

11. The facilitator asks for a volunteer to receive feedback. (If no team member volunteers, the facilitator selects one and asks that the remaining members take their turns in clockwise order.) After all feedback statements have been read aloud and clarified to the feedback recipient's satisfaction, the facilitator instructs those who read statements to give their sheets to the feedback recipient. Then the facilitator either asks for a second volunteer or selects the person who is next in clockwise order. This procedure is repeated until all team members have received feedback. *(Note: This step can produce a great deal of affect, so the facilitator needs to be prepared to intervene appropriately.)*

12. The facilitator leads a discussion based on these questions:

- How did you feel when you gave feedback to your fellow team members? How did you feel when you received feedback?

- What did you discover about what your fellow team members like on the job? What did you discover about what they would change?

- What strengths are represented in this team? How do those strengths benefit the team? How do they benefit the organization?

- How is it beneficial for team members to talk about what they like on the job, what they would change, and what they need from one another?

- What have you learned about yourself as a member of this team?

- What have you learned about your fellow team members that helps you understand better what you need from them?

- What have you learned about the feedback process?

- What have you learned about the connection among people's strengths, what they like on the job, what they would change, and what others need from them?

- How can you use what you have learned to enhance the productivity or cohesiveness of the team?

13. The facilitator makes arrangements for the second session, again explaining that the purpose of that session is to do action planning based on the information just shared. The facilitator gives each team member a copy of the Strengths and Needs Sample Planning Chart; explains that the chart offers a way to display information from completed copies of work sheets A, B, and C; and asks each member to prepare a similar chart in poster (newsprint) size for the action-planning session. In addition, each member is instructed to spend some time thinking and making notes about (a) how he or she can capitalize more on personal strengths and likes and (b) what he or she might be able to do about desired changes and about meeting others' expressed needs. The facilitator emphasizes that each member is to bring the prepared planning chart and the notes to the action-planning session.

Session 2: Action Planning

1. The facilitator asks each team member to post his or her poster-sized planning chart.

2. The facilitator displays the newsprint poster on guidelines for receiving feedback and reviews the content with the team members, urging them to follow these guidelines during the session. This poster remains on display throughout the session. (Five minutes.)

3. The facilitator distributes blank paper, pencils, and clipboards or other portable writing surfaces. The team members are instructed to circulate around the room, reading one another's planning charts. The facilitator encourages the members to jot down notes about agreements they would like to make with one another and any other ideas that occur to them. (Twenty to thirty minutes.)

4. The facilitator reassembles the team and invites the members to share their reactions and the contents of their notes. As ideas are expressed, the facilitator records highlights on newsprint, posts the newsprint, and displays it for the remainder of the session. (Fifteen to twenty minutes.)

5. The facilitator leads a brief discussion about patterns, similarities, and differences in the planning charts and the implications for the team. (Ten minutes.)

6. The team members are asked to spend ten minutes making arrangements to meet with one another during the next hour for the purpose of making agreements and planning whatever action they wish. (Ten minutes.)

7. The facilitator gives each team member a copy of the Strengths and Needs Action-Planning Guide and several sheets of blank paper, announcing that extra copies of the guide and extra blank paper are available if the members need them. The facilitator briefly reviews the action-planning steps, explaining how they fit into the action-planning process, and ensures that the members understand the procedure they are to follow with their partners. (Ten minutes.)

8. The facilitator instructs the team members to spend the next hour meeting with partners to make agreements and to plan action. As the members work, the facilitator monitors their activity, announces the remaining time at intervals, and provides assistance if needed. (One hour.)

9. The facilitator announces the end of the planning time, reassembles the total team, and encourages the members to make arrangements later to do any planning that they did not have time to complete during the session. The members are invited to share some of their one-sentence summaries of the agreements they have reached. As they share, the facilitator records highlights on newsprint. (Ten minutes.)

The Pfeiffer Book of Successful Team-Building Tools

10. The facilitator gives the team members a sheet of newsprint and several different colors of felt-tipped markers and asks them to make a poster that celebrates the strengths of their team. (Ten to fifteen minutes.)

11. After the poster has been completed, the facilitator posts it and invites the team members to share their reactions to making the poster. Afterward the facilitator congratulates the members on their work during the two sessions and encourages them to keep their poster and to display it in their usual meeting room or elsewhere to remind them of the strengths in the team.

Variations

■ The entire activity may be completed as a one-day team-building intervention. In this case one of two approaches may be taken after Session 1, step 12: (a) The homework assignments from step 13 may be omitted, and the team members may be asked to work from their completed handouts; or (b) the facilitator may ask the team members to complete the homework assignments in the team setting and then proceed with action planning. Because either of these two alternatives increases the time required for Session 2, the facilitator may want to omit step 5 from Session 2 and make any other time adjustments necessary.

■ The facilitator or the team leader may collect all completed work sheets, create a planning chart for each team member, assemble the resulting charts into a handout, and distribute copies of the handout for use during Session 2.

■ With a team in which some trust has already been built through team-building activities, this activity may be shortened by using only work sheets A and C. With a team in which no team-building activities have been used, this activity may be shortened by using only work sheets A and B.

Strengths and Needs Work Sheet A

Instructions: Fill out one of these sheets for every other member of your team. Write your name in the "From" blank and the name of the person who is to receive the feedback in the "To" blank. Then spend a couple of minutes writing a brief but specific completion to the statement that follows. Use only the space provided; do not write lengthy paragraphs. Give examples if they would be helpful in explaining what you mean.

Later you will read your statement aloud, clarify your meaning if asked, and then give this sheet to the person.

Here are two sample statements:

- *An area of strength that you bring to the team is* your willingness to help any coworker who needs it. I really appreciated it when you offered to help me proofread the minutes of the department meeting last week, and Alice told me she was grateful when you volunteered to make copies of those minutes.

- *An area of strength that you bring to the team is* your writing ability. When any of us can't find the right word to use in a letter or report, we can turn to you for suggestions.

From ————————————————————————————

To ——————————————————————————————

An area of strength that you bring to the team is:

STRENGTHS AND NEEDS WORK SHEET B

Instructions: Consider the different aspects of your job: task assignments, relationships with coworkers, equipment, systems, procedures, policies, and so on. Then read and complete the following statements, being as specific as you can but using only the space provided.

When you are considering what you like about your job, think about what you find satisfying, motivating, or challenging in a positive sense.

When you are considering what you *would like to change,* think about what you find dissatisfying, demotivating, or stressful.

Later you will read this sheet aloud, clarifying your meaning if asked. Here are two sample statements:

- *What I like about my job is* (1) the large variety of tasks, (2) flexible hours, (3) long-term projects that I can be in charge of and really sink my teeth into, and (4) the opportunity to be mentored by people I respect and admire.

- *What I would like to change about my job is* (1) the amount of time I spend making copies at the copying machine, (2) the frantic pace at deadline time, (3) the lack of privacy and the noise in my office, and (4) the unreliable phone system.

What I like about my job is:

What I would like to change about my job is:

Strengths and Needs Work Sheet C

Instructions: Fill out one of these sheets for every other team member. Write your name in the "From" blank and the name of the person who is to receive the feedback in the "To" blank. Then spend a couple of minutes completing the statement that follows.

Be specific in describing how you would like the person to act and under what circumstances, but do not write lengthy paragraphs; use only the space provided. If you wish, you may explain why you need what you are asking for and/or how the person would benefit by giving you what you need.

Later you will read your statement aloud, clarify your meaning if asked, and then give this sheet to the person.

Here are two sample statements:

■ *What I need most from you is* to get me the new-product descriptions three weeks before the deadline for advertising copy instead of only a week before. Having three weeks to write the copy would mean I wouldn't have to drop everything and race to meet the deadline.

■ *What I need most from you is* to give me some space when you see that I'm upset. It usually takes me at least fifteen minutes to calm down enough to talk about what's bothering me. After some cooling-off time I can be more appreciative of your comments and your concern.

From _____

To _____

What I need most from you is:

STRENGTHS AND NEEDS SAMPLE PLANNING CHART

CHRIS

Strengths	Likes	Desired Changes	Others' Needs
Writing ability Cheerful disposition Willingness to help Understanding of statistics Knowledge of company procedures	Variety of tasks Flexible hours Long-term projects Being mentored	Too much time spent at copying machine Frantic pace at deadline time Lack of privacy and noise in office Unreliable phone system	Submit monthly reports sooner (Fred) Keep voice down when talking on phone (Karen) Give more feedback (Lee) Assist in writing product descriptions (Dale) Devise a handout on customer-service guidelines (Pat)

STRENGTHS AND NEEDS ACTION-PLANNING GUIDE

Action-Planning Steps

1. Define current situation.

2. Define desired change.

3. Describe how success will look or feel.

4. List steps to take.

5. Decide who will take steps.

6. List kinds of help/resources/approval needed.

7. List names of people who might help, provide resources, approve action.

8. Decide who will seek help, resources, approval.

9. Determine a deadline for each step.

10. Arrange to meet periodically to assess progress.

Procedure to Follow with Your Partner

1. Share ideas and suggestions.

2. Plan action.

3. Get feedback from each other about whether planned action would meet needs.

4. Negotiate as necessary.

5. Come to agreement about action to be taken.

6. Use any or all of the above action-planning steps, jotting down whatever information seems pertinent.

7. Summarize what you plan to do in a single sentence.

ANALYZING AND INCREASING OPEN BEHAVIOR: THE JOHARI WINDOW

Philip G. Hanson

Goals

- To describe open and closed behavior in terms of the Johari Window.
- To identify facilitating and inhibiting forces which may affect the exchange of feedback.
- To encourage the development of increased open behavior in the group through facilitated feedback.

Group Size

Eight to twelve participants. Several subgroups may be directed simultaneously.

Time Required

Approximately two and one-half hours.

Materials

- A copy of the Johari Window Self-Rating Sheet for each participant.
- A pencil for each participant.
- A copy of the Johari Window Model Theory Sheet for the facilitator.
- Newsprint and felt-tipped markers for each subgroup.
- A newsprint flip chart and a felt-tipped marker for the facilitator's use.
- Masking tape for posting newsprint.
- A copy of the Johari Window Model (optional).

Physical Setting

A room large enough to accommodate the group or subgroups and to allow subgroups to work comfortably and with minimal noise distraction.

Process

1. The facilitator begins with a lecturette to the total group on giving and receiving feedback, based on the Johari Window Model Theory Sheet. Central to the lecturette, the facilitator will emphasize how decreasing the "Blind Spot" (the area unknown to self) and decreasing the "Facade" (the area unknown to others) will increase the "Arena" (the area known to everyone), thereby fostering openness. The facilitator will also emphasize the role of meaningful feedback in this process.

2. Each participant is given a copy of the Johari Window Self-Rating Sheet and a pencil.

3. The facilitator suggests that one goal participants may have is to discover data about themselves that they were previously unaware of, i.e., "decreasing the Blind Spot." The only way they can do this is to solicit feedback and to be receptive to it. In terms of the Johari Window Model, the vertical line will move to the right as the "Blind Spot" is decreased.

4. The facilitator illustrates the decreasing "Blind Spot" on newsprint using the following model:

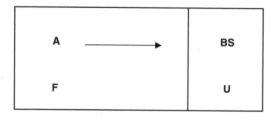

5. The facilitator explains that a scale from one to nine runs across the top of the Self-Rating Sheets, describing the extent to which a person solicits feedback. The participants are asked to think about their last group meeting and about times when they wondered how they were being perceived by other group members.

6. Participants then are asked to look at the scale across the top of the blank window and to find a point on that scale that describes the extent to which they actually solicited feedback in that group session.

The facilitator emphasizes that the participants are not rating how many times they felt the need for feedback but how many times they actually asked for it. The participants then are instructed to draw a vertical line to the bottom of the window from the point they have identified on the top scale.

7. The facilitator suggests that another goal they may have in the group setting is that of becoming more open by disclosing some of the data that they have kept from the group or by giving feedback to others, i.e., decreasing the "facade." The facilitator illustrates how the horizontal line drops when the "facade" is decreased:

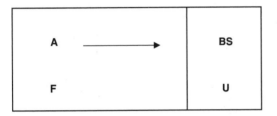

8. The facilitator tells the group to notice how as the "Blind Spot" and "Facade" decrease, the "Arena," or openness to others, increases. He or she then asks them to look at their Johari Window Self-Rating Sheets again and to notice on the left-hand margin a scale running from one to nine, measuring the extent to which a person discloses himself or herself, or gives feedback to the group. The facilitator asks the participants to think back again on their last group meeting(s) and remember how many times during that group session they felt the need to give feedback to other group members, express their own feelings and perceptions about themselves, or take a stand on group issues.

9. The participants are asked to locate on the scale at the left-hand margin the extent to which they actually gave feedback or disclosed themselves to the group. The facilitator emphasizes that they are to rate only the extent to which they actually gave feedback, not how many times they felt like doing so. When they have located the position on the scale they are to draw a horizontal line across the window pane.

10. At this point, the facilitator will illustrate the use of the Johari window by interpreting variously constructed windows.

11. The group or groups are divided into subgroups of three or four, depending upon the size of the group.

12. The facilitator asks the participants to take twenty to thirty minutes to share their windows with the members of their subgroups. They are to ask for feedback as to how they would have been rated in terms of soliciting and giving feedback, thus comparing self-ratings with others' perceptions. When this exchange is complete, they are to begin to identify the forces in their groups that make it easy or difficult to solicit or give feedback. As a subgroup they are to make a list of these facilitating and inhibiting forces, taking about fifteen minutes to accomplish this task. The facilitator supplies newsprint and felt-tipped markers to each subgroup.

13. After approximately forty-five minutes, the facilitator asks the participants to reassemble and to share the information generated by the subgroups. The subgroups are asked to integrate their lists into a final list of forces and in this process discuss what steps the group wants to take in order to increase facilitating forces and decrease inhibiting forces affecting the feedback process. The facilitator may wish to suggest that participants make contracts with one another as a method of increasing the exchange of feedback.

JOHARI WINDOW MODEL THEORY SHEET

The process of giving and receiving feedback can be illustrated through a model called the Johari window. The window was originally developed by two psychologists, Joseph Luft and Harry Ingham, for their program in group process. The model can be looked upon as a communication window through which you give and receive information about yourself and others.

Looking at the four panes in terms of columns and rows, the two columns represent the *self* and the two rows represent the *group*. Column one contains "things that I know about myself;" column two contains "things that I do not know about myself." Row one contains "things that the group knows about me"; row two contains "things that the group does not know about me." The information contained in these rows and columns is not static but moves from one pane to another as the level of mutual trust and the exchange of feedback varies in the group. As a consequence of this movement, the size and shape of the panes within the window will vary.

The first pane, called the Arena, contains things that I know about myself and about which the group knows. It is an area characterized by free and open exchange of information between myself and others. The behavior here is public and available to everyone. The Arena increases in size as the level of trust increases between individuals or between the individual and his or her group and more information, particularly personally relevant information, is shared.

The second pane, the Blind Spot, contains information that I do not know about myself but of which the group may know. As I begin to participate in the group, I communicate all kinds of information of which I am not aware, but which is being picked up by other people. This information may be in the form of verbal cues, mannerisms, the way I say things, or the style in which I relate to others. The extent to which we are insensitive to much of our own behavior and what it may communicate to others can be quite surprising and disconcerting. For example, a group member once commented that every time their facilitator was asked to comment on some personal or group issue, the facilitator always coughed before answering.

In pane three are things that I know about myself but of which the group is unaware. For one reason or another I keep this information hidden from them. My fear may be that if the group knew of my feelings, perceptions, and opinions about the group or individuals in the group, they might reject, attack, or hurt me in some way. As a consequence, I withhold this information. This pane is called the "Facade" or "Hidden Area." One of the reasons I may keep this information to myself is that I do not see the supportive elements in the group. My assumption is that if I start revealing my feelings, thoughts, and reactions, group members might judge me negatively. I cannot find out, however, how members will really react unless I test these assumptions and reveal something of myself. In other words, if I do not take some risks, I will never learn the reality or unreality of my assumptions. On the other hand, I may keep certain kinds of information to myself when my motives for doing so are to control or manipulate others.

The last pane contains things that neither I nor the group knows about me. Some of this material may be so far below the surface that I may never become aware of it. Other material, however, may be below the surface of awareness to both myself and the group but can be made public through an exchange of feedback. This area is called the "Unknown" and may represent such things as intrapersonal dynamics, early childhood memories, latent potentialities, and unrecognized resources. Because the internal boundaries can move backward and forward or up and down as a consequence of soliciting or giving feedback, it would be possible to have a window in which there would be no Unknown. Because knowing all about oneself is extremely unlikely, the Unknown in the model illustrated is extended so that part of it will always remain unknown. If you are inclined to think in Freudian terms, you can call this extension the "Unconscious."

One goal we may set for ourselves in the group setting is to decrease our Blind Spots, i.e., move the vertical line to the right. How can I reduce my Blind Spot? Because this area contains information that the group members know about me but of which I am unaware, the only way I can increase my awareness of this material is to get feedback from the group. As a consequence, I need to develop a receptive attitude to encourage group members to give me feedback. That is, I need to actively solicit feedback from group members in such a way that they will feel comfortable in giving it to me. The more I do this, the more the vertical line will move to the right.

Another goal we may set for ourselves, in terms of our model, is to reduce the Facade, i.e., move the horizontal line down. How can I reduce my Facade? Because this area contains information that I have been keeping from the group, I can reduce my Facade by giving feedback to the group or group members concerning my reactions to what is going on in the group and inside of me. In this instance, I am giving feedback or disclosing myself in terms of my perceptions, feelings, and opinions about things in myself and in others. Through this process the group knows where I stand and does not need to guess about or interpret what my behavior means. The more self-disclosure and feedback I give, the farther down I push the horizontal line.

You will notice that while we are reducing our Blind Spots and Facades through the process of giving and soliciting feedback, we are, at the same time, increasing the size of our Arena or public area.

JOHARI WINDOW SELF-RATING SHEET

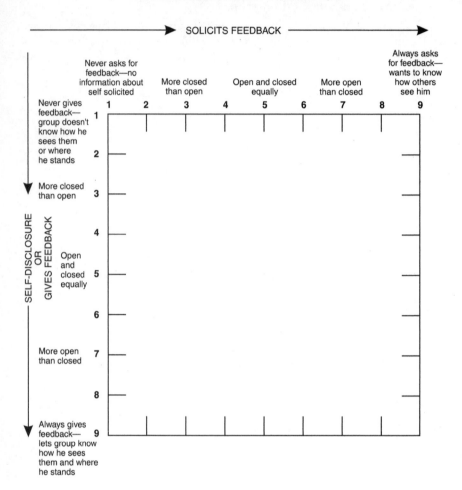

The Pfeiffer Book of Successful Team-Building Tools

Johari Window Mode

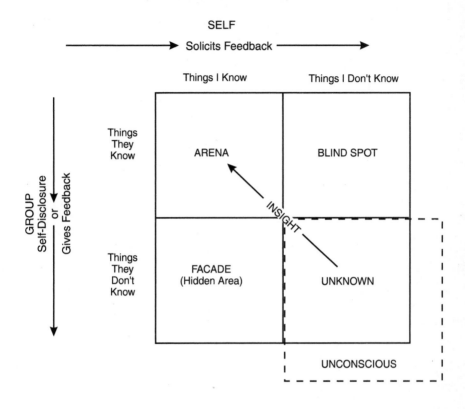

_____

    Requests to reprint the Johari Window Model should be addressed to Mayfield Publishing Company in Mountain View, California.

6 Effective Decision Making

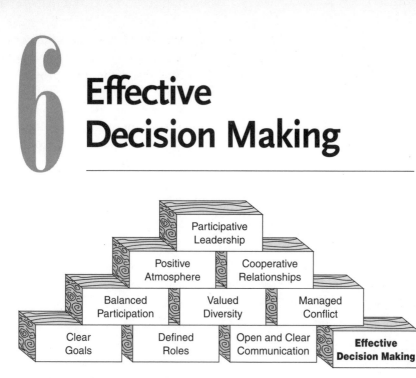

Participative Leadership

Positive Atmosphere | Cooperative Relationships

Balanced Participation | Valued Diversity | Managed Conflict

Clear Goals | Defined Roles | Open and Clear Communication | **Effective Decision Making**

Copyright © 1999 ebb associates inc

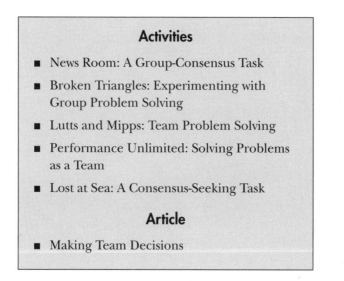

Activities

- News Room: A Group-Consensus Task

- Broken Triangles: Experimenting with Group Problem Solving

- Lutts and Mipps: Team Problem Solving

- Performance Unlimited: Solving Problems as a Team

- Lost at Sea: A Consensus-Seeking Task

Article

- Making Team Decisions

Effective Decision Making is the last building block in the foundation of the model. Without effective decision making, a team impedes how well and how fast it accomplishes its goals. A team can make decisions in many ways, with consensus as the one that is least understood.

143

Five activities hold the key to helping teams be more effective decision makers. Two of these address reaching consensus. The first, "News Room," gives the team a chance to reach consensus under pressure and to discuss the results. The second, "Lost at Sea," is a tried-and-true classic that many of us have heard about. Now you can use it with your teams. Two other activities focus on the process of making decisions. "Broken Triangles" is a modern version of "Broken Squares," an experiential learning activity you may have used in the past. The questions used in processing the activity have a 21st Century focus. The scenario in "Performance Unlimited" can be easily tailored to reflect actual issues a team is experiencing. Finally, "Lutts and Mipps" is a solid classic in which many teamwork issues evolve.

An article, "Making Team Decisions," rounds out this chapter and contains valuable information for you and your teams. It presents seven decision-making methods for teams and introduces you to two tools to enhance team decision making.

NEWS ROOM: A GROUP-CONSENSUS TASK

Heidi Ann Campbell and Heather Jean Campbell

Goals

- To explore the communication processes that emerge in creating a collaborative product.
- To investigate the process of obtaining group consensus.

Group Size

A maximum of three groups with eight to ten participants per group.

Time Required

Fifty to fifty-five minutes.

Materials

- A pack of 3" × 5" index cards with "news" words written on each card for each group.
- A copy of News Room Suggested Word Options for the facilitator.

Physical Setting

A large open space. Tables and chairs for the groups are optional.

Process

1. The facilitator introduces the activity and divides the participants into groups, if need be.

2. The facilitator describes the activity: "You are the editors, writers, and producers for a news program (or news publication) and are under a strict deadline to write a fast-breaking news story on time. A news story typically has multiple authors who must work together to produce one product. Using the information and resources available to you, you must, *as a group*, create a news story within a limited amount

---

of time. The story will be broadcast (or goes to press) in fifteen minutes. As a group, you must select the words to be used and decide on their order of presentation within the news story." (Five minutes.)

3. Each group receives a pack of index cards with "news" words written on each card.

4. The facilitator says that the members of each group are to arrange the word cards to create the story. The group must reach consensus (at least some degree of agreement from each member) on the sequence of words in the story; it may not make decisions by majority rule or voting. Complete sentences are not necessary, but the "basics" of the story should be apparent. The group must use as many words as there are participants in the group. Words may not be used more than once. Each group is to select a spokesperson who will present its story for editorial approval at the end of the activity. The facilitator informs the group of the subject of the story and tells the members that no questions will be answered once the activity starts. (Ten minutes.)

5. As the groups work on the task, the facilitator gives time warnings. When the groups have completed the task or when the time is up, the facilitator asks for a spokesperson from each group to present its story, in turn. (Fifteen minutes plus five minutes per report).

6. The facilitator informs the groups that the producer (or editor-in-chief) says that because of new editorial priorities, the stories are too long. The groups have up to two minutes in which to eliminate three to five words from their stories.

7. When the time is up, the facilitator requests the spokespersons to present the groups' new stories. (Five minutes.)

8. The facilitator leads the group members in processing the activity. The following questions may be used:
   - How did you feel as you went about this activity?
   - Was it easy or difficult to reach consensus on the words in the story? Why or why not?
   - What did you notice about the process as time pressures mounted? As changes had to be made?
   - How does the process of a group creating a single product affect the members' communications?
   - Are you currently involved in any situations in which there are multiple creators? What did this activity teach you that you could apply to those situations?

(Fifteen to twenty minutes.)

Variations

- An entire group or selected members may be designated as "mute" for the activity. To signify a mute person, tie a bandanna or scarf loosely around his or her neck or arm. Additional processing questions could include the following:
  - How was your communication impacted by being mute?
  - Were you able to contribute, or were you ignored?
  - How did you compensate for your limitations?
  - How did you have to think or act differently to communicate nonverbally?
- The words given may be pertinent to a story that is relevant to the group members, based on an issue that they are encountering.
- The re-editing task (steps 6 and 7) may be eliminated.

NEWS ROOM SUGGESTED WORD OPTIONS

Earthquake: tremors, fire, buildings, collapse, shaking, people, warning, destruction, heat, bystanders, hidden, wreckage, rubble, emergency, fleeing, ambulance, broken, homeless, safety, help, no, crash, almost, forever, escape, near, around, call, above, sudden, preparation, evacuation

Example of possible story: Tremors. No warning. Buildings collapse. People escape rubble. Bystanders help homeless. Emergency evacuation.

Search and Rescue Mission: climber, fate, snow, avalanche, helicopter, terrain, ground patrol, search, searchers, rope, leg, arm, hiking, lost, found, broken, fall, suspected, fright, delay, injuries, hope, unknown, almost, fears, continue, help, calculated, mishap, remote, planned, icy, nerves, need, ask, overnight, rescue

Example of possible story: Climber lost overnight. Remote icy terrain. Ground patrol fears mishap. Suspected injuries. Helicopter search. Snow delays rescue. Unknown fears.

Election: opposition, winner, loser, parties, victory, unexpected, planned, votes, counted, narrow, incumbent, shakeup, recall, debate, careful, issues, results, avoided, clear, confused, challenge, victory, election, margin, defeat, decision, speech, rally, plans, announcement

Example of possible story: Incumbent avoided debate. Issues confused. Votes counted. Opposition victory clear.

Broken Triangles: Experimenting with Group Problem Solving

Janet Mills

Goals

- To offer participants an opportunity to experience some of the elements of cooperation in solving a group problem.

- To develop participants' awareness of behaviors that may obstruct or contribute to the solution of a group problem.

- To allow the participants to experience how the completion of a group task is affected by behavioral restrictions.

Group Size

As many as six subgroups of five participants each. If the total group is not divisible by five, one to four participants may be assigned to help the facilitator monitor the activity.

Time Required

Approximately forty-five minutes.

Materials

- One set of broken triangles for each subgroup (prepared in advance; see the Broken Triangles Preparation Sheet for the Facilitator).
- One copy of the Broken Triangles Instruction Sheet for each participant.

Physical Setting

A room large enough for the subgroups to work without being able to see the other subgroups' puzzles. Each subgroup needs a table with five chairs.

Process

1. The facilitator forms subgroups of five participants each and, if applicable, asks the remaining participants to help monitor compliance to the restrictions listed on the instruction sheet. Each subgroup selects one of its members to be captain.

2. Each participant is given a copy of the Broken Triangles Instruction Sheet. The facilitator reads the handout aloud, eliciting and answering questions and ensuring that everyone understands the instructions. (Five minutes.)

3. A set of broken triangles is given to each subgroup captain. The facilitator asks the captains to leave the bags unopened until the signal to begin work is given.

4. The facilitator asks the subgroups to begin. It is important that the facilitator and participant monitors closely observe the process during this activity. Attention should be called to anyone disobeying the rules, and the entire group should be reminded of the specific rule that was broken. (Twenty minutes.)

5. When the last subgroup has completed the task, the facilitator reconvenes the total group and leads a discussion by asking questions such as the following:

   - How focused were you on your subgroup's task, as opposed to completing your own puzzle?

   - Under what conditions were you willing to give up pieces of a finished puzzle? How did you feel about giving pieces away?

   - Which of your behaviors helped you complete the task? Which of your behaviors hindered you?

   - How did you feel about the restrictions imposed on you? How did these restrictions affect your performance? What did you do to overcome those restrictions?

   - Why did some people break the rules? What was the effect of calling attention to those who broke the rules?

   - At work, what kinds of rules and restrictions hinder you and your work group in communicating, solving problems, and achieving goals? What do you do to get past those rules and restrictions?

   - What did you learn during this activity about communicating and cooperating to solve a group problem when restrictions are imposed? What can you do in the future to improve your perform-ance despite restrictions?

(Fifteen to twenty minutes.)

Variations

- Ten-person subgroups may be formed, with two duplicate sets of five triangles each distributed. Subgroups of six to nine members may also be formed; in this case, a broken-triangle set with one triangle for each person would be prepared, with as many duplications of the five tri-angles as necessary.

- When some subgroups have completed their puzzles and others are still working, the facilitator may convene a "consultant group" from those who have finished and ask these participants to come up with one piece of advice for those who are still working. The "consultants" then observe the effect of that advice on the working subgroups. After ten minutes, if all subgroups still have not finished, the consultants may volunteer a second piece of advice. Again, they should observe the effects.

- Extra participants may be assigned to be observers. Or the participants may be assembled into six-member subgroups so that every subgroup has an observer.

- The activity may be conducted with ongoing teams.

This activity is an adaptation of (1) "Broken Squares: Nonverbal Problem Solving" (p. 25) by Tom Isgar, 1968, in *A Handbook of Structured Experiences for Human Relations Training*, Vol. I, by John E. Jones and J. William Pfeiffer (Eds.), San Francisco: Pfeiffer; and (2) Communication Patterns in Task-Oriented Groups" by Alex Bavelas, in *Journal of the Acoustical Society of America*, 1950, *22*, 225–230. Adapted with permission. See also "The Five Squares Problem: An Instructional Aid in Group Cooperation" by Alex Bavelas, in *Studies in Personnel Psychology*, 1973, *5*, 29–38.

BROKEN TRIANGLES PREPARATION SHEET FOR THE FACILITATOR

A set of "broken triangles" is to be given to each subgroup. This set consists of five bundles of poster-board puzzle pieces. Each bundle contains three pieces of the puzzle, and these three pieces are paper clipped together. Each of the five bundles is stored in a sandwich-size, resealable plastic bag. When properly arranged, the puzzle pieces in the set will form five triangles of equal size and shape.

To prepare a set, cut out five squares of poster board, each exactly six inches square. (All five squares of the set must be from the same color of poster board.) Find the midpoint of one side of a square, and create an isosceles triangle (a triangle with two equal sides) by drawing a light line from the midpoint to each of the opposite corners of the square (see Figure 1). Repeat this process for the other four squares. Then cut out all of the triangles. Save the triangles and discard the cutaway pieces of the squares.

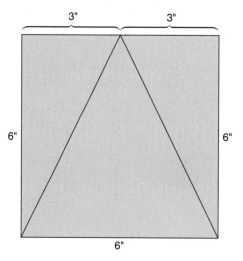

Figure 1. Making an Isosceles Triangle from a Square

Lightly draw lines on each triangle as indicated in Figure 2, and cut on those lines. (Do not reproduce the letters shown in Figure 2; these are for your information only.) The five pieces marked "A" must be exactly the same size. Similarly, the two pieces marked "B" must be exactly the same size, and the two marked "E" must be the same size. Several combinations of puzzle pieces will form one or two triangles, but only one combination will form all five triangles.

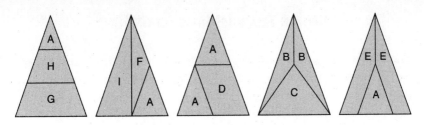

Figure 2. Creating the Final Puzzle Pieces

Repeat the entire process to make as many sets as there will be subgroups. Although all pieces of a set must be made from the same color of poster board, each set should be made from a different color. This precaution will keep pieces from the various sets from getting mixed up.

Into each sandwich-size, resealable plastic bag, place the following bundles of puzzle pieces, paper clipped together:

Bundle 1: A, A, A

Bundle 2: A, A, C

Bundle 3: B, D, E

Bundle 4: F, H, E

Bundle 5: G, B, I

Broken Triangles Instruction Sheet

Your subgroup captain will be given a plastic bag that contains a set of puzzle pieces for forming five triangles. Your captain then will give you and each of the other subgroup members three pieces, paper-clipped together. The three pieces you receive belong to you; you alone will decide whether or not to give any of your pieces to other members of your subgroup.

When the facilitator gives the signal to begin, you and your fellow subgroup members will begin the task of forming *five triangles of equal size and shape.*

The following restrictions are imposed during this activity:

1. There is to be no *verbal* communication of any kind.

2. There is to be no nonverbal communication: no begging, pointing, staring, or emotional displays.

3. Each member must complete a puzzle of his or her own. The members may not create a central communal space for constructing puzzles together.

4. A member may pass only one puzzle piece at a time to another member.

5. Each member must keep at least one puzzle piece at all times.

LUTTS AND MIPPS: TEAM PROBLEM SOLVING*

Editors

Goals

- To study the sharing of information within a team.
- To focus on cooperation in team problem solving.
- To offer the team members an opportunity to observe the emergence of leadership behavior in team problem solving.

Group Size

All members of an ongoing team.

Time Required

Approximately one hour.

Materials

- A copy of the Lutts and Mipps Instruction Form for each team member.
- One set of Lutts and Mipps Information Cards, prepared in advance. To make the cards, the facilitator types each of the twenty-six sentences on a 3" x 5" index card (one sentence per card).
- A copy of the Lutts and Mipps Reaction Form for each team member.
- A pencil for each team member.

Physical Setting

A room with movable chairs so that the team members can be seated in a circle. Writing surfaces of some type should be provided.

---

*The task in this activity is based on a problem by Rimoldi, *Training in Problem-Solving*, Publication No. 21, Loyola University Psychometrics Laboratory.

Process

1. The facilitator distributes copies of the Lutts and Mipps Instruction Form and asks the team members to read this handout.

2. After ensuring that the team members understand the task, the facilitator distributes the information cards randomly. (The team must be given all twenty-six cards.) Pencils are also distributed. Then the team is told to begin its work.

3. After twenty minutes the facilitator interrupts, distributes copies of the reaction form, and instructs the team members to complete the reaction form individually. (Fifteen minutes.)

4. The facilitator announces the solution (See Answer Key, following the Variations for this activity) and then leads a discussion based on the reaction form, encouraging the team members to share information from their completed forms.

Variations

- The facilitator may simplify the problem-solving task by distributing copies of a handout consisting of all twenty-six sentences.

- The facilitator may make the problem more difficult by adding redundant or superfluous information.

- The same activity structure may be used with a problem that is relevant to the team.

Answer Key

All of the following information is derived from the portion of the activity entitled "Lutts and Mipps Information Cards."

A to B: 4 lutts at 24 lutts per wor = $4/24$ wor = $1/6$ = $5/30$ wor

B to C: 8 lutts at 30 lutts per wor = $8/30$ wor

C to D: 10 lutts at 30 lutts per wor = $10/30$ wor

$$\begin{aligned} &5/30 \text{ wor} \\ &+ 8/30 \text{ wor} \\ &+10/30 \text{ wor} \end{aligned}$$

Total = $23/30$ wor

LUTTS AND MIPPS INSTRUCTION FORM

Pretend that lutts and mipps represent a new way of measuring distance and that dars, wors, and mirs represent a new way of measuring time. A person drives from Town A, through Town B and Town C, to Town D.

Your team's task is to determine how many wors the entire trip took. You have twenty minutes to complete this task. Do not choose a formal leader.

You will be given cards containing information related to the task. You may share this information orally, but you must keep your cards in your hands throughout the task.

LUTTS AND MIPPS INFORMATION CARDS

To make a set of cards, type each of the following sentences on a 3" x 5" index card (a total of 26). A set should be distributed randomly among members of each group. Each group must have all twenty-six cards.

1. How far is it from A to B?

2. It is 4 lutts from A to B.

3. How far is it from B to C?

4. It is 8 lutts from B to C.

5. How far is it from C to D?

6. It is 10 lutts from C to D.

7. What is a lutt?

8. A lutt is 10 mipps.

9. What is a mipp?

10. A mipp is a way of measuring distance.

11. How many mipps are there in a mile?

12. There are 2 mipps in a mile.

13. What is a dar?

14. A dar is 10 wors.

15. What is a wor?

16. A wor is 5 mirs.

17. What is a mir?

18. A mir is a way of measuring time.

19. How many mirs are there in an hour?

20. There are 2 mirs in an hour.

21. How fast does the person drive from A to B?

22. The person drives from A to B at the rate of 24 lutts per wor.

23. How fast does the person drive from B to C?

24. The person drives from B to C at the rate of 30 lutts per wor.

25. How fast does the person drive from C to D?

26. The person drives from C to D at the rate of 30 lutts per wor.

LUTTS AND MIPPS REACTION FORM

1. How did the team approach the sharing of information? (What techniques were used?)

2. a. Whose participation was most helpful in the accomplishment of the task?

   b. What particular behaviors were helpful?

3. a. Whose participation seemed to hinder the accomplishment of the task?

   b. What particular behaviors seemed to be a hindrance?

4. What feelings did you experience while the team was working on the problem?

5. What role(s) did you play in the team?

6. a. Who assumed leadership roles during the problem-solving task?

   b. How would you describe the leadership behaviors that emerged?

   c. What were the effects of these behaviors on the completion of the task?

   d. How would you characterize the team members' response to the leadership behaviors that emerged?

7. a. What have you learned about your personal approach to problem solving?

   b. What have you learned about the team's approach?

   c. How can you use what you have learned when the team works on real problems?

PERFORMANCE UNLIMITED: SOLVING PROBLEMS AS A TEAM

James W. Kinneer

Goals

- To encourage the development of group problem-solving skills.
- To encourage the development of group decision-making skills.
- To heighten participants' awareness of how group dynamics affect teamwork.

Group Size

All members of an intact work team.

Time Required

Approximately one hour.

Materials

- One copy of the Performance Unlimited Handout for each participant.
- A pencil and a portable writing surface for each participant.
- A newsprint flip chart and a felt-tipped marker for the facilitator's use.

Physical Setting

Any room in which the group can work comfortably. Movable chairs should be provided.

Process

1. The facilitator explains the goals of the activity. (Five minutes.)
2. Each participant is given a copy of the Performance Unlimited Handout and is asked to read the instructions. The facilitator notes that all of the instructions are on the handout. (Five minutes.)

3. At the end of five minutes, the facilitator instructs the participants that they will have fifteen minutes to make their rankings. (Fifteen minutes.)

4. After fifteen minutes, the facilitator calls time. The spokesperson for the team reports the order in which the team decided to address the problems and provides a brief rationale for the order chosen. The facilitator records the ranking and reasons on the flip chart. (Ten minutes.)

5. The facilitator elicits discussion with questions such as the following:

   - How satisfied are you with the final ranking?

   - How do the decisions reflect the ideas and viewpoints of all members? What process did you use to arrive at the ranking and to determine which ideas to incorporate and which to exclude?

   - What elements of the process pleased you? Displeased you?

   - As you worked together, did some members' opinions conflict? If so, how were the conflicts handled?

   - What are the benefits of working together as a team to solve problems?

   - What are some drawbacks to team efforts in solving problems? How can you overcome some of these drawbacks?

   - How are these five issues handled in this team? How could they be improved?

   (Twenty minutes.)

Variations

- This activity could be used as a team-building activity or as a warm-up to solving a real work issue or problem.

- The scenario in the handout can be revised to reflect actual situations that a team is experiencing.

- The activity may be used with a heterogeneous group.

Performance Unlimited Handout

Instructions: You are a member of Performance Unlimited, a team of highly skilled (and well-paid) performance consultants. Read the scenario below and decide the order in which the five work issues should be addressed by the new team leader. All of the information available is included in this handout.

Read this handout, and feel free to make notes about your ideas. Rank the issues individually. Then the group will rank the issues and provide a rationale for the ranking. Choose a member who will serve as spokesperson. You will have fifteen minutes to make your decisions.

Scenario

Pat has accepted a position as the team leader for a team of computer programmers. This is Pat's first leadership position. The team includes five other members:

- Chris is a twenty-year company veteran with a reputation for being difficult.
- Terry is a competent programmer but lacks self-confidence.
- Kim is soft spoken but impatient.
- Dale is a dynamic person with questionable technical skills.
- Kelly is a recent college graduate with many new ideas and not much follow-through.

Certain issues are present with this team, and Pat must decide on the priorities for addressing these issues.

Issue: Communication

Kelly is full of good ideas but fails to communicate effectively with other members of the team. Even when Kelly does try to communicate, Chris and Kim refuse to listen and dismiss the ideas as those of a newcomer.

Issue: Power

Chris is the informal team leader. Kim and Dale always check in with Chris before following through on Pat's instructions. Kelly disrupts the team by constantly challenging Chris.

Issue: Trust

Chris and Kelly do not trust each other and spend too much time trying to determine each other's motives. In conflicts, Kim and Dale defend Chris's actions while Terry supports Kelly.

Issue: Roles

The team seems to immerse itself in projects without well-defined roles. Frequently, several people work on one part of the project, leaving other parts of the project unattended. Despite this disorganization, the team always manages to deliver the finished project on time.

Issue: Equality of Effort

Often Kelly and Terry put in extra hours. Kim and Chris are willing to do their share but are not willing to work after hours. Dale often leaves early, leaving other members of the team to finish the work.

Pat should address the team's issues in this order:

Individual Ranking	Group Ranking	Rationale
1.	1.	1.
2.	2.	2.
3.	3.	3.
4.	4.	4.
5.	5.	5.

Lost at Sea: A Consensus-Seeking Task

Paul M. Nemiroff and William A. Pasmore

> ## Goals
>
> - To teach the effectiveness of consensus-seeking behavior in task groups through comparative experiences with both individual decision making and group decision making.
> - To explore the concept of synergy in reference to the outcomes of group decision making.

Group Size

Five to twelve participants. Several subgroups may be directed simultaneously. (Synergistic outcomes are more likely to be achieved by smaller subgroups, e.g., five to seven participants.)

Time Required

Approximately one hour.

Materials

- Two copies of the Lost at Sea Individual Work Sheet for each participant.
- A copy of the Lost at Sea Group Work Sheet for each subgroup.
- A copy of the Lost at Sea Answer and Rationale Sheet for each participant.
- Pencils.
- Newsprint and felt-tipped markers.

Physical Setting

Lapboards or desk chairs are best for privacy in individual work. Tables may be used, but the dynamics involved are likely to be different.

Process

1. The facilitator distributes two copies of the Lost at Sea Individual Work Sheet to each participant and asks each person to complete the forms in duplicate. He or she explains that participants are to work independently during this phase. (Fifteen minutes.)

2. The facilitator collects one copy from each participant. The other copy is for the use of the subgroup.

3. The facilitator forms subgroups and directs them to particular work areas in the room. Each subgroup is given a copy of the Lost at Sea Group Work Sheet. The facilitator then reads the instructions to the subgroups, emphasizing that each member of a subgroup should partially agree with the subgroup choices to establish consensus, but that they are not to use such techniques as averaging, majority-rule voting, or trading. He or she stresses that it is desirable that effort be made to achieve success in this task.

4. While the subgroups are engaged in their task, the facilitator scores the individual ranking sheets. The score is the sum of the differences between the "correct" rank for each item and its rank on the Individual Work Sheet (all differences should be made positive and added). Higher scores have greater negative implications. The facilitator then totals all individual scores for each subgroup and divides by the number of members to obtain the average individual score for each subgroup. (Thirty-five minutes.)

5. The facilitator collects the Group Work Sheets and scores them as in step 4, while the participants debrief their consensus seeking. He or she then prepares a chart such as the one on the next page, summarizing the statistics:

6. The facilitator returns all Individual and Group Work Sheets and distributes a copy of the Lost at Sea Answer and Rationale Sheet to each participant. After allowing the subgroups a few minutes to discuss the answers and rationale, the facilitator analyzes the statistics and explains the synergy factor.

7. The facilitator leads a discussion of the comparative outcomes of individual rankings and subgroup consensus rankings. Discussion questions such as the following might be suggested by the facilitator:

   ■ What behaviors helped or hindered the consensus-seeking process?

   ■ What patterns of decision making occurred?

   ■ Who were the influential members and how were they influential?

BEFORE GROUP DISCUSSION

Group	Average Individual Score	Score of Most Accurate Individual
Example	55	45
1		
2		
3		
Average for all groups		

AFTER GROUP DISCUSSION

Group	Score for Group Consensus	Gain/Loss Over Average Individual	Gain/Loss Over Most Accurate Individual	Synergy*
Example	40	+15	+5	Yes
1				
2				
3				
Average for all groups				

*Synergy is defined as the consensus score lower than the lowest individual score in the subgroup.

- How did the group discover and use its information resources? Were these resources fully utilized?

- What are the implications of consensus seeking and synergistic outcomes for intact task groups such as committees and staffs of institutions?

- What consequences might such a process produce in the group's attitudes?

Variations

- Process observers can be used to give feedback about either subgroup or individual behavior.

- A lecturette on synergy and consensus seeking can immediately precede the group problem-solving phase to establish a mental set toward cooperation.

- Each participant can be given only one copy of the Lost at Sea Individual Work Sheet and instructed to score his or her own sheet.

LOST AT SEA INDIVIDUAL WORKSHEET

Name _____

Group _____

Instructions: You are adrift on a private yacht in the South Pacific. As a consequence of a fire of unknown origin, much of the yacht and its contents have been destroyed. The yacht is now slowly sinking. Your location is unclear because of the destruction of critical navigational equipment and because you and the crew were distracted trying to bring the fire under control. Your best estimate is that you are approximately one thousand miles south-southwest of the nearest land.

Following is a list of fifteen items that are intact and undamaged after the fire. In addition to these articles, you have a serviceable, rubber life raft with oars. The raft is large enough to carry yourself, the crew, and all the items in the following list. The total contents of all survivors' pockets are a package of cigarettes, several books of matches, and five one-dollar bills.

Your task is to rank the fifteen items that follow in terms of their importance to your survival. Place the number 1 by the most important item, the number 2 by the second most important, and so on through number 15, the least important.

_____ Sextant

_____ Shaving mirror

_____ Five-gallon can of water

_____ Mosquito netting

_____ One case of U.S. Army C rations

_____ Maps of the Pacific Ocean

_____ Seat cushion (flotation device approved by the Coast Guard)

_____ Two-gallon can of oil-gas mixture

_____ Small transistor radio

_____ Shark repellent

_____ Twenty square feet of opaque plastic

_____ One quart of 160-proof Puerto Rican rum

_____ Fifteen feet of nylon rope

_____ Two boxes of chocolate bars

_____ Fishing kit

LOST AT SEA GROUP WORKSHEET

Group _____

Instructions: This is an exercise in group decision making. Your subgroup is to employ the group consensus method in reaching its decision. This means that the prediction for each of the fifteen survival items must be agreed on by each subgroup member before it becomes a part of the subgroup decision. Consensus is difficult to reach. Therefore, not every ranking will meet with everyone's complete approval. As a subgroup, try to make each ranking one with which all members can at least partially agree. Here are some guides to use in reaching consensus.

1. Avoid arguing for your own individual judgments. Approach the task on the basis of logic.

2. Avoid changing your mind if it is only to reach agreement and avoid conflict. Support only solutions with which you are able to agree at least somewhat.

3. Avoid "conflict-reducing" techniques such as majority vote, averaging, or trading in reaching your decision.

4. View differences of opinion as a help rather than a hindrance in decision making.

_____ Sextant

_____ Shaving mirror

_____ Five-gallon can of water

_____ Mosquito netting

_____ One case of U.S. Army C rations

_____ Maps of the Pacific Ocean

_____ Seat cushion (flotation device approved by the Coast Guard)

_____ Two-gallon can of oil-gas mixture

_____ Small transistor radio

_____ Shark repellent

_____ Twenty square feet of opaque plastic

_____ One quart of 160-proof Puerto Rican rum

_____ Fifteen feet of nylon rope

_____ Two boxes of chocolate bars

_____ Fishing kit

The Pfeiffer Book of Successful Team-Building Tools

Lost at Sea Answer and Rationale Sheet[1]

According to the "experts," the basic supplies needed when a person is stranded in midocean are articles to attract attention and articles to aid survival *until rescuers arrive.* Articles for navigation are of little importance: Even if a small life raft were capable of reaching land, it would be impossible to store enough food and water to subsist during that period of time. Therefore, of primary importance are the shaving mirror and the two-gallon can of oil-gas mixture. These items could be used for signaling air-sea rescue. Of secondary importance are items such as water and food, e.g., the case of Army C rations.

A brief rationale is provided for the ranking of each item. These brief explanations obviously do not represent all of the potential uses for the specified items but, rather, the primary importance of each.

1. **Shaving mirror**
   Critical for signaling air-sea rescue.

2. **Two-gallon can of oil-gas mixture**
   Critical for signaling—the oil-gas mixture will float on the water and could be ignited with a dollar bill and a match (obviously, outside the raft).

3. **Five-gallon can of water**
   Necessary to replenish loss from perspiring, etc.

4. **One case of U.S. Army C rations**
   Provides basic food intake.

5. **Twenty square feet of opaque plastic**
   Utilized to collect rain water, provide shelter from the elements.

6. **Two boxes of chocolate bars**
   A reserve food supply.

7. **Fishing kit**
   Ranked lower than the candy bars because "one bird in the hand is worth two in the bush." There is no assurance that you will catch any fish.

8. **Fifteen feet of nylon rope**
   May be used to lash equipment together to prevent it from falling overboard.

-----

[1]Officers of the United States Merchant Marines ranked the fifteen items and provided the "correct" solution to the task.

9. **Floating seat cushion**
   If someone fell overboard, it could function as a life preserver.

10. **Shark repellent**
    Obvious.

11. **One quart of 160-proof Puerto Rican rum**
    Contains 80 percent alcohol—enough to use as a potential anti-septic for any injuries incurred; of little value otherwise; will cause dehydration if ingested.

12. **Small transistor radio**
    Of little value because there is no transmitter (unfortunately, you are out of range of your favorite radio stations).

13. **Maps of the Pacific Ocean**
    Worthless without additional navigational equipment—it does not really matter where you are but where the rescuers are.

14. **Mosquito netting**
    There are no mosquitoes in the mid-Pacific Ocean.

15. **Sextant**
    Without tables and a chronometer, relatively useless.

The basic rationale for ranking signaling devices above life-sustaining items (food and water) is that without signaling devices there is almost no chance of being spotted and rescued. Furthermore, most rescues occur during the first thirty-six hours, and one can survive without food and water during this period.

MAKING TEAM DECISIONS

Kristin Arnold

Abstract: Making decisions is one of the most important team responsibilities. Team members must not
only make the most effective and appropriate decisions, but they must make decisions that will be supported by everyone on the team. This article presents
seven decision-making methods for teams. It focuses
on consensus, the most misunderstood, yet often the
most needed method, providing suggestions for more
efficiently reaching consensus.

$\mathbf{H}$ow do teams make decisions? If you took a poll, most team members would say "by consensus"—without really knowing what consensus is or how to build a true team consensus. Most traditional teams use only one or two strategies to make decisions. However, high performing teams use a wide range of decision-making options, from one person (usually the team leader or expert) deciding to the entire team agreeing wholeheartedly, depending on the time available, involvement desired, expertise available within the team, and the need to develop the team. Several methods and the advantages and disadvantages of each are shown in Figure 1. Let's define each of these ways teams make decisions and some reasons why each may be successful.

Command Decisions. With this method, the team leader or expert decides. This method is useful when a decision must be made quickly and the leader is in control of the situation. The key here is for the leader to explain the decision and the reasons for making the decision to other team members as soon as possible.

Leader Decides with Input from Individuals. The advantage of obtaining input is that the leader does not have to bring all the team members together; yet he or she does collect information from them before making a decision. As information is collected, the key is for the leader to explain the criteria for making the decision, how others will be involved, and what type of input is needed (ideas, suggestions, information).

Leader Decides with Input from Team. By gathering the team together, the leader creates opportunities for creativity, synergy, and buy-in. However, the process does take more time and may create conflict if the leader makes a decision that is against the team's recommendation. The key is for the leader to explain the criteria for making the decision, how the team will be involved, what type of input is wanted, and the time available for discussion. In addition, the leader must clearly state up front that he or she will make the decision.

Majority Vote. Majority vote is useful when the issue is relatively inconsequential or the team is stuck. The advantage is that Americans are fairly

Method	Disadvantages	Advantages
Command decisions	• May not consider expertise in the group. • Limited implementation commitment. • Disagreement and resentment may decrease effectiveness.	• Efficient when leader has all information. • Fastest of all methods.
Leader decides with input from individuals	• Leader must explain criteria and input multiple times, resulting in increased chance for miscommunication. • No chance for group brainstorming of new ideas. • May not have complete buy-in from team members after decision.	• Do not have to gather all team members together. • Not much time needed from members.
Leader decides with input from team	• May not create commitment to implementation. • May create competition among group members. • Members may tell leader what they think he or she wants to hear. • Potential for group think.	• Uses entire group as a resource. • Gains benefit of group discussion. • Members can play off one another's ideas. • Takes less time.
Majority vote	• May leave minority dissatisfied. • Decision lacks total commitment. • May not utilize resources of team.	• Good for fast decision when consensus is not important. • Closes discussions that are not important.
Minority rule	• No widespread commitment. • Unresolved conflict may have future implications.	• Useful when all cannot meet. • May be opportunity for delegation. • Useful for simple, routine decisions. • Opportunity to use experts.
Unanimous agreement	• Very difficult to reach.	• May be necessary for most critical decisions.
Consensus	• Takes a great deal of time and psychological energy. • Time pressure must be minimal. • Potential for weak decision.	• Produces innovative, high-quality decisions when done well. • Elicits commitment from all. • Uses all resources. • Future decision-making ability of group is enhanced.

Figure 1. Decision-Making Methods Employed by Teams

comfortable with a hand vote. The key is for the leader to ensure that everyone understands what they are voting on and the rules involved *before* the actual vote is taken.

If the team must make a decision among many choices, ¾-inch round labels can be used to prioritize. The leader can post the list on a flip chart and give each participant one vote per item. If the leader desires, team members can be given more than one label and allowed to vote for more than one item or to place all labels beside just one item. This produces a more dramatic visual representation of the team's preferences. Also, the leader could use two different colors of label so that team members could vote for first and second preferences. The results in this case could resemble Figure 2.

Minority Rule. Minority rule is a standard default for routine team decision making and useful for less important issues. It does, however, require a team member to have the courage to speak up with an opposing viewpoint. From a positive perspective, the team may request a subject-matter "expert" in the group to make a decision. The key is that the team must support this method of decision making and the decision reached.

Unanimous Agreement. The hardest way to reach a decision is by unanimous agreement. This strategy is not recommended unless all team members must agree, as in matters of life or death.

Consensus. When there is consensus, everyone can live with *and* support the decision, but it is not necessarily everyone's first choice. Leaders use consensus for important issues when the team must learn about all the alternatives and issues, and then implement the decision. Reaching consensus increases the likelihood and ease of successfully implementing a decision.

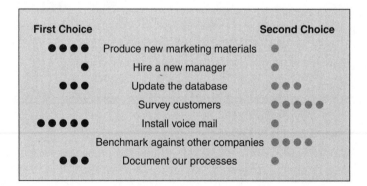

Figure 2. Making a Team Decision by Affixing Labels

Consensus is not the same as unanimity, wherein a decision is everyone's first choice. Nor is it a compromise, whereby each person makes concessions to achieve a team decision. As Robert Ludlum said, a compromise is "a decision which pleases no one, except in knowing that no one else got what they wanted either." Consensus is a process. The team *builds* a consensus—striving to reach a decision that best reflects the thinking of *all* team members. Consensus is a bigger, better decision that is built from the input of each and every team member.

When a team decides to make a decision by consensus, the leader must explain exactly what consensus means and why it is important for the team to reach it. The leader must ensure that all team members understand the issue and the most important aspects of the decision. To prevent confusion, he or she must take the time to define terms, as well as identify and outline any constraints (e.g., time, financial, resources, political). The leader must remind each member to participate fully in the discussion and that each has equal power to support or block any proposals. Finally, the team must agree on a "fallback" decision-making strategy in case consensus cannot be reached. For a group of peers, the fallback strategy is usually to use majority vote. When the leader is part of the group, the fallback strategy may be to defer to the leader.

To build a consensus, the leader *must* hear from everyone on the team. Many teams do this by soliciting opinions from everyone in the group or by brainstorming every possible option and then looking for opportunities to combine, create, and synergize the items into a better idea.

The following questions can be used to help a team be more creative before trying to reach consensus:

- "All of these items are possible. Do we have to choose only one?"
- "Is there any way we can use the best features of all of our options?"
- "What would happen if we added/deleted features of several options. Would that move us closer to what we want?"
- "Could we try out several options in parallel before we commit to just one?"

Team energy increases as new ideas and possibilities surface. Using a trial-and-error approach appears chaotic; however, it is well worth it if a team builds a new, synergistic alternative based on the best of the best.

When it appears that a team has reached a decision, the leader usually takes a "straw poll" to see how close or how far apart the team members are. The leader reminds the team at this point that this is not a final vote, but simply a way to determine how much work must be done to build consensus. These sentence starters can be used:

- "It sounds as though we are making progress. Let's check that out with a quick straw poll to see how close we are to a consensus. We'll go right around the table. Sally?"

- "Let's see if everyone either can agree with or can agree to support the most popular alternative. Let's start with Emile and go around the room."

Record the responses and summarize the results. If everyone can live with and support the alternative, then the team has reached a consensus.

Try this quick, fun approach to testing for consensus: the "Five L Straw Poll." Give each person a Post-it™ Tape Flag. Draw the "Five L" scale on a flip chart, as shown in Figure 3. Describe each "L" as you write it. Say something like "You *loathe* it or hate it. You will *lament* it and moan about it in the parking lot. You can *live* with it. You can *like* it. Or you can really *love* it."

Now ask the team members to think silently about the proposed alternative. Then ask them to place their tape flags on the flip chart, building a bar chart, such as the one in Figure 4.

Ask if the team believes there is a consensus, that is, the alternative received at least a "live with" or better vote. In the event there are votes that are in the "loathe" or "lament" categories, the leader must check with the team to see why people have voted that way, being careful not to pick on a specific person, but hearing feedback from team members.

If your team cannot reach consensus, try these sentence starters:

- "There seems to be a lot of support for this alternative. What would it take for *everyone* to support it?"

- "What is getting in the way of some team members' ability to support this alternative? What could we do to meet those needs?"

Integrate the feedback and create another, better alternative! Continue to build agreement for the decision until there is true consensus, that is, when everyone can live with *and* support the decision. Four criteria must be met before a decision can be declared to have been made by consensus.

1. All team members must have had an opportunity to provide input.

2. All team members must believe that they were heard and understood.

3. Everyone must be able to state the decision clearly.

The Pfeiffer Book of Successful Team-Building Tools

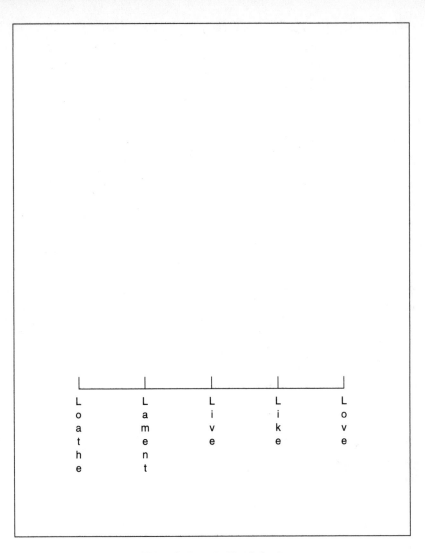

Figure 3. Sample Five L Scale

4. All team members must agree to support the decision in what they say and what they do.

If time runs out, the leader must decide whether to postpone the decision for another time or whether to fall back to another decision-making method. If a leader uses the fallback decision option frequently or for many key decisions, something is happening that must be addressed. Many times, the "something" is happening outside of the group or is beyond the team's control.

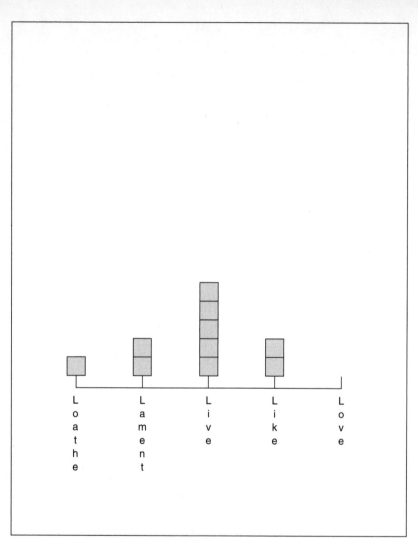

Figure 4. Sample Five L Bar Chart

By building a consensus, team leaders have a greater chance of producing a better quality decision, a more cohesive team, and smoother implementation of the decisions that are made.

The Pfeiffer Book of Successful Team-Building Tools

7 Balanced Participation

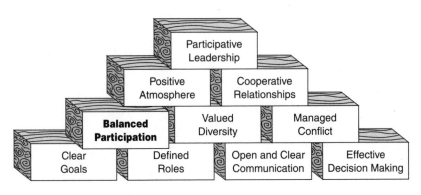

Copyright © 1999 ebb associates inc

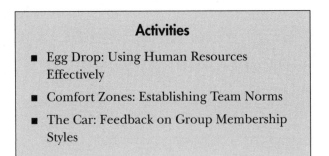

Activities

- Egg Drop: Using Human Resources Effectively

- Comfort Zones: Establishing Team Norms

- The Car: Feedback on Group Membership Styles

Balanced Participation begins the next level of the model, building on the foundation row. Participation is almost as important as communication. Without it, there is no team. Participation goes beyond just doing something to be involved. It means that team members encourage the opinions, ideas, and involvement of others. Team participation is influenced by the leader's behavior and by the participants' expectations.

This chapter contains three enjoyable experiential learning activities to explore team members' participation. All three require the active participation of *all* members of the team. This requirement alone could give you, the team builder, a discussion starter. "Egg Drop" analyzes the effective use of members of a team. "Comfort Zones" will help teams establish the norms that identify the extent of participation. "The Car" examines members' styles, examines the team's operating style, and explores ways to improve the team's functioning.

Egg Drop:
Using Human Resources Effectively

Douglas Bryant

<table>
<tr><td>

Goals

- To help participants to analyze the use of human resources within a group.

- To allow participants to study the relationship between managers and workers in carrying out a task.

- To demonstrate the impact of the communication process on assigning and carrying out a task.

- To allow participants to study the effects of positive and negative reinforcement.

</td></tr>
</table>

Group Size

Twelve to twenty-four participants, divided into subgroups of six members each.

Time Required

Two hours.

Materials

- One copy of the Egg Drop Rule Sheet for each participant.
- One copy of the Egg Drop Materials Requisition for each participant.
- One copy of the Egg Drop Observation Sheet for each subgroup's observer.
- A clipboard or other portable writing surface for each observer.
- A pencil for each participant.
- One egg for each subgroup.

- Twenty paper plates.

- Twenty plastic bowls.

- Fifty sheets of paper toweling.

- Twenty small Styrofoam® plates.

- Twenty Styrofoam® cups.

- Forty plastic coffee stirrers.

- Forty plastic drinking straws.

- Twenty plastic cups.

- Twenty large Styrofoam® plates.

- Forty index cards.

- Forty paper clips.

- Forty rubber bands.

- Several rolls of masking tape.

- Two boxes of facial tissues.

- A pocket calculator for the facilitator.

- A newsprint flip chart and a felt-tipped marker.

- Masking tape for posting newsprint.

Physical Setting

A room large enough for subgroups to work without disturbing one another. The room also should be equipped with a wall clock.

Process

1. The facilitator introduces the goals of the activity. The participants are told that they will assemble into subgroups to design and build a structure that will support an egg as it is dropped from a height of approximately eight feet. The facilitator states that any subgroup that completes the project within budget and without breaking its egg will be considered successful. Then the facilitator distributes copies of the Egg Drop Rule Sheet and reviews the rules with the entire group. (Ten minutes.)

2. The participants are asked to form subgroups of six members each.

3. The facilitator distributes copies of the Egg Drop Materials Requisition and pencils and then announces that each subgroup will have

ten minutes to choose an observer, managers, and workers. (Ten minutes.)

4. The facilitator gives each observer a copy of the Egg Drop Observation Sheet, a pencil, and a clipboard or other portable writing surface and reviews the instructions *(but not the questions)* on the observation sheet with the entire group. (Five minutes.)

5. The facilitator gives each subgroup an egg, asks the subgroups to begin, and reminds the observers to keep track of the time. The facilitator monitors subgroup activities and assists as necessary. While the subgroups are in the construction phase, the facilitator calculates the total costs of the materials that each subgroup requisitions and records that information on newsprint. (Forty-five minutes.)

6. After forty-five minutes, the facilitator calls time and reassembles the entire group. He or she posts the newsprint listing the materials costs for each subgroup. Each observer is asked to add the amount of penalties that his or her subgroup incurred as well as the costs of the subgroup's design and construction time and to announce whether the subgroup completed its task within budget. (Ten minutes.)

7. Each subgroup's structure is tested by having one of its managers stand on a chair and drop the egg from a height of approximately eight feet. (The facilitator marks the height on newsprint so that each subgroup drops its egg from the same point.) The structure is considered successful if the egg does not break, and each successful subgroup is congratulated. (Ten minutes.)

8. The observers are asked to take turns reporting their observations. (Ten minutes.)

9. The facilitator debriefs the activity by asking the following questions:

- How did you feel about how you acquired your role?

- Who influenced decisions most? How was that influence exerted? How did you react to that influence?

- How did you feel as your subgroup worked on designing and building its structure?

- Which human resources (including yourself) were used wisely? Unwisely?

- What have you learned about the effective use of human resources? Given what you have learned, what would you do differently if you were to repeat this activity?

- If you could rewrite the rules of this activity, what would you change? How would your changes contribute to a more effective use of human resources?

- How does this experience relate to your own work process? How can you apply what you have learned to improve your own work process?

(Twenty minutes.)

Variations

- If sufficient time is available, the subgroups may be asked to repeat the activity using the rewritten rules.

- The facilitator may have the subgroups compete with one another by stipulating that the winning subgroup will be the one whose structure is successful (egg does not break) and who built its structure at the lowest cost.

EGG DROP RULE SHEET

In the upcoming activity, your subgroup's task is to design and build a structure that will support an egg as it is dropped from a height of approximately eight feet.

Your budget for completing the task is $3,000. The materials you may choose for construction purposes are listed on the Egg Drop Materials Requisition, which includes prices for these materials. In addition, as indicated below, your subgroup will be charged for the positions of observer, manager, and worker.

If the egg does not break when dropped and you stay within budget, you will have completed the task successfully.

Choosing Observer, Managers, Workers

You and your fellow subgroup members may choose roles in any way you wish. Note the following costs of the different positions:

Manager = $200 each

Worker = $100 each

Observer = $ 75 each

Note: Your subgroup must have one observer.

Designing the Structure

1. Managers design a construction plan.

2. Workers may not participate in the design process in any way.

3. Workers and managers may look at but not touch the resource materials.

Building the Structure

1. Once the design has been completed, your subgroup may request the materials it needs from the facilitator by completing and submitting a copy of the Egg Drop Materials Requisition. The subgroup is charged the indicated amounts for chosen materials.

2. All materials must be requested at one time; however, in the event that a requested item is not in stock, your subgroup may revise its requisition.

3. Your subgroup may begin the construction phase whenever it is ready.

4. Managers may offer instructions, ideas, and feedback, but they *may not touch the resource materials*. Workers are to build the structure, but they *may not use their own ideas*.

5. If either infraction in item 4 occurs, the observer will penalize the subgroup $100 for each occurrence.

> Note: The total time allotted for design and construction is forty-five minutes.

Egg Drop Materials Requisition

Budget: $3,000

Manager   # _____   @ $ 200.00 each

Worker   # _____   @ $ 100.00 each

Observers (1)   # _____   @ $ 75.00

Design Time (actual minutes)   # _____   @ $ 2.50 per minute

Construction Time (45
minutes minus Design Time)   # _____   @ $ 5.00 per minute

Paper Plate   # _____   @ $ 50.00 each

Plastic Bowl   # _____   @ $ 100.00 each

Paper Towel   # _____   @ $ 25.00 each

Small Styrofoam Plate   # _____   @ $ 75.00 each

Styrofoam Cup   # _____   @ $ 50.00 each

Coffee Stirrer   # _____   @ $ 5.00 each

Plastic Drinking Straw   # _____   @ $ 7.50 each

Plastic Cup   # _____   @ $ 175.00 each

Large Styrofoam Plate   # _____   @ $ 125.00 each

Index Card   # _____   @ $ 10.00 each

Paper Clip   # _____   @ $ 1.00 each

Rubber Band   # _____   @ $ 2.00 each

Tape (inches)   # _____   @ $ 1.00 per inch

Pencil   # _____   @ $ 2.00 each

Facial Tissue   # _____   @ $ 3.00 each

EGG DROP OBSERVATION SHEET

Instructions: Your role is to observe the members of your subgroup and make notes on their behavior using the questions below as a guide. Also track the time for the design phase and for the construction phase, and note any penalties that occur. You may *not* offer input or help during design or construction.

1. How did your subgroup decide who would assume which roles? What were the key considerations?

2. How did the manager(s) approach the task? What process did the manager(s) use?

3. Did the manager(s) look at the process from the workers' point of view? How?

4. What type of communication did the manager(s) engage in with the workers?

5. How was the design communicated to the workers?

6. How did the manager(s) and workers give one another positive or negative reinforcement?

7. How did the workers follow instructions? What were their reactions?

8. How effectively did the workers use their time?

9. How did the workers work as part of the team?

	Begin	End
Design Time		
Construction Time		
Penalties		

The Pfeiffer Book of Successful Team-Building Tools

COMFORT ZONES: ESTABLISHING TEAM NORMS

Chris C. Hoffman

Goals

- To foster effective team performance.

- To acquaint team members with the concept of norms.

- To provide an opportunity to establish the practice of explicitly discussing not only how things should be done in the team but also how things actually are done.

- To provide team members with a relatively low-risk opportunity for self-disclosure.

- To foster interpersonal communication in the team.

Group Size

All members (at least three and no more than ten) of an ongoing work team, a task force, or a project team. This activity is best used with a newly formed team, an ongoing team that is experiencing difficulties in interpersonal relations, or a team that is becoming self-directed.

Time Required

Two to three and one-half hours, depending on the number of team members and the depth of discussion following each norm.

Materials

- A copy of the Comfort Zones Work Sheet for each participant.
- A pencil for each participant.
- A clipboard or other portable writing surface for each participant.
- Newsprint poster sheets patterned after Figure 1, prepared in advance by the facilitator.

Goals and Objectives

1	2	3	4	5	6	7

Reactions:

Openness

1	2	3	4	5	6	7

Reactions:

Conflict Resolution

1	2	3	4	5	6	7

Reactions:

(Continue this format for the remaining norms.)

Figure 1.   Team Norms Summary Poster Format

- A newsprint flip chart and a felt-tipped marker.
- Masking tape for posting newsprint.

Physical Setting

Any room in which the participants can work comfortably. It is preferable that the participants be able to see one another as well as the facilitator and the newsprint posters.

Process

1. The facilitator introduces the activity to the participants with comments such as the following:

   "Virginia Satir (1967), who has done extensive work with families, states that every individual grows up with unspoken assumptions and rules learned from parents about how families should operate and what family life should be like. Similarly, individuals, in their roles as workers, develop unspoken assumptions and rules about work life—and particularly about the life of the work "family," the team—from past work experiences and, ultimately, from family-of-origin experience.

"If the members of a team do not talk about their assumptions and if those assumptions differ, the team members inadvertently violate one another's expectations. Teamwork, satisfaction, and productivity can suffer. Consequently, it is a good idea to develop team "norms," which are rules about what constitutes normal or acceptable behavior for team members. When everyone in the team makes similar assumptions (shares the same norms), team-member interactions tend to be smoother.

"The activity that you are about to participate in is designed to help you and your fellow members enhance your functioning as a team by developing an understanding of everyone's assumptions, agreeing on which of those assumptions will govern behavior in your team, and declaring those assumptions to be your team's norms."

(Five minutes.)

2. The facilitator distributes copies of the Comfort Zones Work Sheet, pencils, and clipboards or other portable writing surfaces; reads the instructions on the work sheet aloud; answers any questions about the task; and then asks the participants to complete the work sheets on their own. (Ten to fifteen minutes.)

3. The facilitator displays the newsprint posters patterned after Figure 1 and asks one of the participants for the number of his or her comfort zone for the first norm, Goals and Objectives. After writing an "X" in the appropriate box on the poster, the facilitator asks the participant to read what he or she wrote concerning reactions that occur when others operate outside his or her comfort zone. As the participant reads, the facilitator records key words or phrases on the poster.

4. The procedure described in Step 3 is repeated until the facilitator has recorded all participants' information for the first norm. (Five to ten minutes for Steps 3 and 4.)

5. The facilitator leads a discussion about the following:

   ■ *A summary of the reactions that occur when teammates operate outside one another's comfort zones.* (This discussion should be nonjudgmental: Everyone has a right to his or her feelings. If people have differing expectations of one another, they need to develop ways to work together so that all of their needs are met as much as possible.)

- *The implications that this pattern of comfort zones has for the team.* (The pattern is intended as a starting point for discussion. In general, a team whose members have similar zones will have an easier time dealing with the issues involving a particular norm, whereas a team whose members have widely scattered comfort zones will have more work to do in terms of understanding and appreciating differences. Also important to note is a situation in which the leader or another key member has a comfort zone that is quite different from the zones of the other members.)

The facilitator assists the participants in establishing a team norm (*in terms of behaviors that the participants will/will not engage in*) for the first item, and the norm is recorded on newsprint. If there is wide divergence in comfort zones, the participants may need some help with conflict management during this step. During this discussion the facilitator should focus on helping the participants to make "I statements" about their feelings, to make clear requests of one another, and to respect differences within the team. (Ten to twenty minutes.)

6. The facilitator asks the participants to select four more norms to concentrate on during the session, explaining that the remaining ten norms on the Comfort Zones Work Sheet will be addressed in subsequent team meetings.

7. The process described in Steps 3, 4, and 5 is repeated four times to establish team norms for the four selected items. (One to two hours.)

8. The facilitator reviews the five team norms established by the participants. The newsprint sheet listing these recorded norms is given to one of the participants to reproduce and distribute to all participants in handout form. (Ten minutes.)

9. The facilitator leads a discussion by asking the following questions:

- How do you feel about the norms established by the team thus far?

- How do you feel about the process by which you arrived at these norms?

- What have you learned about norms? What have you learned about establishing team norms?

- How will you monitor adherence to the norms you establish? How will you address norm "violations"? What process will you set up to review norms from time to time (when new members join the team, when the team's mission or assignments change radically, and so on)?

(Fifteen minutes.)

10. The facilitator assists the participants in making arrangements for future sessions at which they will review the ten remaining items on the Comfort Zones Work Sheet and establish norms for those items. (The facilitator's presence at future sessions is helpful but not essential.)

Variations

■ To shorten the time required and proceed directly to the activity's focus, the facilitator may collect the completed work sheets, ask the participants to take a break, and spend the break time charting the results. After the break the facilitator should return the work sheets to their owners so that the participants can take notes.

■ The activity may be extended into a full-day intervention by helping the participants to establish norms for all fifteen items on the Comfort Zones Work Sheet.

■ Although this activity addresses key norms, it does not deal with all areas in which a team might want to establish norms. Therefore, at some point the participants may consider what other issues or behaviors would be useful to clarify and may make arrangements to establish norms about these issues or behaviors. In this case the facilitator should elicit the participants' suggestions, record them on newsprint, make arrangements for a session to address these issues or behaviors, and give the newsprint to one of the participants to keep and bring to the future session.

■ The activity may be followed with a lecturette and discussion about the norms that characterize high-performance teams. See, for example, Isgar (1989).

■ The activity may be used in connection with diversity training. In this case the facilitator should emphasize the point that people enter the workplace with different assumptions about work life.

■ The Comfort Zones Work Sheet may be used to evaluate how the participants actually behave in terms of established norms. Such evaluation may be done as a separate activity or in conjunction with this activity.

References

Isgar, T. (1989). *The ten minute team.* Boulder, CO: Seluera Press.

Satir, V. (1967). *Conjoint family therapy.* Palo Alto, CA: Science and Behavior Books.

COMFORT ZONES WORK SHEET

Norms are standards of behavior that each member of a team is expected to follow. They reflect the team's values about work.

Following is a list of fifteen topics or behavioral areas about which teams develop norms. Each topic on the list includes a continuum with a brief description of possible norms at opposite ends. For each of these topics, everyone has a "comfort zone" that represents the level of behavior in a team that is the most helpful to that person in terms of getting work done.

Consider each topic on this work sheet and follow these instructions:

- Circle the number that best describes your own personal "comfort zone."

- In the space below each continuum, write a few words about the reactions you have when other members of your team function outside your comfort zone for that behavioral area.

GOALS AND OBJECTIVES

All goals and objectives should be determined from above.

All goals and objectives should be determined by team consensus.

| 1 | 2 | 3 | 4 | 5 | 6 | 7 |

Reactions:

OPENNESS

People should "stick to the facts." Focus should be strictly business; talking about feelings is not appropriate

People should talk a lot about personal issues and feelings and should often disclose parts of their lives outside work.

| 1 | 2 | 3 | 4 | 5 | 6 | 7 |

Reactions:

CONFLICT RESOLUTION

It is always best to avoid
conflict at any cost.

It is always best to confront every
conflict openly and work it through.

| 1 | 2 | 3 | 4 | 5 | 6 | 7 |

Reactions:

ORIENTATION TO HIERARCHY

Hierarchy helps; people should
always go through the boss.

Working as a team of peers helps;
people should go ahead and do it
and then—maybe—tell the boss.

| 1 | 2 | 3 | 4 | 5 | 6 | 7 |

Reactions:

MUTUAL SUPPORT

I am at my best when I
am working on my own.

I am at my best when
people rely on one another.

| 1 | 2 | 3 | 4 | 5 | 6 | 7 |

Reactions:

REPORTING WITHIN THE TEAM

Only the headlines
should be reported.

Hands-on detail
should be reported.

| 1 | 2 | 3 | 4 | 5 | 6 | 7 |

Reactions:

PROBLEM SOLVING/DECISION MAKING

All decisions should be made by the team leader.

All decisions should be made by the team as a whole.

1	2	3	4	5	6	7

Reactions:

LEADERSHIP

In the final analysis, one person should lead.

Leadership roles should be shared.

1	2	3	4	5	6	7

Reactions:

EXPERIMENTATION/CREATIVITY

People should use the regular, tried-and-true ways.

People should make a habit of trying anything new, no matter how unusual or different.

1	2	3	4	5	6	7

Reactions:

CONTROL AND PROCEDURES

People should always follow established procedures to get work done.

People should bypass established procedures whenever possible to get work done.

1	2	3	4	5	6	7

Reactions:

SELF-EVALUATION

The team should never evaluate its functioning or process.

The team should frequently evaluate its functioning and process.

| 1 | 2 | 3 | 4 | 5 | 6 | 7 |

Reactions:

WORKING OVERTIME

People should finish their work during regular hours; having to work overtime means that work has not been scheduled properly.

People should work a lot of overtime; working overtime shows dedication, loyalty, and professionalism.

| 1 | 2 | 3 | 4 | 5 | 6 | 7 |

Reactions:

MEMBER WHO DOES NOT PULL HIS OR HER WEIGHT

A member who does not pull his or her weight should be transferred or fired so that the team is not damaged further.

A member who does not pull his or her weight should be coached and/or retrained, no matter how much of the team's time and energy is required.

| 1 | 2 | 3 | 4 | 5 | 6 | 7 |

Reactions:

NURTURING/RENEWAL

Nurturing the team   The team frequently makes
wastes productive time.   time to nurture itself.

   1   2   3   4   5   6   7

Reactions:

INDIVIDUAL RECOGNITION

Recognition should be   Recognition should be
public and highly visible.   quiet, private, low-key.

   1   2   3   4   5   6   7

Reactions:

THE CAR:
FEEDBACK ON GROUP MEMBERSHIP STYLES

Alfred A. Wells

Goals

- To allow the team members to obtain feedback on their perceived role functions and membership styles.
- To enable a team to examine its operating style and to plan changes.
- To encourage and practice giving and receiving feedback.

Group Size

All members of an ongoing team.

Time Required

One hour and fifteen minutes.

Materials

- A copy of The Car Parts Sheet for each team member.
- A copy of The Car Work Sheet for each team member.
- A pencil for each team member.
- A newsprint flip chart and a felt-tipped marker.

Physical Setting

A room with writing surfaces for the team members.

Process

1. The facilitator introduces the activity as an opportunity for the team members to practice giving and receiving feedback on their perceived

role functions and membership styles. The facilitator provides the rationale for and gives an overview of the activity. The facilitator explains that by receiving feedback from many people about one aspect of our behavior, we can better determine the accuracy and usefulness of the feedback. The facilitator says that, following the feedback session, the team members will examine the role functions in their team and determine whether they need to add to or modify their behaviors in the team in order to improve its functioning. The facilitator also tells the team members that the initial feedback in this activity is to be given anonymously. (Five minutes.)

2. Each team member is given a copy of The Car Parts Sheet, a copy of The Car Work Sheet, and a pencil. The facilitator reads aloud the functions of the various car parts, ensuring that all members understand these functions. Then each team member is told to think of the team as a car and to determine which team member, if any, performs each of the sixteen functions and to write that member's name next to the appropriate number on the work sheet. The team members are told to consider themselves as well as other members when making their decisions; they are also told that some names may be used more than once and some names may not be used at all. In addition, the facilitator asks the team members *not* to write their names on their work sheets. (Ten minutes.)

3. The facilitator collects the work sheets and asks the team members to spend a few minutes discussing their reactions to the activity thus far. (Five minutes.)

4. While the team members are engaged in discussion, the facilitator tabulates the work sheets on a newsprint chart listing the names of all team members. The facilitator notes how many times each member was nominated for each of the role functions (see the example in Figure 1).

5. The newsprint chart is posted where all team members can see it. The facilitator states that although the actual sources of the feedback on the work sheets may remain anonymous, the members are to use this information as a basis for giving one another feedback and for exchanging general reactions to the membership roles represented in the team. The facilitator provides the following guidelines for giving feedback:

   ▪ The feedback is to be *descriptive*, not judgmental.

   ▪ The feedback is to describe *behavior*, not to guess at the intentions underlying the behavior.

The Pfeiffer Book of Successful Team-Building Tools

Group I	
Member	*Function and Times Nominated*
Pat	Gas - 5 Engine - 4 Wheels - 1
Dale	Headlight - 6 Mud Guard 3
Lee	Baggage - 4 Hood Ornament - 2

Figure 1.   Example of Tabulation Chart

- The feedback is to be *specific*, not general.

- The feedback is to be related to the members' *behaviors in the team.*

The facilitator asks the team members to start and guides them through the feedback process. (Twenty minutes.)

6. At the conclusion of the feedback phase, the team members are instructed to share their reactions to the feedback and to discuss how it has affected their perceptions of themselves *in terms of their roles in the team.* (Ten minutes.)

7. The team members are asked to reflect silently for a few minutes on what the feedback implies about how they interact and on how they could change their own behavior so that the team's interpersonal dynamics and functioning might be improved. The facilitator invites the team members to jot down a few notes on the reverse side of their parts sheets, if they wish. (Five minutes.)

8. The facilitator elicits comments about the manner in which the team currently operates in terms of membership roles and how the team's functioning could be improved in this regard. (Ten minutes.)

9. The team members are encouraged to formulate contracts for desired changes and to establish procedures for reviewing their progress in this area at a specific time in the future. (Ten minutes.)

Variations

- If specific problem areas in the team's functioning are identified, sub-groups may be formed to discuss individual problem areas and to make specific suggestions for improvement.

- After step 9 the team members may form pairs. The members of each pair contract to help each other in implementing personal plans for improvement.

THE CAR PARTS SHEET

The Car Parts Sheet

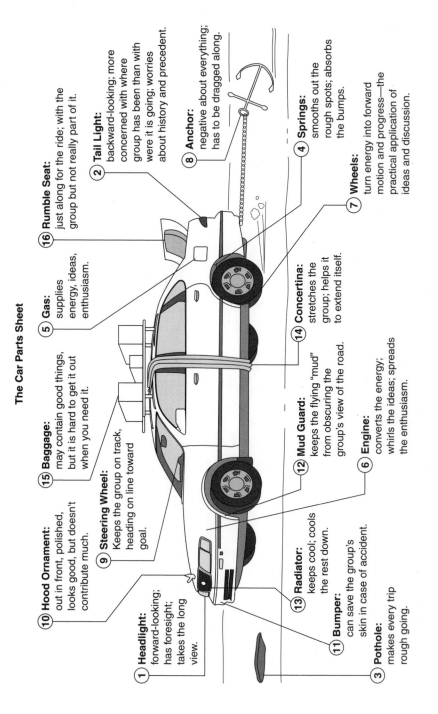

1 Headlight: forward-looking; has foresight; takes the long view.

2 Tail Light: backward-looking; more concerned with where group has been than with were it is going; worries about history and precedent.

3 Pothole: makes every trip rough going.

4 Springs: smooths out the rough spots; absorbs the bumps.

5 Gas: supplies energy, ideas, enthusiasm.

6 Engine: converts the energy; whirls the ideas; spreads the enthusiasm.

7 Wheels: turn energy into forward motion and progress—the practical application of ideas and discussion.

8 Anchor: negative about everything; has to be dragged along.

9 Steering Wheel: Keeps the group on track, heading on line toward goal.

10 Hood Ornament: out in front, polished, looks good, but doesn't contribute much.

11 Bumper: can save the group's skin in case of accident.

12 Mud Guard: keeps the flying "mud" from obscuring the group's view of the road.

13 Radiator: keeps cool; cools the rest down.

14 Concertina: stretches the group; helps it to extend itself.

15 Baggage: may contain good things, but it is hard to get it out when you need it.

16 Rumble Seat: just along for the ride; with the group but not really part of it.

THE CAR WORK SHEET

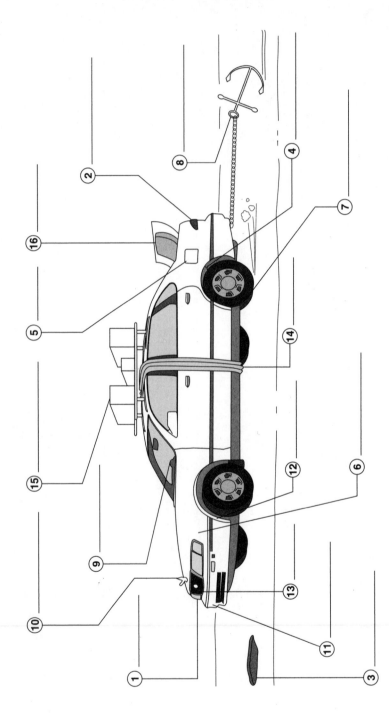

Valued Diversity

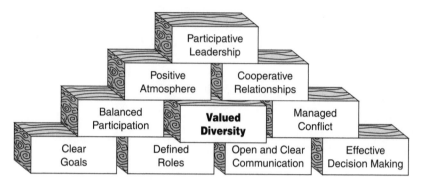

Copyright © 1999 ebb associates inc

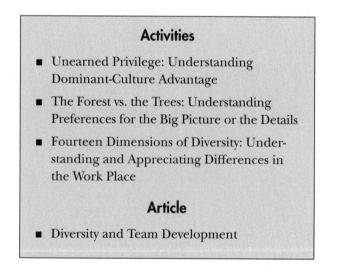

Activities

- Unearned Privilege: Understanding Dominant-Culture Advantage

- The Forest vs. the Trees: Understanding Preferences for the Big Picture or the Details

- Fourteen Dimensions of Diversity: Understanding and Appreciating Differences in the Work Place

Article

- Diversity and Team Development

Valued Diversity is at the heart of the ten boxes of the model. It is also at the heart of effective teamwork. Valued diversity means that team members value one another for their unique contributions, perceptions, and ideas.

Diversity can be an uncomfortable topic, and "Unearned Privilege" is an activity that may produce discomfort. It may hit a bit too close to home, as it focuses on unearned advantages or opportunities in the workplace. Diversity is also about understanding and appreciating others' preferences. "The Forest vs. the Trees" aids team members in understanding and appreciating individuals who have big-picture and detail orientations. Diversity goes much further than either of these, and "Fourteen Dimensions of Diversity" helps teams explore these other dimensions.

The article, "Diversity and Team Development," provides a way to think about the diversity of race, gender, and nationality as it applies to team members at different stages of a team's development. You might consider making copies of this article to provide for the team with which you are working.

Unearned Privilege: Understanding Dominant-Culture Advantage

Julie O'Mara and Aja Oakman

Goals

- To acquaint participants with the concept of "privilege" as it pertains to diversity (unearned advantage or opportunity afforded members of the dominant culture).

- To provide an opportunity for participants to identify, examine, and study examples of privilege in the workplace.

- To develop participants' awareness that privilege is inherent in organizations.

- To explore how awareness of privilege can encourage the effective use of human resources in participants' organization(s).

Group Size

Twelve to thirty participants of diverse backgrounds (racial, ethnic, gender, sexual orientation, age, ability/disability, and/or work group). All participants should be members of the same organization.

(*Important Note for the Facilitator:* This activity may produce a high level of affect. It is advised that you use the activity only if you have extensive experience in dealing with diversity issues. Also, the activity is best positioned in a diversity program that is at least one day long and in which topics such as prejudice, discrimination, and stereotyping are addressed in depth early. Under these circumstances the activity is best used in mid-afternoon to late afternoon, after the participants have acquired some background in and understanding of diversity issues. In preparation for answering questions and leading discussion, the facilitator should study the references listed after "Variations.")

Time Required

Approximately one hour and thirty minutes.

Materials

- Copies of the Unearned Privilege Theory Sheet for all participants.
- A flip-chart poster listing the following questions:
  - To what degree do you believe the statements on the handout are experienced by people in your organization? In your department or unit?
  - What examples of "white privilege" have you experienced, observed, or heard about?
- Masking tape for posting.
- A flip chart and markers for each subgroup and for the facilitator.

Physical Setting

A room large enough for subgroups of four or five members each to work without distracting one another. Movable chairs should be provided; a table for each subgroup is optional.

Process

1. Introduce the activity by defining "privilege" as it relates to diversity and by reviewing the goals. State that the concept of privilege may be new to some and may cause some persons to feel uncomfortable and/or resistant. Emphasize that the concept of privilege is complex and that the focus of this activity is to open the door to basic understanding of privilege. (Five minutes.)

2. Form subgroups of four or five persons each, ensuring that the members of each subgroup represent a variety of diversity dimensions (race, ethnicity, gender, sexual orientation, age, ability/disability, or work group). Ask the members of each subgroup to convene at a different table or to form their chairs into a circle. Give each subgroup a flip chart and several felt-tipped markers.

3. Distribute copies of the theory sheet and ask participants to read it. (Five minutes.)

4. Display the poster of prepared questions. Explain that members of each subgroup will have fifteen minutes to discuss briefly their re-

actions to the twenty theory-sheet statements and then to concentrate on their responses to the posted questions. Ask each subgroup to appoint a recorder to list responses to the posted questions on the flip chart. Monitor the subgroups as they work to ensure that they do not get stuck on the reaction phase and have plenty of time to respond to the posted questions. (Spending no more than five minutes on reactions works well.)

5. Ask the members of each subgroup to choose:

   - One statement they believe is especially true;

   - One example that they discussed in support of one of the statements; and

   - One statement they believe is *not* true (unless they cannot identify one).

   Explain that the recorder should record each subgroup's choices; then the subgroup should appoint a spokesperson to share those choices with the total group, as well as any highlights of their discussion. Again monitor the subgroups as they work, reminding them periodically of the remaining time. (Fifteen minutes.)

6. After fifteen minutes call time and reconvene the entire group. Ask the spokespersons to take turns reporting; limit each subgroup to three minutes. When denials of privilege are brought up, immediately facilitate a discussion on the subject. (*Note:* It is not uncommon for white persons to deny the existence of privilege. They may not feel particularly privileged in their lives or in the organization; they may believe that education and training in diversity issues and equal opportunity employment have reduced or eliminated disparate treatment. Emphasize that although they may not feel privileged individually and personally, as members of the dominant culture they possess both power and opportunity and, thus, have advantages that have not been earned.) (Twenty-five minutes.)

7. Explain that now each subgroup is to meet again to select one of the following dominant cultures in North American organizations and to choose two or three examples of unearned privilege for that group:

   - Men

   - Heterosexuals

   - People without disabilities

   Ask the recorders to list the examples on their flip charts. State that each subgroup has ten minutes to complete this task and then ask the subgroups to begin. Monitor their work, keeping them apprised of the remaining time. (Fifteen minutes.)

8. After ten minutes call time and reconvene the entire group. Ask the spokespersons to take turns presenting examples; limit each spokesperson to two minutes. After each spokesperson reports, ask for brief questions or comments from participants. (Twenty minutes.)

9. To conclude, lead a discussion based on the following questions:

   - What are your key learnings on privilege as it pertains to diversity?

   - Why might some persons in a dominant culture deny they have unearned privilege?

   - How does unearned privilege impact your organization?

   - How might you use what you have learned during this activity in your work life?

   (Ten minutes.)

Variations

- Instead of using the theory sheet as a handout, give a lecturette on its first few paragraphs (not including the twenty statements) and then distribute copies and form subgroups. (*Note:* This variation may produce an especially high level of affect; if so, extra time may be needed to process this affect.)

- After Step 6 lead a concluding discussion, thereby limiting the focus to white privilege only.

- To ensure that all three categories in Step 7 are covered, either assign a category to each subgroup or ask each subgroup to list examples for every category.

- In Step 9 ask participants to discuss actions that the organization can take to minimize the negative impact of privilege.

References

Cose, E. (1993). *Rage of a privileged class: Why are middle-class blacks angry?* New York: HarperCollins.

Kendall, F. (1997). *Barriers to clarify or what keeps white people from being able to see our privilege.* Unpublished manuscript. Albany, CA: Kendall and Associates (510) 559-9445.

Kendall, F. (1997). *Understanding white privilege.* Unpublished manuscript. Albany, CA: Kendall and Associates (510) 559-9445.

Maier, M. (1997). *Invisible privilege: What white men don't see.* Teaneck, NJ: The Diversity Factor.

McIntosh, P. (1992). White privilege and male privilege: A personal account of coming to see correspondences through work in women's studies." (pp. 70–81). In M.L. Anderson & P.H. Collins (Eds.), *Race, class and gender.* Belmont, CA: Wadsworth.

UNEARNED PRIVILEGE THEORY SHEET

"Privilege" as it pertains to diversity is the unearned advantage or opportunity one receives just because one is a member of a dominant culture. Being in the dominant culture means you hold power and have unearned access to opportunities and, often, but not always, are in the majority. *Random House Webster's Unabridged Dictionary* (2nd ed., 1998) defines privilege as "a right, immunity, or benefit enjoyed only by a person beyond the advantages of most."

In North America, the privilege afforded white people is the most prevalent type of unearned advantage. Privilege is also commonly experienced by men, heterosexuals, and persons without disabilities.

It is important to distinguish between earned and unearned advantage. For example, earning a higher salary or having access to resources because one holds a doctoral degree is *earned* privilege. The distinction between earned and unearned can become muddied, however. Some individuals in a dominant culture (a group in power) may be accepted into a doctoral program more readily because of their race, gender, or sexual orientation. Thus, while they truly earned the degree and therefore merit the rewards it brings, unearned privilege may have played a role in their gaining acceptance into the graduate program from which they earned that degree.

People who have unearned privilege often are unaware they have it. But those who do not have privilege usually are very aware when others have it. Persons who have this kind of privilege take certain things for granted and consider them normal. For example, heterosexuals frequently and without concern put a spouse's photo on their desk, while most gays/lesbians/bisexuals probably think twice before displaying a photo of their same-sex partners. To do so may cause anxiety and discomfort. To do so may even cause someone in the organization to deny gays and lesbians promotional opportunities.

Among the goals of diversity work are (1) to develop people's understanding of the concepts of earned and unearned privilege, (2) to enable all individuals access to earned privilege, and (3) to mitigate the unearned privilege that some members of organizational populations have.

The following statements, each of which should be prefaced with the phrase "If I am white," represent the typical attitudes and feelings experienced by white persons in North America:

If I am white ...

1. I am not concerned that people may think I was hired to mirror work-force demographics or fill a quota, rather than for my abilities.

2. and I must relocate for my job, I need not limit my choice of neighborhood, I need not fear that I may be unwanted by my neighbors, and I need not feel I stand out because of my race.

3. I do not worry that people may assume I am incompetent or ignorant because of my race.

4. I need not think that my choices of clothing might be considered too "ethnic."

5. I do not feel obligated to contribute (time, effort, money, or other resources) to the betterment of the white community, nor do I feel obligated to mentor others of my race so that they may succeed in their endeavors.

6. I do not suspect that I might be mistaken for another white person who works in the same organization.

7. and I am being considered for a promotion, I am not concerned that I will be denied the promotion if there are other white people with the same experience and qualifications who have already filled the "slots" allotted for white persons.

8. and I lend my luxury car to my teenage child, I need not fear that the police may see my child driving and assume the car was stolen.

9. and I do not receive a promotion, I do not assume that my race was a factor.

10. and I have a few cocktails at a party sponsored by the organization, people do not necessarily assume I am an alcoholic.

11. I do not consider it unusual for my race to be well-represented at all organizational levels, and I am secure in the fact that I belong where I am in the organization.

12. it is not assumed that I know specific demographics and techniques to serve or market to others of my race.

13. and I am engaging in casual discussion with co-workers, I do not feel uncomfortable when negative comments and jokes are made about my race.

14. I do not worry that my promotability rests on having the "right" accent.

15. and I go into work after hours dressed in casual clothing that might be considered inappropriate for the work environment, I do not worry about being mistaken for someone who is there to do maintenance work or cleaning.

16. and I speak to a high-ranking person at my company, I am likely to be speaking to someone of my race.

17. and I excel in a special project or receive an award for my accomplishments, people do not mention my race.

18. and I travel for business, I do not feel that people will look at me in surprise or think it unusual if I fly first class.

19. and I am invited to make a significant presentation to a large audience and that presentation is not well-received, I do not feel that my performance reflects negatively on others of my race.

20. people do not assume that I only do certain types of work, such as computer programming, gardening, convenience store clerking, or taxi driving.

For most people, learning about unearned privilege is a long-term process. It is a difficult topic for most persons who have unearned privilege because the denial of its existence is strong. For example, many white persons do not believe that having white people in charge of hiring contributes to the hiring of white people, rather than the hiring decision being based entirely on skill. This is not to say that being white is the only reason someone is hired; however, race may contribute.

The subject of privilege is a complex one, and you are encouraged to research it further and broaden your understanding of the issues involved. Doing so will increase your effectiveness, both within your organization and in your private life as well.

THE FOREST VS. THE TREES: UNDERSTANDING PREFERENCES FOR THE BIG PICTURE OR THE DETAILS

Bonnie Jameson

Goals

- To assist participants in becoming aware of their own and others' preferences for "the forest" (the big picture) or "the trees" (the details).

- To help participants to understand that both perspectives (the forest and the trees) are valuable in a group and that both may also cause conflict in a group.

- To help participants to understand what each type of person needs from the other in order to work together.

Group Size

Sixteen to thirty-two participants, assembled into a maximum of three "Forest" and three "Trees" teams of four to eight members each. The teams may vary in size, but there should be the same number of teams for each perspective (one Forest team and one Trees team, two Forest teams and two Trees teams, or three Forest teams and three Trees teams).

Time Required

One hour and twenty to forty minutes.

Materials

- A copy of The Forest vs. the Trees Theory Sheet for each participant.

- A copy of The Forest vs. the Trees Team-Selection Sheet for each participant.

- Several sheets of paper and a pencil for each participant.

- A clipboard or other portable writing surface for each participant.
- A flip chart and a felt-tipped marker for each team.
- A roll of masking tape for each team.

Physical Setting

A room large enough for the teams to work without disturbing one another. Movable chairs must be provided, and plenty of wall space must be available for posting newsprint.

Process

1. The facilitator introduces the goals of the activity.

2. The facilitator distributes copies of The Forest vs. the Trees Theory Sheet and discusses the content with the participants. (Five minutes.)

3. The facilitator distributes copies of The Forest vs. the Trees Team-Selection Sheet and instructs each participant to select a team—either Forest or Trees—based on the characteristics listed on this sheet. The "Forest" participants are asked to assemble in one end of the room and the "Trees" in the other. (Five minutes.)

4. The facilitator assembles the teams, making sure that there are as many Forest teams as Trees teams. The teams need not have (and probably will not have) the same numbers of members.

5. The participants are given paper, pencils, and clipboards or other portable writing surfaces. The members of each team are instructed to work individually to list what they perceive to be the behaviors of the opposite kind of team. (Forests generate perceptions of the behaviors of Trees; Trees generate perceptions of the behaviors of Forests.) (Five minutes.)

6. The facilitator gives each team a flip chart, a felt-tipped marker, and masking tape. The members of each team are asked to share their perceptions about behaviors while one member records these perceptions on the flip chart. The participants are encouraged to add any new ideas about behaviors that arise during this sharing. (Fifteen minutes.)

7. The facilitator instructs each team to choose a spokesperson to report the team's data, reassembles the entire group, and asks the spokespersons to take turns reporting. Each team's flip-chart paper is posted and stays in place so that all participants can see it during the next step. (Five to fifteen minutes; time varies depending on the number of teams reporting.)

8. The facilitator asks the teams to reassemble and to brainstorm what they want and need from the opposite kind of team when they are working together on problem-solving and planning tasks. (Forests generate wants and needs from Trees; Trees generate wants and needs from Forests). The facilitator clarifies that each team is to appoint a recorder to write members' ideas on the flip chart. (Ten minutes.)

9. The members of each team are instructed to prioritize their top five wants and needs from the brainstormed list. (Ten minutes.)

10. The facilitator again instructs each team to choose a spokesperson to report the team's data, reassembles the entire group, and asks the spokespersons to take turns reporting. Each team's flip-chart paper is again posted and remains in place during the concluding discussion. (Five to fifteen minutes; time varies depending on the number of teams reporting.)

11. The facilitator leads a total-group discussion based on these questions:

   ■ What new insights do you have about the Forest perspective? About the Trees perspective?

   ■ How have the two perspectives and their associated behaviors led to conflict in group meetings that you have attended? How have the two perspectives and their behaviors contributed positively to group meetings?

   ■ How have your assumptions about the Forest perspective changed? How have your assumptions about the Trees perspective changed?

   ■ How will you use your new understanding of the two perspectives in future meetings? How can you share your understanding with others? What might you do differently to work better with people whose perspective is the opposite of yours?

   (Twenty minutes.)

Variations

■ After step 7 the facilitator may encourage the Forest and Trees team members to ask for clarification of any perceptions of behavior that they do not understand.

■ This activity may be used with the *Myers-Briggs Type Indicator* or the Time-Management Personality Profile on page 149 in *The 1995 Annual: Volume 2, Consulting.*

■ The process described in this activity may be used for any dimension of the *Myers-Briggs Type Indicator* or another inventory on time management.

THE FOREST VS. THE TREES THEORY SHEET

Important issues can be looked at from two separate points of view: the "Forest" (or big-picture) perspective and the "Trees" (or detail) perspective. People with a Forest perspective are concerned with the future; they look at things with a wide-focus lens and generate global scenarios about what might happen. Those with a Trees perspective are concerned with immediate problems; they look at things with a narrow-focus lens and concentrate on specific details. Current research in the field of psychological type suggests that an individual generally has a strong preference for one perspective or the other and that his or her communication patterns are based on that preference.

Organizational leaders need to understand and be comfortable with both perspectives. For example, both perspectives are important in strategic planning. The visioning portion of strategic planning, which involves determining a future-oriented mission, values, and goals, requires the Forest or big-picture perspective. A team of policy makers must answer the global questions "why?" and "what?" in establishing the organization's purpose and the general means by which it will meet that purpose.

The operational portion of strategic planning, which involves determining the specific outcomes and action plans necessary to achieve the long-range goals, requires the Trees or detail perspective. The policy makers must figure out "what" tasks must be performed, "by when," and "who" is responsible for each task that contributes to achieving the long-term goals.

However, the Forest and Trees perspectives can clash and often do, leading to miscommunication, misunderstandings, interpersonal conflict, stress, ineffective meetings, and other negative results. It is important to realize that both perspectives are essential to organizational functioning and that neither is inherently superior to the other.

The Forest vs. the Trees Team-Selection Sheet

Instructions: Please select the Forest perspective or the Trees perspective based on your preference for the characteristics listed below.

Trees Perspective	Forest Perspective
• Wants facts and details right away.	• Needs to understand the purpose (why something has to happen) before working on a solution.
• Prefers working on one aspect of a problem at a time.	• Needs an overview of the entire problem before discussing details.
• Prefers not to envision a possible future or scenario of the future.	• Needs to see and imagine possible scenarios for the future.
• Is bored with too much theory or abstraction.	• Wants theory to be verified.
• Wants to go directly to the action stage and implementation of a chosen solution.	• Prefers to envision how the situation will look at its best in the future before developing specific outcomes.

FOURTEEN DIMENSIONS OF DIVERSITY: UNDERSTANDING AND APPRECIATING DIFFERENCES IN THE WORK PLACE

Sunny Bradford

Goals

- To help participants understand that diversity is multidimensional and applies to everyone.
- To assist participants in exploring which of the dimensions of diversity have special relevance to their own identities.
- To stimulate appreciation of the value of diversity in the workplace.

Group Size

Fifteen to thirty participants in groups of approximately five members each.

Time Required

One hour and ten minutes to one and one-half hours.

Materials

- A copy of the Dimensions of Diversity Diagram for each participant.
- A copy of the Dimensions of Diversity Work Sheet for each participant.
- A pencil for each participant.
- An overhead transparency or a flip chart drawing of the Dimensions of Diversity Diagram.[1]
- An overhead projector (if a transparency is used).

---

[1]Diagram from *Workforce America! Managing Employee Diversity As a Vital Resource* by M. Loden and J. Rosener, 1991, Burr Ridge, Illinois: Irwin, p. 20. Used with permission of the McGraw-Hill Companies.

Physical Setting

A room large enough for subgroups to work without disturbing one another. A writing surface and movable chair should be provided for each participant.

Process

1. The facilitator begins by showing an overhead transparency or flip chart drawing of the Dimensions of Diversity Diagram and gives a copy of the Dimensions of Diversity Diagram and a pencil to each participant. The following explanatory comments are made:

   ■ Diversity is a multidimensional phenomenon. Its dimensions represent major aspects of people's backgrounds and identities, which make them similar to and different from one another. In the workplace, diversity refers not only to race and gender but to many other significant characteristics as well. These different dimensions represent an array of contributions that people can make because of their various outlooks and differences.

   ■ Each person is a complex mix of many dimensions. We all have other characteristics that are not in this diagram, but the ones that do appear in the diagram are some of the most fundamental aspects of who we are and how we experience the world.

   ■ The six dimensions in the center circle are called "primary" because they are central aspects of our identities and greatly impact our values and perceptions. Some of them are present at birth, and some have a significant impact on how we are socialized as children. Also, other people frequently respond to or make judgments about us based on their assumptions regarding "who we are" in terms of these dimensions. Most of the major "isms" are based on the elements in the center: racism, sexism, ageism, etc.

   ■ The dimensions in the outer circle are called "secondary" because they are characteristics that we can modify and because their presence or absence does not usually change our core identities. However, for some people, certain dimensions in the outer ring exert a fundamental influence on their identities and world views (e.g., their incomes, religious beliefs, and military experiences).

   ■ The diversity dimensions are significant in an organizational context. For example, consider how the work expectations and priorities of a twenty-three-year-old, first-time employee might compare to those of a fifty-five-year-old employee who has worked for the organization for eighteen years. Or consider the work-related goals and experiences of a recent immigrant to the United States who speaks English as a second language and has worked in several countries, compared to those of a native-English speaker who has not worked or traveled outside the United States.

■ Because people all are unique, each of us could draw a personal diversity diagram showing which of these fourteen dimensions are especially relevant to his or her core identity at this time in life. For one person, his or her gender or race might be very significant; to another person, such factors may be less important than sexual orientation or physical characteristics. For some people, characteristics on the outer circle of the diagram might be central to their identities today. Respecting differences means recognizing that the individual coworkers, customers, and clients with whom we interact will have different perceptions, values, concerns, and life experiences based on the various dimensions of diversity that have been salient in their lives.

(Ten minutes.)

2. The participants are formed into subgroups of approximately five members each, with each subgroup representing as much gender, race, culture, and age diversity as possible.

3. The facilitator announces the goals of the activity and hands out a Dimensions of Diversity Work Sheet to each participant. The facilitator briefly reviews the three questions on the work sheet. (Option: To establish an atmosphere of openness, the facilitator may give brief examples of how he or she would personally answer one or two of the questions.) The participants are told that they will have ten minutes in which to fill out the work sheets individually. *[Note to the facilitator:* Be sure to be familiar with the fourteen dimensions and be prepared to answer questions that might arise, such as how race and ethnicity overlap or how generational differences can shape people's perceptions.] (Fifteen minutes.)

4. When all participants have finished filling out the work sheet, the members of each subgroup are invited to report their answers to their subgroup. One person in the subgroup gives his or her answer to question 1, another person gives his or her answer to question 1, and so on, until all group members have explained their answers to all work sheet questions. Before the participants start their reporting, the facilitator provides the following suggestions:

- There are no right or wrong answers; each person will have unique responses to the questions.

- When you share your answers, please explain the reason that you said what you did.

(Thirty to forty-five minutes.)

5. The facilitator calls time and reassembles the total group. Some of the following questions can be used to elicit the participants' reactions to the experience:

- Was it easy or difficult for you to select the three most important aspects of your core identity? What made it easy? What made it difficult?

- How did some of you respond to the first question? Which three dimensions did you identify as part of your core identity?

- How many of you found that some dimensions of diversity are more (or less) salient to you now than they were ten years ago? Why was this?

- What did some of you list as special contributions you bring to the workplace because of your diversity? What have you come to appreciate about the special contributions of others?

- What have you learned about diversity? What have you learned about diversity in the workplace?

- How might you apply the understanding you gained about diversity at work?

(Fifteen to twenty minutes.)

Variations

- In Step 1, examples relevant to the organization's employee-diversity or customer-diversity mix may be used to illustrate the organizational significance of the diversity dimensions.

- In Step 1, the material may be presented as an interactive lecturette by asking the group a few questions. For instance, before explaining the primary/secondary distinction, the facilitator may ask participants what the six elements in the center have in common or why they might be considered "primary."

- If the group consists of people who work together (an intact work group or committee), the activity may be used to help members move to greater trust and a deeper appreciation of their differences. For

The Pfeiffer Book of Successful Team-Building Tools

such a group, questions such as the following may be added to the work sheet or used in the debriefing:

- What dimensions of your own diversity do you think others at work (peers, clients, customers) see first when they interact with you? Why is this?

- What aspects of your own diversity do you wish your coworkers understood better? Why are they important to you?

- What diversity dimensions or aspects of yourself do you express most fully (authentically) at work? What aspects are not fully expressed or are masked?

Reference

Loden, M., & Rosener, J. (1991). *Workforce America! Managing employee diversity as a vital resource.* Burr Ridge, IL: Irwin.

Fourteen Dimensions of Diversity Diagram[1]

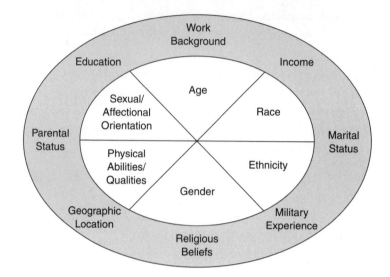

Primary Dimensions of Diversity

The primary dimensions of diversity are those basic characteristics that are inborn and/or that greatly affect how you are socialized. These dimensions shape your self-image, your world view, and how others perceive you. At the core of your identity and life experience, they continue to exert powerful impacts throughout your life.

Age: the number of years you have been alive and the generation in which you were born.

Race: the biological groupings within humankind, representing superficial physical differences, such as eye form and skin color. Race accounts for .012 percent difference in a person's genetic heredity.

Ethnicity: identification with a cultural group that has shared traditions and heritage, including national origin, language, religion, food, customs, and so on. Some people identify strongly with these cultural roots; others do not.

---

[1]Diagram from *Workforce America! Managing Employee Diversity As a Vital Resource* by M. Loden and J. Rosener, 1991, Burr Ridge, Illinois: Irwin, p. 20. Used with permission of the McGraw-Hill Companies.

Gender: biological sex as determined by XX (female) or XY (male) chromosomes.

Physical Abilities/Qualities: a variety of characteristics, including body type, physical size, facial features, specific abilities or disabilities, visible and invisible physical and mental talents or limitations.

Sexual/Affectional Orientation: feelings of sexual attraction toward members of the same or opposite gender, such as heterosexual, gay/lesbian, or bisexual.

Secondary Dimensions of Diversity

The secondary dimensions of diversity are those characteristics that you acquire and can modify throughout your life. Factors such as income, religion, and geographic location may exert a significant impact in childhood, but most of the others are less salient than the core dimensions. However, all of these characteristics add another layer to your self-definition and can profoundly shape your experiences.

Education: the formal and informal teachings to which you have been exposed and the training you have received.

Work Background: the employment and volunteer positions you have held and the array of organizations for which you have worked.

Income: the economic conditions in which you grew up and your current economic status.

Marital Status: your situation as a never-married, married, widowed, or divorced person.

Military Experience: service in one or more branches of the military.

Religious Beliefs: fundamental teachings you have received about deities and your internalized experiences from formal or informal religious practices.

Geographic Location: the location(s) in which you were raised or spent a significant part of your life, including types of communities, urban areas versus rural areas, and so on.

Parental Status: having or not having children and the circumstances in which you raise your children (single parenting, two-adult parenting, and so on).

FOURTEEN DIMENSIONS OF DIVERSITY WORK SHEET

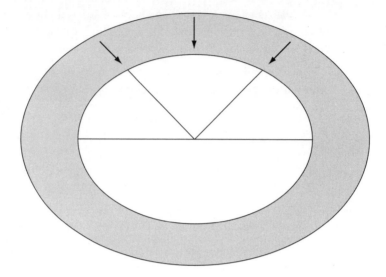

Review the Dimensions of Diversity Diagram. Then fill out the blank diagram above by responding to the following:

1. Which dimensions of diversity are part of your core identity? In other words, which of the fourteen dimensions belong in *your* inner circle? Place the three most central aspects on the top row of the inner circle above. Why are these three dimensions especially important aspects of your identity?

The Pfeiffer Book of Successful Team-Building Tools

2. For many people, aspects of identity change over the years. Would you have selected the same three dimensions ten years ago? If not, what has changed?

3. Now think of yourself at work. What are two or three special contributions that you bring to the workplace because of your own diversity? Think in terms of any of the fourteen dimensions of diversity.

DIVERSITY AND TEAM DEVELOPMENT

Claire B. Halverson and Guillermo Cuéllar

Abstract: The changing nature of work, coupled with
the changing composition of the work force, has put
a great deal of pressure on organizations to adapt. A
major response is the formation of diverse, interdependent work teams. This article discusses the complexities of the development of a team through three
stages: infancy, adolescence, and adulthood (Weber,
1992). The climate issues, interpersonal issues, task
issues, and leadership issues that face a multicultural
team at each stage of development are described and
contrasted with those of monocultural teams. The
focus is on diversity of race, gender, and nationality
as it applies to team members at different stages of
development of their social identity. Other issues,
such as sexual orientation, physical/development
ability, and socioeconomic class are equally as important, but, for the purpose of brevity, will not be
the focus of this article. Issues that need to be addressed by consultants and team leaders who are
helping teams to overcome the threats—and benefit
from the challenges—of diversity are identified.

The changing nature of work has put a great deal of pressure on organizations to adapt. This change is a result of the following factors:

- specialization of human resources;
- limited physical resources, which requires increased synergy and coordination;
- increased complexity of problems, which demands high-quality creative solutions; and
- rapidly changing markets and technologies.

To respond to these factors, organizations are changing from depending on individuals to perform discrete tasks to utilizing high-performance teams that accomplish work interdependently.

The composition of the work force also is changing; it is increasingly diverse. This is the result of changes in immigration patterns, lifestyles, economic pressures, and legal demands.

Although there historically has been diversity of race,[1] gender, and/or ethnicity/nationality in many organizations, roles generally were segregated so that teams were homogeneous. An example of this is the Bell Telephone Company, which, in the 1960s, was the first corporation brought before the U.S. Supreme Court for a violation of affirmative action. Its record was not worse than other corporations at the time, but it was the largest employer. At that time, EuroAmerican men who worked at Bell were technicians, African American men were janitors, and EuroAmerican females were operators. Later, EuroAmerican women moved to clerical positions, and African American women became operators. Today at Bell, as at many other organizations, jobs are integrated into teams that are diverse in terms of race, gender, nationality, sexual orientation, age, and physical ability.

---

[1]The authors wish to acknowledge that "race" is a sociological construct based on people's perceptions, not a biological reality, inasmuch as no one characteristic can group people of the world according to distinct racial categories.

Developmental Stages of Social Identity

A multicultural team is likely to be confronted with issues related to the developmental stages of social identity of members and their consciousness of racism and sexism (Halverson, 1982; Jackson and Hardiman, 1983). These stages can be generalized to other types of social diversity. The stages are described as follows.

Dependent

The team members who have dominant status in society (whites, men) and those who have subordinate status (people of color, women) accept the standards and judgments of the dominant status group. Racism and sexism are ignored, and problems are perceived as resulting from actions of individual members of the subordinate-status group or the overt bigot/chauvinist. Relationships are "one up-one down," reflecting the power dimensions of society.

Counterdependent

Dominant-status group members realize the institutional nature of oppression and their privileged status. This is often accompanied by guilt and inability to be authentic with members of subordinate-status groups. People of color, women, and foreign-born nationals redefine themselves according to the standards and values of the group. They usually experience anger at what they have given up and how they have been treated during their dependent stage. Their choices often are in reaction to the norms of the dominant group.

Independent

At this stage, both dominant- and subordinate-status group members actively work against the established values of oppression. Relationships are authentic and collaborative across groups. There is open dialogue about problems related to diversity.

Multicultural teams often are composed of individuals who are at different stages of development in their consciousness of their social identity. This affects the development of the team.

Developmental Stages of Teams

Stage I: Infancy

Climate

During this forming stage, individuals seek to create a safe environment for their interactions and they establish basic criteria for membership. As they form, multicultural teams must manage a more complex range of issues than monocultural teams. The familiar patterns of compatibility are layered with an array of cultural differences and values. For example, simple things that individuals take for granted in a homogeneous group, such as common norms related to the pacing of speech, use of silence, and type of emotional expression may not be present in a diverse group.

If dominant- or subordinate-status team members are in the dependent stage, they may be unaware of the complexities of diversity and assume that all members should conform to the dominant-status norms. Subordinate-status members in the counterdependent stage may be angry at attempts to establish conformity. Others may be aware of the complexities but feel awkward and confused about how to work with the differences. In monocultural teams the climate is polite; in multicultural ones politeness can be exaggerated to awkwardness.

Interpersonal Issues

Individuals usually are tentative and polite in order to be included in a team. In multicultural teams, they progressively discover more complex and difficult issues that affect inclusion. They look for solutions to ease the uncertainty of their interactions.

Dominant-status members are easily included, and subordinate-status members may be consciously or unconsciously excluded. Members of subordinate status (e.g., people of color, women, recent immigrants) may need a longer period of time in which to develop trust. This is because they may have been excluded in the past, their abilities may have been questioned, and they may be struggling with the cost of relinquishing their cultural norms and values in order to be accepted. They may tend to take a low participatory role, either to observe the stage of consciousness of dominant-status members and ascertain their own safety or, if they are new to the country, to understand the cultural norms.

If members of the dominant culture attempt to include others in their participation, their actions may be perceived as insensitive and impolite because they do not understand the perceptions, values, and cultural behavioral patterns of the subordinate-status members. For example, they may not understand the preference of many Asians to hold back on participation, to speak only if something important needs to be said, and to allow intervals of silence.

Cultural differences related to individualism/collectivism and task/relationship are crucial here. For example, individualism and task orientation have been documented (Halverson, 1993; Hofstede, 1984) as being deep cultural values in the dominant-status group in the United States. Team members with these values find it difficult to join with others and often prefer to work by themselves. They want to start on the task right away and consider time spent in developing relationships to be time wasted. Members from more collectivist and relationship-oriented cultures assume that the group has a higher value than individual needs and preferences. They consider it important to spend time connecting at the beginning of meetings. EuroAmericans who try this often find that the task can be accomplished in the same amount of time. Differences such as these represent cultural patterns.

Cultural patterns are different from stereotypes because groups are not rigidly categorized; preferences, not innate characteristics, are identified. Even if a person has a preference for one thing, he or she is capable of the alternative.

Task Issues

In the first stage, little work is done, and that which is accomplished often is not of good quality. If decisions are made, they are often rushed and represent the desires of the dominant culture.

In Stage I, it is important for the team to agree on its goals and purpose. For a multicultural team, a compelling goal that transcends individual differences is even more crucial than it is for a monocultural group.

Identifying the skills of individual members also is important. Assumptions and stereotypes may exist about roles members should take in accomplishing the work. For example, it may be assumed that Asian Americans may be good technicians but not good leaders.

Leadership Issues

In Stage I, team members are uncomfortable with ambiguity and need to establish leadership. Multicultural teams often follow a path of least resistance and form around the leadership of the dominant-culture members. Group members collude with the leadership to ignore differences and to suppress discomfort. A dynamic of social conformity or "groupthink" emerges, and members choose loyalty to the team even if the leadership is not providing a realistic appraisal or an effective course of action.

The degree to which these dynamics occur varies according to the extent of diversity in the team and the developmental stages of consciousness of the leader and team members.

Leadership is critical to creating an environment that is either inclusive or exclusive. When leadership fails to address inclusion needs, the team will not achieve the level of safety necessary to move past the stage of infancy. A "revolving door syndrome" may occur as subordinate-status members join the team and then leave.

Stage II: Adolescence

Climate

During the second stage, politeness wears off and conflict emerges openly or is hidden under the surface. In multicultural teams, members of the dominant-status group (e.g., whites and men) are apt to be unaware of the conflicts felt by members of the subordinate-status groups (e.g., people of color and women).

Interpersonal Issues

In any team, issues of subgrouping, alliances, and infighting occur in Stage II. In multicultural teams, subordinate-status members frequently are excluded from forming effective relationships with dominant-status members. They may be excluded because they do not share the same jokes, language, style of communicating, social habits, or work style. Or they may be excluded because of feelings of hostility and unwillingness to accept them. Men, whites, and U.S. nationals may fear that they will have to change because of the subordinate-status group members, but they often do not believe they *should* have to change.

If members of subordinate-status groups form relationships among themselves, they are accused of subgrouping and of not becoming part of the team. Subordinate-status group members can experience anxiety and stress if there is pressure to conform in order to belong to the team.

Task Issues

In the adolescent stage, a team needs to focus on how realistic its goals are and what norms and procedures should be used in accomplishing them. Creating common norms is more complicated in multicultural teams because of culturally different patterns of behavior regarding decision making, conducting meetings, communication, and conflict management. For example, the dominant cultural style of problem solving in the United States is linear and emphasizes rational thought processes; however, many other cultures value circular and holistic processes that include intuition.

A team often will find it easier to continue with business as usual and use norms that reflect the culture of the dominant-status group. This happens particularly when there is only token representation of subordinate-status groups. However, differences need to be addressed in a way that allows all to contribute and the team to benefit from the richness of diversity.

Leadership Issues

In the adolescent stage, leadership is resisted by most teams. In multicultural teams, this struggle is apt to be less overt. Because white male leadership may be taken for granted, it may be harder to challenge it. In self-directed teams, it may seem easy and natural to have the leadership fall to, or be taken over by, white men. White women frequently assume traditional roles and support white male leadership. If the leader is a member of a subordinate-status group, for example, a Hispanic female, she may be bypassed or ignored, or there may be a rebellion against her leadership.

Stage III: Adulthood

Climate

The third stage is characterized by interpersonal support and high energy for accomplishing the task. The energy and creativity can be higher in a multicultural team than in a monocultural one (Adler, 1991).

Interpersonal Issues

Emotional conflict in this stage is reduced by patching up previously conflicting relationships. There is a strong sense of group identity and expression of interpersonal support. Differences continue to be expressed, but there are agreed-on methods for managing them. Relationships are functional.

Task Issues

The team may be harmonious but unproductive after it has faced the issues of conflict in the adolescent stage. If so, the team must be realigned with its goals. When this is accomplished, it can be highly productive, drawing on the diverse skills of all team members and no longer hindered by stereotypes and assumptions.

Multicultural teams at this stage can be more productive than monocultural teams because they can benefit from the following:

- increased creativity from different points of view,
- a decreased tendency to conform to ideas without questioning their validity,
- special insights and observations resulting from the previous exclusion of subordinate-status members,
- the opportunity to rethink norms and processes, and
- strengths stemming from cultural patterns of members of subordinate status as well as those of dominant-status members.

Increased creativity is particularly important when the team is working on tasks that require an expanded understanding of the problem and new solutions. For example, one team with a member who spoke English as a second language finally recognized its need to slow down and to paraphrase and summarize more frequently so the member could understand. When it adopted this norm for the non-English speaker, the team found that all benefited with increased understanding.

Leadership Issues

In the adult stage, there is less attention to status hierarchy, and the leadership skills of various team members are utilized. Lines of authority are followed, not circumvented. Different styles of leadership are recognized and valued. For example, women's experience in listening and supporting is recognized and valued as important to team building and coaching.

CONCLUSION

Many multicultural teams do not move beyond the initial stage of infancy and, thus, are less effective than monocultural teams. Stereotypes abound, and differences are treated as problems rather than as potential benefits. Whites and men, at the dependent stage in their consciousness of racism and sexism, may not realize that people of color and women do not feel included and that their skills are not being used.

In working with multicultural teams, the team leader or consultant needs a high level of awareness relative to the issues of a diverse work force. A clear vision is needed of what diversity and equality mean in a team and how the dynamics related to dominant- and subordinate-status groups can negatively impact the team. Specific guidelines around safety and participation need to be developed so that members of subordinate groups can be included as full participants on their own terms. Members' differing needs for addressing task and interpersonal issues should be acknowledged.

The adolescent stage is more intense and complex in multicultural teams than in monocultural teams, because of the difficult issues of racism, sexism, and other forms of discrimination. The team leader or an outside consultant must help the team to resolve conflicting needs in order to develop synergistic norms.

The team needs to set aside time to discuss its processes relative to diversity. Addressing conflict is complicated by differences in individual and cultural styles of conflict management. For example, whites and men may be reluctant to accept direct feedback from people of color and women. Differences in emotional expression also may abound. Skills in giving and receiving feedback, process observation, active listening, and problem solving may need to be developed.

Multicultural teams in the adult stage often will perform better than monocultural teams. The danger for multicultural teams is that differences will be ignored and conflict will be unresolved; the opportunity is their high potential to be creative and productive.

References

Adler, N. (1991). *International dimensions of organizational behavior.* Boston, MA: Kent.

Halverson, C.B. (1982). *Training and stages of consciousness of racism and sexism in the world of work.* Paper presented at the OD Network 1982 Conference, Breakthroughs: Creating a World That Works, Lake Geneva, WI.

Halverson, C.B. (1993). Cultural context inventory. In J.W. Pfeiffer (Ed.), *The 1993 annual: Developing human resources.* San Francisco, CA: Pfeiffer.

Hofstede, G. (1984). Motivation, leadership, and organization: Do American theories apply abroad? In D.A. Kolb, I.M. Rubin, & J.M. McIntyre (Eds.), *Organizational psychology.* Englewood Cliffs, NJ: Prentice-Hall.

Jackson, B.W., & Hardiman, R. (1983). Racial identity development: Implications for managing the multiracial work force. In R.A. Ritvo &

A.G. Sargent (Eds.), *The NTL managers' handbook.* Arlington, VA: NTL Institute.

Jackson, B.W., & Holvino, E. (1986). *Working with multicultural organizations: Matching theory and practice.* Proceedings of the OD Network 1986 Conference, New York.

Weber, R.C. (1982). The group: A cycle from birth to death. In L. Porter & B. Mohr (Eds.), *NTL readings book for human relations training.* Arlington, VA: NTL Institute.

Managed Conflict

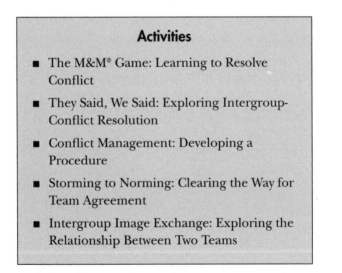

Copyright © 1999 ebb associates inc

Activities

■ The M&M® Game: Learning to Resolve Conflict

■ They Said, We Said: Exploring Intergroup-Conflict Resolution

■ Conflict Management: Developing a Procedure

■ Storming to Norming: Clearing the Way for Team Agreement

■ Intergroup Image Exchange: Exploring the Relationship Between Two Teams

Managed Conflict is one of the most difficult team issues to address, yet it is a very important one. Managed appropriately, conflict increases creativity, encourages the team to look at all points of view, and can lead to consensus decisions. It often leads to higher quality decisions and allows team members to express their true feelings. Poorly managed conflict can lead to a team's destruction. Unfortunately, most teams do not plan how they will manage conflict until after they have an explosive experience.

Although conflict can be one of the most difficult team issues to deal with, it can also be the most rewarding for both the team and the team builder. I am excited to present the five activities in this chapter. "The M&M© Game" acquaints team members with conflict-resolution strategies. Be sure to check out the suggested readings. If you haven't read at least Blake and Mouton, Fisher and Ury, Hersey, Blanchard, and Natemeyer, and Thomas and Kilman, you are not prepared for a conflict-management activity.

"They Said, We Said" provides a process and behaviors for resolving intergroup conflicts that can be tailored to each group. "Conflict Management" helps a team develop its own procedure for managing conflict. "Storming to Norming" presents a way to model effective conflict resolution and set the stage to develop team ground rules. "Intergroup Image Exchange" is an activity that I have used with dozens of teams that are wrestling with a "we/they" issue. This activity will serve you well when working with a split team.

THE M&M® GAME:
LEARNING TO RESOLVE CONFLICT

Gerald V. Miller

Goals

- To observe individual and team conflict resolution when resources are unequal.
- To acquaint the participants with conflict-resolution strategies.
- To offer the participants an opportunity to experience and compare the effects and outcomes from different conflict-resolution strategies.

Group Size

Twenty to thirty participants, as written, but could be played by any number.

Time Required

Approximately one hour.

Materials

- An M&M® Game Conflict-Resolution Lecturette Sheet for the facilitator.
- An M&M® Game Keys to Processing Sheet for the facilitator.
- One M&M® Game Goals and Rules overhead transparency.
- A one-pound package of M&M®s plain candy.
- One copy of the M&M® Game Conflict-Resolution Paired Discussion Sheet for each participant.
- A pencil or pen and paper for each participant.
- An overhead projector and blank transparencies.

- A flip chart and markers.
- An accurate timer or watch.

Physical Setting

A room large enough so that all participants can move freely around the room while negotiating conflict-resolution strategies with one another.

Process

1. Prior to the session, read the M&M® Conflict-Resolution Lecturette Sheet and develop a lecturette to present to participants. Make a copy of the M&M® Game Goals and Rules on an overhead transparency or on a flip chart, and read through the M&M® Game Keys to Processing Sheet to be sure you understand the nuances of the game and are prepared for the ensuing discussion.

2. After participants are seated, pass the bag of M&M®s around and instruct them to take three M&M®s each, but not to eat them. While the participants are passing the bag, introduce the topic of conflict resolution by giving a lecturette on the topic of conflict resolution from the M&M® Game Conflict-Resolution Lecturette Sheet.

3. Ask the following questions to encourage discussion, writing their answers on the flip chart:

   - How would you define conflict? *(Suggested response:* A state of disharmony between seemingly incompatible ideas or interests.)

   - What does the word "resolution" conjure up in your mind? *(Suggested response:* A course of action to solve a problem, a solution.)

   Be sure to bring out that each person has a different style of dealing with conflict. Remind participants that all styles are appropriate to use at various times.

4. Display the M&M® Game Goals and Rules overhead transparency or flip chart and explain the game. Answer questions, but do not discuss strategy. Make sure that no one starts until you say, "Go!" Tell participants that you will be the time keeper, and that they will have five minutes to complete the game. Tell them to "go." (Ten minutes.)

5. Give a one-minute warning. After five minutes, stop the game. Ask participants to return to their seats.

6. Use the following questions to process the activity.

   - What happened during the game?

- What techniques did you use or see others use to acquire M&M®s?

- Did you consider joining forces with another participant? Why or why not?

- How might your strategy have changed if you had formed teams?

- How did you interpret the goal? How did the words "as possible" affect your working toward the goal?

- Did you try bargaining? Did it work? Why or why not?

- What would have been the result if everyone had collaborated? Would that have been a better result? Why or why not?

(Fifteen minutes.)

7. Give a copy of the M&M® Game Conflict-Resolution Paired Discussion Sheet, paper, and a pen or pencil to each participant. Have them form pairs and find a quiet location to complete the questions together. (Twenty minutes.)

8. When the pairs have finished, reconvene the large group and conclude with a discussion summarizing the activity, using these questions:

- What did you learn about conflict and conflict resolution from doing this activity?

- If you were to do this activity again, what would you do differently?

- What did you learn from this activity about how you handle conflict?

- How might you handle conflict differently in the future?

(Ten minutes.)

Variations

- This activity can be adapted to acquaint the participants with using bases of power.

- Instead of the discussions in pairs, role plays could be developed.

Suggested Readings

Blake, R.B., & Mouton, J.S. (1970). The fifth achievement. In *The Journal of Applied Behavioral Science, 6*(4), 413–426.

Fisher R., & Ury, W. (1981). *Getting to yes: Negotiating agreement without giving in.* New York: Penguin.

French, J.R.P., Jr., & Kruglaski, W. (1975). The bases of social power. In
D. Cartwright (Ed.), *Studies in social power.* Ann Arbor, MI: Institute
for Social Research.

Hall, J. (1969). *Conflict management survey.* Houston, TX: Teleometrics.

Hersey, P., Blanchard, K.H., & Natemeyer, W.E. (1979). *Situational leadership: Perception and the impact of power.* Escondido, CA: Leadership
Studies.

Karp, H.B., (1985). *Personal power: An unorthodox guide to success.* New York:
AMACOM.

Mauer, R. (1996). *Beyond the wall of resistance: Unconventional strategies that
build support for change.* Austin, TX: Bard Books.

Raven, B.H., & Kruglanski, W. (1975). Conflict and power. In P.G. Swingle
(Ed.), *The structure of conflict.* New York: Academic Press.

Robert, M. (1982). Conflict management style survey. In J.W. Pfeiffer &
L.D. Goodstein (Eds.), *The 1982 annual for facilitators, trainers, and
consultants.* San Francisco, CA: Pfeiffer.

Thomas, K.W. (1967). Conflict and conflict management. In M. Dunnette
(Ed.), *Handbook of industrial and organizational psychology* (Vol. 2).
New York: John Wiley & Sons.

Thomas, K.W., & Kilmann, R.H. (1974). *Thomas-Kilmann conflict mode instrument.* Tuxedo, NY: XICOM, Inc.

Wiley, G.E. (1973). Win/lose situations. In J.E. Jones & J.W. Pfeiffer
(Eds.), *The 1973 annual handbook for group facilitators.* San Francisco,
CA: Pfeiffer.

M&M® Game Conflict-Resolution Lecturette Sheet

Instructions: Use the information below as a basis for introducing the topic of conflict resolution. You may give a lecturette directly from this sheet or add whatever material you desire.

Conflict

Conflict is one of the more potent of human interactions. It can either facilitate growth or bring harm to the people involved. Perhaps because of its potency, "conflict" has become a loaded word, carrying many negative connotations. There are many popular misconceptions of the meaning and purpose of conflict. People think of conflict as negative, but it may actually be positive and enhance one's strength, clarify one's purpose, or encourage action.

Conflict is a daily reality. Whether at home or at work, our needs and values continually and invariably come into opposition with those of others. Some conflicts are relatively minor, easy to handle, or capable of being overlooked. Others, however, require a strategy for successful resolution to avoid lasting enmity.

The ability to resolve conflict successfully is probably one of the most important skills that you can possess. Yet there are few formal opportunities to learn conflict-resolution skills. This experiential learning activity provides you with such an opportunity.

Like any other human skill, conflict resolution can be taught; like other skills, it consists of a number of important subskills, each separate and yet interdependent. These skills must be assimilated at the cognitive level. Ask yourself: Do I understand how conflict can be resolved? And also at the behavioral level: Can I resolve specific conflicts?

M&M® Game Keys to Processing Sheet

Processing the Game

1. A key point that will come up is that participants will not think in terms of forming teams to achieve their goals, but rather in terms of competition—leading to conflict. There will most likely be an assumption that the word "you" is singular, rather than plural. Be sure to discuss this point (making assumptions) thoroughly.

2. Another concept that is hard for participants to understand is that simply having the most of a certain color does not cause them to win. The goal is to "collect as many of the same color as possible." Therefore, if an individual or team acquires four blue M&M®s and there are only four blue M&M®s available during the game, then they have met the goal. Brown is the predominate color in a bag of M&M®s. Individuals or teams collecting brown candies generally believe that they have won because they have the highest number. *This is only true if they have all the brown M&M®s that were out during the game.* This calls for a discussion of clarifying rules prior to forging ahead with a game.

3. Participants should also learn that when individuals or teams primarily use compromise or bargaining in this game, they cannot win because of the unequal distribution of the colors of M&M®s. With bargaining, one eventually has nothing to trade, if he or she does not possess the color the other person needs. The game can be won by an individual, but because of limited time and variation in color, one person would probably have to use sheer force of will to win.

4. Collaboration and team effort are needed to "win." Teaming up on a particular color will ensure a win-win result. If everyone chooses collaboration to resolve the conflict, it is possible for many teams to win. It is also possible for the large group to collaborate, that is, to agree to share all the M&M®s and simply divide them by color category.

5. As stated above, it is possible for one individual to win the game by going for a particular color and using strong force of will on the other group members. However, that strategy will only work in the short term, as others will resent such behavior. The conflict will not be resolved, but probably will escalate.

M&M® GAME GOALS AND RULES

Goal:

In the next five minutes you are to collect as many of the same color M&M®s as possible.

Rules:

1. Do not start until I say, "Go!"

2. How you achieve the goal is up to you.

3. Do no bodily harm!

4. You may only use the M&M®s that are out at this time.

M&M® Game Conflict-Resolution Paired Discussion Sheet

Instructions: Spend twenty minutes with your partner discussing the following and writing down your answers:

1. List words that describe how you deal with conflict, for example, collaborate, submit, accommodate others' needs, persuade, force, fight, flee, compete, avoid, bargain, compromise:

   _____

   _____

2. What do these words tell you about your conflict-resolution style?

   _____

   _____

3. What insights or learnings about your conflict-resolution style did you have during the activity?

   _____

   _____

4. Which of these insights is potentially the most useful to you in the future? Why?

   _____

   _____

5. As a result of your key discoveries, what will you:
   - Continue doing?

   _____

   _____

   - Start doing?

   _____

   _____

   - Stop doing?

   _____

   _____

THEY SAID, WE SAID:
EXPLORING INTERGROUP-CONFLICT RESOLUTION

Jason Ollander-Krane and Neil Johnson

Goals

- To offer the participants a process and be-haviors for resolving intergroup conflicts.
- To provide the participants with an oppor-tunity to practice or observe intergroup-conflict resolution in a safe environment.

Group Size

All members of two ongoing work teams.

Time Required

One hour and forty minutes.

Materials

- Blank paper, a pencil, and a clipboard or other portable writing sur-face for each of four volunteers (see Step 7).
- A newsprint flip chart and a felt-tipped marker.
- Masking tape for posting newsprint.

Physical Setting

A room that will accommodate a group-on-group configuration. A group-on-group configuration consists of two groups of participants: One group forms a circle and actively participates in an activity; the other group forms a circle around the first group and observes the first group's activity. In this activity, four participants engage in a role play in the inner circle while the remaining participants observe in the outer circle. Movable chairs should be provided for the participants, and plenty of wall space should be available for posting newsprint.

Process

1. The facilitator introduces the goals of the activity.

2. The participants are asked to contribute examples of intergroup-conflict issues or situations that they have experienced or are experiencing. The facilitator clarifies that the examples *need not* involve these two particular teams, but *may* involve these two teams if the participants wish; however, the examples must be situations that the participants would not object to role playing. As the participants contribute sample conflict situations, the facilitator records the highlights of each situation in neutral terms on newsprint. He or she then posts each completed newsprint sheet. (Ten minutes.)

3. The facilitator chooses one of the conflict situations and asks for two volunteers from each work team. The volunteers are instructed to be seated in a circle in the middle of the room with the remaining participants seated around them.

4. The volunteers from one work team role play one side of the situation, and the volunteers from the other work team role play the other side of the same situation. The volunteers are asked to spend ten minutes role playing the chosen situation and coming to some resolution of it. The remaining participants serve as observers and are asked to note their impressions of behaviors that helped and those that hindered resolving the conflict. (Ten minutes.)

5. After ten minutes the facilitator stops the role play and asks the four volunteers to discuss answers to the following questions:

   ■ How do you feel about the resolution of the role play?

   ■ What did you agree to?

   ■ Which behaviors helped to resolve the conflict? Which behaviors hindered resolution?

   As the volunteers discuss their answers, the facilitator writes their comments on newsprint. After the volunteers have completed their discussion, the observing participants are asked to contribute their impressions about what was agreed to, which behaviors helped, which behaviors did not help, and the resolution of the role play; these comments also are recorded. All newsprint is posted so that the participants can review the content later. (Twenty minutes.)

6. The facilitator makes the following comments about the process involved in resolving intergroup conflict:

"When two groups disagree and are unable to resolve their differences, it is often because each individual group's needs were not listened to or met. A successful approach to intergroup conflict resolution provides two things: (1) an opportunity for each group to state and clarify what it needs and (2) a commitment from each group to listen to and try to understand the other group's needs.

"After both groups have stated and clarified their needs and listened to and understood the other group's needs, the two groups explore through back-and-forth dialogue how to meet both sets of needs. They look for opportunities to meet both groups' needs simultaneously. Also, they explore the reason behind each group's needs: Why does the other group want a particular thing? What will that thing provide? Sometimes discovering the reasons behind needs can be the key to a successful resolution.

"Once a resolution has been determined, both groups should summarize aloud what they have agreed to do. Sharing summaries ensures that both groups are taking away the same action plan and are committed to carrying out that plan."

As the facilitator talks, he or she outlines this process on newsprint, posts the newsprint prominently, and then elicits and answers questions about the process. (Ten minutes.)

7. The facilitator chooses another situation to role play using the process just described; he or she asks for two different volunteers from each work team. The new volunteers are instructed to be seated in the inner circle. In addition, all four volunteers are given blank paper, a pencil, and a clipboard or other portable writing surface. Volunteers are told that they will spend a couple of minutes making notes on his or her own team's needs *before* beginning the role play and instructed to make notes on the other team's needs *during* the role play. The facilitator reminds the volunteers to make sure their teams' needs are stated and understood, to make sure they hear and understand the other team's needs, and to explore ways of meeting both sets of needs.

8. After allowing a few minutes for the volunteers to make notes, the facilitator asks them to spend ten minutes role playing the new situation. (Approximately fifteen minutes.)

9. After the role play has been in progress for ten minutes, the facilitator stops it and invites the four volunteers to discuss answers to the same questions asked in connection with the previous role play:

- How do you feel about the resolution of the role play?

- What did you agree to?

- Which behaviors helped to resolve the conflict? Which behaviors hindered resolution?

Again the facilitator writes the volunteers' comments on newsprint. Subsequently, the observers share their impressions about what was agreed to, which behaviors were helpful, which behaviors were not helpful, and the resolution of the role play; these comments also are recorded. All newsprint is posted next to the sheets with the comments on the previous role play. (Twenty minutes.)

10. The facilitator leads a discussion comparing the two role plays and concluding the activity. The following questions may be helpful:

- How did the second role play compare with the first in terms of the role players' feelings about the resolution?

- What similarities and differences did you see in the two role plays?

- What have you learned about useful behaviors and processes in conflict resolution?

- What behaviors do you plan to use the next time you are involved in an intergroup-conflict situation?

(Fifteen minutes.)

Variations

- Prior to the session, the facilitator may ask the participants to write summaries of intergroup-conflict situations that they have experienced, are experiencing, or have observed. Then these situations may be read in the total group and used as the basis for the choices of role-play situations.

- After Step 10 the facilitator may ask the participants who have only observed so far to choose another situation and role play it. At least one participant should observe each role play and share feedback with the role players afterward.

- The participants can be taught the effective conflict resolution process before they begin the role plays.

- The activity can be used with a group other than two intact work teams.

CONFLICT MANAGEMENT: DEVELOPING A PROCEDURE

Lawrence C. Porter

Goals
■ To acquaint the team members with some guidelines for resolving a conflict with another person by giving useful feedback.
■ To help the team members to develop their own procedure for managing conflict.

Group Size

All members of an ongoing team, assembled into subgroups of two or three members each.

Time Required

One hour and forty minutes to two hours and fifteen minutes.

Materials

- A copy of the Conflict Management Suggestion Sheet for each team member.
- Blank paper and a pencil for each team member.
- A newsprint flip chart and a felt-tipped marker for each subgroup.
- Masking tape for posting newsprint.

Physical Setting

A room with movable chairs for the team members. If tables are not available for the individual subteams, the facilitator may substitute clipboards or other portable writing surfaces. Plenty of wall space should be available for posting newsprint.

Process

1. The facilitator distributes copies of the Conflict Management Suggestion Sheet and asks the team members to read the sheet. (Ten minutes.)

2. The facilitator reviews the content of the suggestion sheet with the team members, eliciting and answering questions as necessary. (Ten minutes.)

3. The team members are asked to assemble into subgroups of two or three members each. The facilitator distributes blank paper and pencils, gives each subgroup a newsprint flip chart and a felt-tipped marker, and instructs each subgroup to write a set of guidelines for conflict management that their team can use. The facilitator clarifies that the ideas presented in the handout can serve as a useful starting point and that the subgroups may approach this task in any way they wish; for example, they may borrow ideas from any or all sections of the handout, modify these ideas, write entirely new guidelines, or combine the handout ideas with their own. The facilitator explains that after all subgroups have completed the task, the subgroups will take turns displaying their guidelines on newsprint, presenting these guidelines to the total team, and explaining their reasons for including specific ideas. (Twenty to thirty minutes.)

4. After the subgroups have completed their task, the facilitator reconvenes the total team and asks the subgroups to take turns presenting their guidelines and their reasons for choosing as they did. All displayed newsprint remains posted throughout this step and the next. (Fifteen to twenty minutes.)

5. The facilitator reviews the posted information with the team members and assists them in achieving consensus about which guidelines they want to adopt for their team. *Note to the facilitator: Consensus means that all members can at least "live with" each item. Guidelines not accepted consensually will not be used. Aim for fewer guidelines rather than pressuring the team to accept items agreeable only to some people.* (Thirty to forty-five minutes.)

6. When the team members have reached consensus, they work together to record the final guidelines on newsprint.[1] Then the facilitator gives the newsprint list to a volunteer to reproduce and distribute to all

---

[1]It is vital to involve the team members in the writing task because this helps to build their ownership of the guidelines.

The Pfeiffer Book of Successful Team-Building Tools

team members soon after the session. The facilitator also suggests posting a copy in the room where the team usually holds its meetings.

7. Before adjourning, the facilitator asks the following questions:

- It is vital to involve the team members in the writing task because this helps to build their ownership of the guidelines.

- What were your thoughts and reactions as your subgroup was developing guidelines? What were your thoughts and reactions while the total team was working on guidelines?

- Which specific guidelines would have been useful in managing conflicts or disagreements that arose during this activity?

- What differences did you notice between the handout guidelines and the guidelines that your team ultimately adopted? How do you account for those differences?

- What did you learn about managing conflict? What did you learn about developing procedures for a team to use?

- How can you ensure that the guidelines will be used? How can you ensure that they will be evaluated periodically? What obstacles might get in the way of using the guidelines? What might motivate you to use them?

Variations

- The focus may be placed on personal guidelines (what each team member can do) or organizational guidelines (how to handle conflict within the organization).

- At the beginning of the activity, the facilitator may ask the team members to write about the guidelines that appear to be followed (those that are implicit) in the team and the consequences of those guidelines.

- The facilitator may conclude the activity with a role play that demonstrates the use of feedback guidelines and develops a win-win solution.

CONFLICT MANAGEMENT SUGGESTION SHEET

A Procedure for Managing Conflict

The following procedure has been shown to be helpful in managing conflict in an organizational setting:

1. Do not ignore something that bothers you. Work on the issue involved before the situation becomes intolerable to you. However, if needed, a cooling-off period may be established, with an agreed-on time to deal with the issue later.

2. Talk directly to the other person involved. Work with the other person to try to solve the issue yourselves.

3. If your organization has a human-resource professional on staff, ask that professional for suggestions on how to approach the other person or for suggestions on how to define the issue. Be sure to check back with the professional for feedback or perspectives on the result.

4. If the solution you work out involves a potential change of work procedure, get the approval of your manager before you implement the change.

5. If someone approaches you with an issue, be willing to work on it. You may also wish to seek the help of a human-resource professional in clarifying your point of view.

6. If an individual begins to complain to you about another person who is not present, encourage that individual to talk directly with the other person instead. This approach to handling conflict is much more positive and discourages the perpetuation of rumors, false information, and so on.

7. If, after you have tried to work on the issue on your own with the other person involved—and there has been no change and the conflict still exists—ask for help from a human-resource professional.

Things To Keep in Mind Before Working on an Issue

Before you attempt to resolve an issue with another person, consider these suggestions:

1. Be sure that there is a real problem and that you are not just in a bad mood.

2. Try to identify the real issue or opportunity rather than just the symptoms or personalities.

3. Be prepared to work toward a mutually agreeable solution, not just toward "winning."

4. Remember that it is all right to disagree and that the other person is not "bad" if he or she disagrees with you.

5. Keep some perspective. Relationships are not destroyed but can even be enhanced by working toward a mutually satisfactory solution to a conflict.

Things To Keep in Mind While Working on an Issue

The following reminders may be helpful as you work with another person to resolve an issue:

1. Look for a "win/win" solution: an arrangement whereby both you and the other person involved "win."

2. Do your best to put yourself in the other person's shoes.

3. Be willing to "own" part of the problem as belonging to you. (Avoid thinking "That's not *my* problem.")

4. Remember that talking about your feelings is more effective than acting them out.

5. Establish a common goal and stay focused on it.

6. Be persistent in coming to a satisfactory solution if the issue is really important to you.

7. Use the guidelines listed below under "Giving Feedback."

8. At the end of the discussion with the other person, summarize what has been decided and who will take any next steps.

Giving Feedback

Giving "feedback" is a way of helping another person to consider changing his or her behavior. Feedback is communication to a person that gives that person information about how he or she affects you. Used properly, it can be a helpful "guidance-control" mechanism that the feedback recipient can use in altering his or her behavior.

Here are some guidelines for giving useful feedback:

1. *Describe the other person's behavior; do not judge it.* Describe your own reaction to the behavior. Avoid "judging" language so that the other person will feel less defensive.

2. *Use specific rather than general terms.* Do not say, "You are dominating." Say instead, "Just now when we were discussing the issue, you didn't listen to what I said but kept right on talking."

3. *Consider the needs of the other person as well as your own needs.* Feedback can be destructive when it serves only the needs of the person who gives it and fails to consider the needs of the person who receives it, such as saying "Shut up and listen" rather than listening to the other person's question or issue.

4. *Discuss behavior that the other person can do something about.* Frustration is only increased when a person is reminded of some shortcoming over which he or she has no control (for example, stuttering).

5. *Be aware that feedback is more effective when requested than when "dumped."* The person who requests feedback is more likely to appreciate it and consider it carefully than the person who has not requested it.

6. *Give feedback as soon as possible after the behavior has occurred.* Feedback is most useful and has the greatest impact when it follows the behavior in a timely fashion. However, you may sometimes want to wait so that you can calm down, avoid embarrassing the person in front of others, and so on.

7. *Check to make sure that what you have said is clear.* After you have given feedback, ask the other person to try to rephrase what you have said.

STORMING TO NORMING: CLEARING THE WAY FOR TEAM AGREEMENT

Beverly J. Bitterman

Goals

- To normalize a conflict or confusion a team is experiencing.
- To model effective conflict resolution.
- To set the stage for development of team ground rules for behavior.

Group Size

Any size intact team.

Time Required

Over a period of one to two weeks:

- Sixty-minute manager meeting.
- Two-hour meeting with team.
- Sixty-minute post-team meeting with manager.

Materials

- Flip chart or whiteboard.
- Felt-tipped markers.
- Post-it® Notes and pens or pencils for team members.
- Masking tape.

Physical Setting

A room large enough for each of the formal meetings, with tables arranged in a circle or U shape.

Prior to the Session

1. Meet with the manager of the group to let him or her know that you are aware that the team is experiencing some lack of productivity due to conflict or confusion.

2. Ask the manager to explain some of the specific concerns or issues he or she is having with the team. The following issues are examples of concerns you might hear:

   - Poor communication among team members, such as some people feeling out of the loop.
   - Talking behind others' backs.
   - Lack of respect for authority.
   - Emails critical of other team members.
   - Inconsistency in the team's approach or results.
   - Members not meeting quality standards.

3. Take copious notes, writing the issues in the manager's own words.

4. Explain the approach you propose to use, which would include the following:

   A. Team will meet together.

   B. You will acknowledge the difficult situation and create a vision for a team that is performing at high standards and having fun doing it.

   C. The team will establish ground rules.

   D. The team will address four questions: What is going well right now? What would you like more of? What would you like less of? What are some recommendations you have for moving forward?

5. Assure the manager that you will help to create a safe space for the conversation. The manager may choose to attend the meeting or to be present for the beginning and then leave. You and the manager will need to decide the best course of action.

6. Tell the manager that, by beginning this process, he or she is implying his or her commitment to listen to the team concerns and recommendations and to act on reasonable recommendations. Reassure the manager that he or she need not feel obligated to meet all of the recommendations, but that the team will still expect open and honest discussion about all their recommendations. Advise the manager that some of the recommendations may be beyond the manager's au-

thority to implement and that a more senior manager may need to be consulted.

Process for Team Meeting

1. Meet with the team. Provide a vision for success. Welcome them and thank them in advance for their participation. Let them know that team "storming" is to be expected and creates an opportunity to advance the team to a higher level of performance. Within the context of the organization and the team's role, paint as vivid a picture as possible of what high performance may look like. For example, "I'm looking in my crystal ball, and six months from now I see a group of energetic and enthusiastic individuals who are communicating with each other, anticipating each other's actions, and picking up the slack like an NBA basketball team (or football team, comedy improv group, camp counselors, etc.). By enabling your team to be more successful, your contribution to the company will be enhanced, you will have the opportunity to reach our company goals, and leaders in the company could come to recognize your capabilities."

2. Let them know that ground rules will be set to make the environment safe. Begin by asking them what behaviors they propose to change to create a more effective meeting. Expect to see the following list. If you don't get the whole list, you can fill in the rest:

   - One person speaks at a time.
   - What is said in the room stays in the room, specifically, no direct quotes, no repeating what someone said in the session.
   - Cell phones are silenced.
   - All participate for best results.
   - It is OK to pass if you feel you do not want to contribute.
   - We will end on time.
   - You will get feedback as to next steps by [fill in date].

3. Pass out Post-it Notes and pens or pencils. Ask participants to write one thought on each note for each of the following questions. Let them know they can write more than one thought for each question.

   - What is going well with your group or team?
   - What would you like to see more of?
   - What would you like to see less of?

   Give them time to complete the task. (Fifteen minutes.)

4. Post three flip-chart pages, one for each question. Ask them to come up and stick their notes to the appropriate charts.

5. Next, divide the participants into three groups. Assign one flip-chart page to each small group and have them group the ideas into themes on each chart. This gives everyone the opportunity to understand the pervasiveness of a given view. (Fifteen minutes.)

6. Call time and ask each group to state the themes they see. At this point, members may volunteer to clarify their points or add to a view. If not, seek to start some dialogue by asking:

   ■ What observations can you make based on the themes you see?

   ■ What stands out for you as a pivotal theme—one that, if addressed, would move the team forward? Think of a rock placed behind a car wheel to keep it from rolling down a hill. All that is necessary to get the car moving is to remove one rock. What is your rock?

   (Thirty minutes.)

7. Invite them to continue looking at what actions or agreements could be put into place to move the group toward being a high-performing team. At this point, you may no longer need the Post-its. Participants may be comfortable enough to share their ideas out loud with the group. That is ideal. If you feel some people are not sharing, you may wish to implement another strategy to pull them in. Ideas include:

   ■ Use a wand or ball and ask each person to think of an idea to share. Now pass the item and have each person share when the item comes to him or her.

   ■ Start a piece of paper at three points in the room with a question listed on top. One person writes an idea and passes it to the next person to advance the thought.

   ■ Ask them to move into groups of three to come up with three ideas per group. One person shares the ideas for each group, and they are written on a flip chart.

8. Reinforce the ideas given and express appreciation for the participation of the group. Note what recommendations are fully within the ability of the group to implement (e.g., agreement to treat each other with respect, focus on issues and behavior, disagree in private, etc.). (Fifteen to thirty minutes.)

9. Tell them that you will consolidate the ideas and requested changes that are beyond the control of the group. Let them know when they will hear back from you.

10. Conclude by making action plans for the ideas that are within the control of the group.

Process for Follow-Up Meeting

1. Prior to the meeting, determine whether the facilitator or the manager will be the primary leader for this meeting. The other will be in a supportive role.

2. Convene the group and thank everyone for their participation in the process. Let them know what positive changes have already been experienced.

3. Summarize the recommendations from the team's initial meeting for the manager.

4. Let the team members know the timeline for any changes that are going to be implemented by management.

5. Let them know what cannot be addressed at this time. If you are able to, share the rationale for any decisions that management has made.

6. Invite the group to share any ideas they have had since the previous meeting and ask if they have had any problems trying to implement changes. Ask for suggestions they could follow through on in the future, for example, a small committee or volunteers could be appointed to oversee the agreed-on changes. Ask for volunteers to create action plans where necessary. Let them know that the process will now be followed in their regular team meetings.

Variations

■ During the first meeting with the team, ask them to create a vision for success.

■ More formalized group guidelines could be developed.

■ Other types of training could be held, such as role clarification or listening skills.

Intergroup Image Exchange: Exploring the Relationship Between Two Teams

Editors

Goals

- To assist the members of two teams in improving the relationship between the two teams.
- To assist the team members in exploring how teams interact with each other.

Group Size

Two teams or subteams of up to thirty members.

Time Required

Approximately three and one-half hours.

Materials

- Two newsprint flip charts and felt-tipped markers.
- Masking tape.

Physical Setting

One room large enough to seat the members of both teams and with adequate wall space for posting newsprint sheets. Another room should be provided nearby (so that the teams can meet in separate rooms for their private work).

Adapted from *A Handbook of Structured Experiences for Human Relations Training* (Vol. III, Rev.), edited by J.W. Pfeiffer and J.E. Jones, 1974, San Francisco, CA: Pfeiffer.

Process

1. In a general meeting, the consultant discusses the goals and the schedule.

2. The consultant asks each team to meet separately for one hour to generate the following sets of data on sheets of newsprint: (1) How team members see themselves, (2) How they think the other team sees them, and (3) How they see the other team. The consultant asks each team to select at least one spokesperson to present the data. Each team is provided with a newsprint flip chart and several felt-tipped markers, and the individual teams are instructed to assemble in separate rooms. During this time the consultant travels from room to room, assisting as necessary. (One hour.)

3. The consultant reassembles the two teams and asks the spokesperson of one team to post and explain the data on how the team thinks it is seen by the other team. The consultant asks the other team members to listen, but not respond. Their goal is to understand the perceptions of the other team. (Five minutes.)

4. The consultant asks the spokesperson of the other team to post and explain the data on how his or her team sees the first team. (Five minutes.)

5. The consultant asks the spokesperson of the first team to post and explain the data on how his or her team sees itself. (Five minutes.)

6. The consultant asks the spokesperson of the second team to post and explain the data on how this team thinks it is seen by the first team. (Five minutes.)

7. The consultant asks the spokesperson of the first team to post and explain the data on how the first team sees the second team. (Five minutes.)

8. The consultant asks the spokesperson of the second team to post and explain the data on how the second team sees itself. (Five minutes.)

9. The consultant asks the two teams to meet separately again, in their separate rooms, for one hour to respond to the data and to plan how to process it. The consultant monitors the activities in each room, assisting as necessary. (One hour.)

10. In a third general meeting, members of the two teams share their reactions to the feedback. The consultant leads a discussion on how to diagnose the way the two teams are interacting. (Thirty minutes.)

11. The consultant helps the members make contracts across the teams to improve relationships. The consultant records these contracts on newsprint and gives them to one of the team members for reproduction and distribution to all members of both teams.

Variations

- The individual team members may be asked to write down their perceptions before the team meetings.

- After Step 10 the teams may separate again and respond to two questions: (1) What our team will do differently, and (2) What both teams could do differently.

- The teams may direct their attention to critical incidents in the history of the relationship between the two teams. They may be restricted to a list of adjectives only as feedback.

- The process may be carried out in a series of meetings over a period of days or weeks.

10 Positive Atmosphere

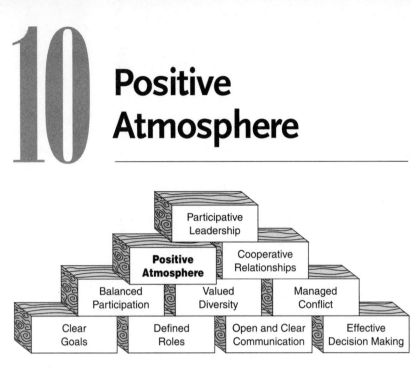

Copyright © 1999 ebb associates inc

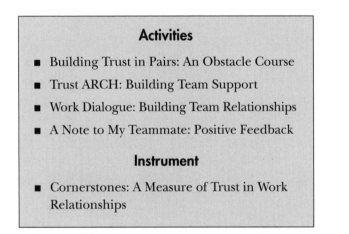

Activities

- Building Trust in Pairs: An Obstacle Course
- Trust ARCH: Building Team Support
- Work Dialogue: Building Team Relationships
- A Note to My Teammate: Positive Feedback

Instrument

- Cornerstones: A Measure of Trust in Work Relationships

A *Positive Atmosphere* requires a climate of trust and openness. It also means that the team members are comfortable enough to take risks, be creative, and make mistakes. Building trust and openness is not just something a facilitator can conduct in a team-building session. These activities can also be used in staff meetings to initiate or to enhance a positive atmosphere. Think of a positive atmosphere as the end product that may occur much later. That is one of the reasons that Positive Atmosphere is near the top of the model.

The four activities and one instrument presented in this chapter will all lead to a more positive atmosphere. "Building Trust in Pairs" is a typical trust-walk activity. It is enhanced by the questions that the guides and the walkers complete at the end of the activity. In addition, the lecturette that accompanies the exercise is a valuable resource. "Trust ARCH" not only identifies characteristics that are important to building trust, but it explores actions to increase trust in the future. "Work Dialogue" presents a series of sixty-four questions that can be used to build positive working relationships between members of the team through openness and disclosure. "A Note to My Teammate" provides team members an opportunity to practice giving and to experience receiving positive feedback—an individual step toward a positive atmosphere for the whole team. "Cornerstones" is a powerful tool to use to measure three dimensions of trust.

BUILDING TRUST IN PAIRS: AN OBSTACLE COURSE

Valerie C. Nellen and Susan B. Wilkes

> ## Goals
>
> - To experience the feeling of being in a trusting relationship.
> - To identify the factors contributing to trust between individuals.
> - To apply a model of trust within the context of the activity, in preparation for future use at work.

Group Size

Five to seven pairs.

Time Required

Approximately one and one-half hours.

Materials

- Blindfolds for half of the participants.
- A length of wood (at least four inches wide and five feet long).
- Several large, empty cardboard boxes (such as those in which food or beverages are commonly delivered) approximately 24 inches long by 12 inches wide by 16 inches deep.
- Several sets of jacks.
- A large sign that says "Travelers' Wall."
- Enough Building Trust Guide Instruction Sheets for half of the participants to have one each.
- Enough Building Trust Traveler Instruction Sheets for the other half of the participants to have one each.

- Enough Building Trust Questions for Guides Sheets for half of the participants.

- Enough Building Trust Questions for Travelers Sheets for the other half of the participants.

- A copy of the Building Trust Lecturette for the facilitator.

- Pens or pencils for all participants.

Physical Setting

Two separate rooms: one that has chairs in a circle or U-shape around a table and another that is empty and out of sight of the participants. The second room should have one wall that has an open door on it and at least five feet of wall space to one side of the door.

Process

1. Prior to the arrival of participants, prepare the two rooms. In one, arrange the chairs in a circle or a U-shape around a table. The participants should not be able to see the second room while sitting in the first room.

   The second room should be empty and large enough to allow at least twelve people to move around freely. Set up the following areas within the second room with as much space between them as possible:

   - Lay the length of wood on the floor, with ample space on either side of it.

   - Place several empty boxes in line with one another, with at least two feet between boxes. Boxes should not be against the wall.

   - Strew the jacks about in a three-foot by three-foot section of the floor.

   - Mark a five-foot section of wall next to an open door by posting the "Travelers' Wall" sign.

   - In one corner of the room, leave an open space with enough room for one person to turn around in a circle with his or her arms spread.

2. Welcome the group in the room furnished with chairs and a table. Introduce the activity with the following remarks:

   During this activity, we will start with an experiential segment and finish with a group discussion and processing session. You will work in pairs and be assigned one of two roles, either "guide" or "traveler." You will receive written instructions for your role in addition to this explanation.

Each pair will consist of one guide and one traveler. The guide will lead the traveler, who will be blindfolded. Each of you should carefully review the written instructions for your role.

If you are undertaking this activity as pre-existing dyads (for example, manager and employee or experienced and new co-worker), the roles of guide and traveler should be assigned according to your work relationships. For those who are part of a larger group that has been randomly paired, the roles of guide and traveler can be arbitrarily assigned.

You will be given a few minutes to read your instruction sheets and ask any questions. Please take care not to share the contents of your instruction sheets with those who have a different role than you do.

3. Have each pair identify its traveler and its guide. Provide the appropriate instruction sheet to each person. Allow time for the participants to read their instructions. (Five minutes.)

4. Tell the participants that they will have approximately twenty minutes in which to complete the experiential part of the activity. Encourage them to take their time. The goal is not to race through the steps, but to give all guides and travelers a chance to participate fully in the experience.

Say that when the members of a pair have completed the experiential segment, they should return to the first room and remove the travelers' blindfolds, pick up the Building Trust Question Sheets for their respective roles, and take their time answering the questions. Let the pairs know that they can begin the task when they are ready. (Thirty minutes.)

5. While the pairs are completing the activity, place the Building Trust Questions for Guides and Questions for Travelers Sheets in two stacks at one end of the table. As pairs return to the room, direct them to the appropriate sheets and give them pencils or pens. Tell them that they have about ten minutes to answer the questions. (Ten minutes.)

6. When everyone has completed the activity and has had a chance to answer the questions, reconvene the large group and process the experience with the following questions:

   ■ How did you feel during this activity?

   ■ The travelers were in vulnerable situations, dependent on their guides. Do you ever feel as though you are in a similar situation at work? Can you provide an example?

- How do you define trust?
- How is trust achieved?
- What did the guides do to encourage trust?
- How could what you have learned during this activity help you as a leader or follower back on the job?

(Fifteen minutes.)

7. If the discussion is not as comprehensive as you would like it to be, deliver the Building Trust Lecturette at this point and then continue asking processing questions, as follows:

- How can trust be built in a setting in which risk and vulnerability exist?
- What can you take back to the workplace from this activity?

(Thirty minutes.)

Variation

- Additional obstacles, based on work-related metaphors, can be added.

BUILDING TRUST GUIDE INSTRUCTION SHEET

Instructions: Welcome to the Blindfolded Obstacle Course! As a "guide," your task is to lead a "traveler" in your care safely through a series of experiences that he or she would not be able to navigate alone. You may complete this task by speaking and/or by physically leading the traveler. It is important, however, that you act as a guide rather than as a proxy. In other words, your role is to facilitate the traveler's navigation of the path and the obstacles, rather than to perform the tasks for him or her.

Above all else, it is your responsibility to protect your traveler. While you are leading the traveler through the obstacles, his or her physical safety supersedes all other concerns.

When your traveler is ready to begin, your first task is to blindfold him or her securely before leaving the room. The traveler should not be able to see through the blindfold at all, but do not make the blindfold restrictive or uncomfortable.

Guide the traveler from the room that you are in now to the room in which an obstacle course has been set up. This should take some time, as your traveler will be adjusting to being blindfolded and will move tentatively.

There are five tasks for you to guide the traveler through. These can be completed in any order and should be navigated with an eye to where other participants are and how you can most easily move from one to the next. Again, please remember that you are *guiding* the traveler and *describing* the tasks, but he or she is responsible for performing each task. The five tasks are as follows:

- Lead the traveler to the section of wall marked "Travelers' Wall." Instruct the traveler that there is a wall in front of him or her, but that a passage can be found through the wall. The traveler's task is to find the door and pass through it.

- Guide the traveler to the section of the room where the floor is strewn with jacks. The traveler's task is to walk across the entire section of floor, from one end to the other, without stepping on anything.

- Bring the traveler to the length of wood. The traveler's task is to step onto the wood and to walk from one end to the other, without falling off.

- Lead the traveler to a corner of the room with nothing in it. Spin the traveler around at least six times. The task is for the traveler to then walk to the center of the room while dizzy.

- Guide the traveler to the line of boxes. Guide the traveler as he or she walks from one end of the line of boxes to the other, stepping over the boxes as though they are hurdles.

When the traveler has completed all of the tasks, guide him or her back to the first room. There, you can remove the blindfold and then each of you is to fill out the appropriate Building Trust Questions Sheet for your role.

BUILDING TRUST TRAVELER INSTRUCTION SHEET

Instructions: As a traveler, your task is to perform a series of five tasks on an obstacle course while blindfolded. Your guide will describe each task to you and will facilitate your performance, as you will not be able to see through your blindfold. Although the guide's role is to be helpful to you, it is important that you actually perform the tasks by yourself.

While performing the tasks, you are free to ask for and to receive help from your guide through either spoken instructions or physical assistance. It is very important that you pay attention to your guide's facilitation of your performance. Note his or her method of instruction and remember things that are helpful or unhelpful to you.

Your physical safety is unquestionably the most important priority during this activity. If at any time you feel that your well-being is in jeopardy (whether due to personal factors or to severely inattentive guidance), you may opt out of finishing the activity, although the obstacles that you will be navigating are not inherently dangerous.

When you are ready to begin the activity, your guide will blindfold you securely. You should not be able to see through the blindfold at all, but the blindfold should not be restrictive or uncomfortable. Your guide will then lead you out of the room and through your five tasks.

When you have completed all of the tasks, your guide will lead you back to this room. There, you can remove the blindfold and each of you can fill out the Building Trust Questions Sheet for your role.

Building Trust Questions for Guides Sheet

What were some of your thoughts and feelings as you read the instructions, prior to putting a blindfold on the traveler?

_____

_____

_____

_____

Did you use spoken instructions or physical assistance or both with your traveler?

_____

_____

_____

_____

Did your method of assistance change with different activities?

_____

_____

_____

_____

What was the easiest part of the experience to guide your traveler through? What made it easy?

_____

_____

_____

_____

What was the most difficult part? What made it difficult?

_____

_____

_____

_____

Which of your actions as a guide did the traveler respond to best?

_____

_____

_____

_____

_____

Which of your actions as a guide were not successful for your traveler?

_____

_____

_____

_____

_____

Did your relationship with your traveler change during the experience? In what way?

_____

_____

_____

_____

_____

How did trust factor into the activity? What did you do to build trust?

_____

_____

_____

_____

_____

How did the obstacle course metaphorically represent some common expressions?

_____

_____

_____

_____

BUILDING TRUST QUESTIONS FOR TRAVELERS SHEET

What were some of your thoughts and feelings as you read the instructions, prior to being blindfolded?

_____

_____

_____

What did it feel like to be blindfolded?

_____

_____

_____

What were some feelings that you had about the experience or toward your guide while performing the tasks?

_____

_____

_____

What things did your guide do that were very helpful?

_____

_____

_____

What were some unhelpful things that your guide did?

_____

_____

_____

What do you wish your guide had done that he or she did not do?

_____

_____

_____

Did you ask for help? In what way? Did you receive what you needed from your guide?

_____

_____

_____

_____

Do the feelings that you had during this activity remind you of feelings you have had on the job? In what way are the situations similar?

_____

_____

_____

_____

Did your relationship with your guide change during the experience? In what way?

_____

_____

_____

_____

How did trust factor into the activity? What did your guide do to build trust?

_____

_____

_____

_____

Do any common expressions come to mind to describe the obstacles you faced?

_____

_____

_____

_____

_____

BUILDING TRUST LECTURETTE

What exactly does it mean to trust? In terms of relationships, trust is the extent to which a person is confident in and willing to act on the basis of the words, actions, and decisions of another. Trust includes the very important element of allowing oneself to be vulnerable, based on the assumption that the trusted person will provide protection. Travelers today willingly entered situations that they could not have negotiated alone, trusting that their Guides would see them through safely.

Where does trust come from? Trust has a three-part foundation. The first is *competence*. We are all more likely to trust someone who demonstrates an ability to perform whatever task is at hand. In today's activity, the Travelers were unable to determine whether their Guides were competent or not, as they were blindfolded and could not judge. The Travelers were forced to rely on Guides' competence nonetheless. Travelers recognized that it was the only way to complete the tasks. In general, we as Guides acknowledge someone's competence by delegating important tasks to them and then not checking up to make sure the work is being done properly.

The second piece of the foundation of trust is *consistency*. We are all more inclined to trust someone who demonstrates consistent behavior: telling the truth, demonstrating integrity in word and deed, and honoring commitments. When someone is consistent, we say that we can count on or depend on him or her. We place faith in the statements of consistent people without independently verifying their actions. This level of behavioral predictability is vital to trust. During this activity, Travelers learned to trust Guides who were consistently correct in leading them through the tasks.

The third basis for trust is *care*. When a person demonstrates that he or she cares about our well-being and is willing to put our welfare ahead of his or her concerns, we feel safe. We willingly risk being emotionally, financially, or otherwise vulnerable with a person whom we trust to look out for our needs and keep our secrets. During this activity, the degree of care Guides had was readily apparent to Travelers.

When all three of these components of trust are found in a relationship, we can say that we trust the other person. When one element is missing, we may trust the person in a limited way, but we do not fully give ourselves over to the other person.

The obstacles for this activity were purposely chosen as metaphors of common situations we may encounter. Travelers found themselves "up against a wall," "overcoming hurdles," "negotiating rough ground," "walking on the edge," and "not knowing which way to turn."

The Pfeiffer Book of Successful Team-Building Tools

TRUST ARCH: BUILDING TEAM SUPPORT

Mary B. Wacker

Goals

- To discuss actions and behaviors that create trust and undermine trust in groups.
- To identify characteristics that are important to building trust.
- To identify current and future actions that will increase trust in relationships.

Group Size

Several groups of four to six people from the same organization.

Time Required

Approximately ninety minutes.

Materials

- One copy of the Trust ARCH Handout for each participant.
- One copy of the Trust ARCH Work Sheet for each participant.
- One copy of the Trust ARCH: What You Can Say handout for each participant.
- One copy of the Trust ARCH Action Planning Sheet for each participant.
- A pen or pencil for each participant.
- A flip chart and felt-tipped marker for each group.
- Masking tape.

Physical Setting

A room large enough for participants to work in groups without disturbing one another. Tables for groups to meet and record responses on worksheets and flip charts. Wall space is required for posting flip-chart sheets.

Process

1. Introduce the session by stating that trust is an important element of effectiveness for groups and individuals who work together.

2. Ask the participants why trust is important. Discuss their responses for about 5 minutes. You may also record their responses on a flip chart and post it on the wall. (Five minutes.)

3. Ask participants how they would define trust. Discuss their responses and record them on a flip-chart page and post it on the wall.

4. Distribute a copy of the Trust ARCH Handout to each participant. Introduce the handout by discussing the following key points:

   ■ As we have discussed, trust is a building block for communication and effectiveness between individuals and within groups.

   ■ Architecturally, an ARCH is a type of opening that withstands pressure and is stronger than a square or rectangular opening. Therefore, an ARCH can be a metaphor for a relationship that is strong and withstands pressure. The ARCH is also an acronym for four essential elements of trust, as described on the handout.

   (Five minutes.)

5. Read the Trust ARCH Handout to the group and ask participants for a work-related example for each element. (Ten minutes).

6. Distribute one Trust Arch Work Sheet to each participant, along with a pen or pencil. Read the directions to participants. Divide participants into groups of four to six individuals, preferably those who work together. Give each group a flip-chart page and marker. Ask each group to discuss the four elements of the Trust ARCH and to list four specific examples from their work groups that create trust and four that undermine trust. (Ten minutes.)

7. Have each group post its flip-chart page of trust behaviors and have a representative read the group's list to the rest of the participants. (Ten minutes.)

8. Discuss with the groups what trust-building behaviors are important to add to their interactions with each other. Discuss behaviors that un-

The Pfeiffer Book of Successful Team-Building Tools

dermine trust that they can agree to stop. Capture important agreements on flip-chart pages. (Ten minutes.)

9. Ask participants how they might approach someone about a behavior that is undermining trust. Ask them what they might say to the person. Distribute a copy of Trust ARCH: What You Can Say to each participant. Ask participants to review the handout and identify what phrases they might be comfortable using with one another. Identify other phrases that might be added to the list. (Ten minutes.)

10. Distribute a copy of the Trust ARCH Action Planning Sheet to each participant. Give participants five minutes to complete the worksheet. Remind them to pay particular attention to what they can do in the future to build trust within their work teams.

11. Depending on the size of the group, either conduct a round robin asking participants to report actions they will commit to doing, or have participants share their commitments within their small groups. (Ten to fifteen minutes.)

12. Lead a concluding discussion of the importance of honoring trust and building commitments; the importance of participants openly asking for what they need from each other; and the importance of communicating about actions that undermine trust. Consider asking the following questions:

    ■ What have you learned about the rule of trust in your work group?

    ■ How will you follow through on the commitments you made today?

    ■ What do you need from one another to be able to meet these commitments?

    ■ Where else can you apply what we have talked about today?

    (Ten minutes.)

THE TRUST ARCH HANDOUT

Building effective teams requires that you create relationships based on trust. Four behaviors required to support the Trust ARCH, representing relationships based on trust, are

ADAPTABLE—to be flexible in your approach toward others. This requires an awareness of and appreciation for individual differences and non-judgmental acceptance of other people and situations. It might be expressed in the following way: "I communicate and act in ways that meet your needs."

RELIABLE—consistent follow-through on commitments and promises. This requires "owning" and communicating one's expectations to others, telling people what you will do, and then doing it. It might be expressed as: "I do what I say I'll do."

COMPETENT—effective technical and interpersonal skills. This requires the ability to act on something by using appropriate resources and problem-solving skills. It could be expressed as: "I know what to do."

HONEST—to inspire believability. Requires the ability to share information and be direct while still maintaining confidentiality when appropriate. This could be expressed as follows: "I tell it like it is."

TRUST ARCH WORK SHEET

Group Activity

From your own experiences, identify several examples of behaviors that CREATE TRUST in the workplace and several behaviors that UNDERMINE TRUST in the workplace. Be specific. For example, rather than say something like "Respect each other," list several specific ways RESPECT can be demonstrated through behaviors, such as "Critique ideas but don't criticize people."

Creates Trust	Undermines Trust

TRUST ARCH: WHAT YOU CAN SAY

Here are some ideas on how to begin a conversation to resolve a problem and increase trust between you and another person. Remember that your tone of voice and non-verbal behavior are also important in creating a climate that supports open, honest communication.

"I'd like to check out something with you. In our meeting I thought. . . . How did you see it?"

"This isn't working very well for me. How is it working for you?"

"I'd like to take a risk and tell you how I felt about. . . ."

"I'm uncomfortable with what is happening right now."

"What's most important to you in this situation? Here is what's important to me about it."

"How can we do this in a way that meets your needs? Is there a way we can meet both our needs?"

"What do you need right now?"

"Is this your understanding of what we agreed to do?"

"What do we want to do next time to resolve this problem?"

TRUST ARCH ACTION PLANNING SHEET

	What I Do Now	What I'll Do in the Future
Adaptable		
Reliable		
Competent		
Honest		

WORK DIALOGUE:
BUILDING TEAM RELATIONSHIPS

Judith F. Vogt and Karen L. Williams

Goals

- To explore the sequence of building from interpersonal to team relationships.

- To provide an opportunity to enhance work relationships through mutual openness and disclosure.

- To allow the participants to practice interpersonal skills related to sharing personal information, taking risks, listening, and giving and receiving feedback.

Group Size

Up to ten pairs of participants. Participants should know one another and have worked together, either as members of an ongoing team or from having worked together in cross-functional teams.

Time Required

Approximately two and one-half hours.

Materials

- A copy of the Work Dialogue Instructions for each participant.
- A copy of Work Dialogue Booklet for each participant. (*Note to the facilitator:* Prepare each Work Dialogue Booklet by cutting along the dashed lines. Assemble the pages in order and staple them along the left side to form a booklet.)
- Newsprint flip-chart paper and felt-tipped markers for each subgroup.
- Masking tape for posting newsprint.

Physical Setting

A room, series of rooms, or outdoor area in which the pairs can communicate in relative privacy. Also, a space in which all participants can work in groups of three to five members each, with wall space for posting flip-chart "products."

Process

1. The facilitator introduces the activity by discussing the following points:

   - Today's organizations have shifted (or are shifting) to work relationships based on employee empowerment and participation, teams and groups, interdependence, process orientation, continuous learning, and quality.

   - For example, work relationships occur in self-managed work teams, temporary (or project) teams, total quality management teams, etc.

   - Such relationships require that people be able to deal productively with others in face-to-face situations. Whether working in short- or long-term work groups, individuals need interpersonal skills, understanding of group dynamics, the ability to work creatively with others for extended periods, and the ability to handle ambiguity in both relationships and tasks.

   - To meet the demands of team and group work, people need to have experience and confidence in the skills of relationship building, including being open, taking risks, giving and receiving feedback, listening, and clarifying expectations.

   (Five minutes.)

2. The facilitator has the participants form pairs by any convenient method, asking them to pair up with persons whom they do not know as well as others. (Five minutes.)

3. One copy of the Work Dialogue Instructions and one Work Dialogue Booklet are distributed to each participant. The facilitator reviews the instructions with the participants. (Five minutes.)

4. Each pair is directed to proceed to a private area and to follow the instructions. The participants are told what time to return to the common meeting room. (One and one-half hours.)

5. When the total group has reassembled, the facilitator helps the participants to process the experience by encouraging them to share

what they have learned about themselves. [*Note:* One of the guide-lines is confidentiality. It is imperative to ensure that this norm is maintained by permitting each person to talk only about himself or herself, not about his or her partner.] The processing questions may include the following:

- What was this experience like for you? How did it change as the time progressed?

- What did you discover about yourself by engaging in this dialogue? What did you discover about the relationship with your partner?

- What did you learn from this process about building work rela-tionships? What skills are important in building relationships?

(Ten to fifteen minutes.)

6. After the experience has been processed for individual learnings, the facilitator shifts the focus to implications of the experience for group and team work. The participants are instructed to form groups of three to five members each, depending on the size of the total group (threes if the total group is small and fives if it is large). Dialogue part-ners should not be in the same group. Each group is given two sheets of flip-chart paper and felt-tipped markers. The discussion groups are asked to extract and list implications for teams resulting from the dialogue experience. The facilitator encourages the participants to focus on the *process* of the dialogue experience. [Once again, partic-ipants are reminded not to discuss their dialogue partners' reactions or comments.] (Twenty minutes.)

7. Masking tape is distributed. Each group, in turn, is asked to post its list of implications and briefly to describe the highlights of its dis-cussion. (Ten to twenty minutes.)

8. The facilitator leads a concluding discussion based on the follow-ing questions:

- What are some ways to build team relationships? What things would inhibit building team relationships?

- What can you apply immediately to a team in which you are a member?

Variations

- If this activity is being used as a team-building activity or with an ongo-ing work group, the group can then establish norms or expectations for itself for the future based on its members' learnings. The norms can be posted and used periodically as a process check for the group's progress. It is important to emphasize here that relationships are dynamic and that norms and expectations are likely to change over time to accommodate new conditions.

- The participants might want to develop a matrix listing various types of teams and the group-relationship factors that they perceive as particularly salient for those teams. This would help facilitators, leaders, and group members to focus future relationship and team-building activities.

- Pertinent lecturettes (e.g., on group development, the Johari Window, the concept of a "psychological contract," or group norms) can provide team members with a greater understanding of the potential of groups that recognize interpersonal competence in group development and group work.

- Dialogue partners can maintain their relationship throughout a workshop or back on the job as "helping pairs." Periodically, they can get together to explore experiences or concerns relevant to their earlier discussions. It is important to clarify that group-based issues should be brought back to the group for resolution. However, the pair discussions can provide support or insight to members prior to their taking personal observations to the group.

- Self- and/or group-assessment tools can be used as a follow-up to the dialogue. These can help to strengthen each person's self-learning and/or the group's functioning.

- The dialogue can be utilized in team settings. Two options are possible. First, if members have minimal interpersonal or group skills, it is suggested that dialogue partners complete the booklet first. After Step 5, each dialogue pair selects two sentence stems that they think are essential for the team to discuss. Each pair describes why it selected the items. Once the team has had an opportunity to discuss at least one item from each pair, it can return to Step 6 and continue.

  A second option for utilizing the dialogue as a team activity requires that group members have good interpersonal skills, especially in terms of openness and trust. Steps 2, 3, and 4 can be replaced by a team dialogue (a group of sixteen is the maximum size). First, the group discusses the introductory comments for clarity and implications. Then each member starts the discussion of an item by completing the stem. Others follow if they want to. Once discussion slows down for that item, another group member starts discussion of the next item by completing the stem; again other members participate if they choose to. This process continues through all the items or until the allocated time has expired. All members should have an opportunity to initiate an item and to participate in the open discussion. If this is not happening, the facilitator may want to break the group into smaller groups or even pairs, so that each person can participate and learn from the process.

■ The activity can be ended after Step 5, after adding a concluding discussion question such as "What have you learned from this experience that you can apply to the team as a whole?"

WORK DIALOGUE INSTRUCTIONS

About This Dialogue

The conversation that you are about to begin is intended to help you develop more effective work relationships. Tasks are accomplished more effectively if people who work together have the ability to exchange expertise, ideas, points of view, feelings, and attitudes.

It is also important that you be able to clarify expectations and assumptions that you make about one another in relation to the work to be done. Furthermore, the system's (team, group, division, or organization) culture emerges from interactions that members have with one another.

One purpose of this discussion is to foster greater understanding of others at work. By telling about yourself and by sharing perceptions with another person, you will be working toward a higher level of trust. Trust is the foundation for effective group work, especially in settings that demand coordination, teamwork, creativity, and quality.

Guidelines for This Dialogue

1. The booklet consists of a series of open-ended statements. You and your partner will take turns, each completing the next statement orally. Focus your discussion around work-related issues.

2. All of this discussion is confidential. Do not repeat later what your partner has said during the dialogue.

3. Do not look ahead in the booklet.

4. Do not skip items. Consider each statement in the order in which it is presented.

5. You may decline to respond to any statement.

When you and your partner have finished reading this introduction, turn the page and begin.

Following Up

The items are intended to open a dialogue that can be carried on in your work relationship. You may wish to make definite plans to continue this exchange in the future. Some activities that you may consider follow:

- Go through this dialogue booklet again after about six months.
- Schedule meetings to discuss items and your relationship.
- Contract with each other for support in changing your behavior at work.

Usually, I am the kind of person who . . .   1

I want to become the kind of person who . . .   2

When I am feeling anxious in a new work situation, I usually . . .   3

I am happiest at work when . . .   4

My greatest area of growth at work is . . .   5

I am resistant when . . .   6

I usually react to negative criticism by . . .   7

I usually react to supportive remarks by . . .   8

To me, belonging to a team means . . .   9

When I am in a new work group, I . . .   10

Briefly discuss how the dialogue is going.   11

When things aren't going well at work, I . . .   12

Basically, the way I feel about my work is . . .   13

When I think about your responsibilities, I think that . . .   14

The most important skill in developing work relationships is listening. To im- 15
prove your ability to hear each other, follow these steps: the person whose turn
it is completes the following item in two or three sentences; the listener then para-
phrases in his or her own words what the speaker has said; then the listener com-
pletes the same item, and the other partner paraphrases what he or she has heard.

As a member of a team, I expect . . .   16

When each of you has had a turn, share what you may have learned about   17
listening. During this dialogue, you may wish to continue the development
of your listening capabilities by paraphrasing what your partner has said.

At work, I'm best at . . .   18

In conflict situations between people at work, I usually . . .   19

The thing I like best about you is . . .   20

I prefer to receive feedback about myself and my work . . .   21

The ways I prefer to receive information are . . .   22

The kinds of task information I value are . . .   23

I prefer to work with people who . . .   24

My first impression of you was . . .   25

I think you see me as . . .   26

What I think you need to know about working with me is . . .   27

The Pfeiffer Book of Successful Team-Building Tools

Ten years from now, I . . .   28

I joined this organization because . . .   29

The next thing I'm going to try to accomplish at work is . . .   30

The next step in my career development seems to be . . .   31

Faced with a conflict between the goals of the organization   32
(division) and your own welfare, I predict that you would . . .

My own personal goals are to . . .   33

The worst coworker I ever had . . .   34

When I ask for help at work, I . . .   35

When someone helps me at work, I . . .   36

Have a brief discussion of how this dialogue is going so far. How open   37
are you being? How do you feel about your participation up to this point?

The emotion I find most difficult to control at work is . . .   38

When I offer help at work, I . . .   39

Your work seems to be . . .   40

The best colleague I ever had . . .   41

Listening Check: Paraphrase your partner.   42

The worst boss I ever had . . .   43

When I am approaching a deadline, I . . .   44

What team work means to me is . . .   45

I think my goals and your goals can be achieved if . . .   46

I think you could help me to . . .   47

Have a brief discussion of what your responses to the last few items say   48
about what you believe to be valuable in work relationships and teams.

I think our personal goals and our organization's goals can be   49
mutually achieved if . . .

I think of terms such as "boss," "supervisor," and "manager" as . . .   50

The best leader I ever worked with . . .   51

When I see you work with others, I . . .   52

In a work group, I am most comfortable when my colleagues . . .   53

In a work group, I feel most comfortable when leadership . . .   54

My impression of you now is . . .   55

In a work group, I usually get most involved when . . .   56

Listening check: Paraphrase your partner.   57

In ambiguous, unstructured situations, I . . .   58

I like to be a follower when . . .   59

When I have to work with others to accomplish goals, I . . .   60

My position in this organization . . .   61

I would like my role in the organization/team to . . .   62

Together we can . . .   63

Have a brief discussion of your participation in and reactions to this   64
conversation.

A NOTE TO MY TEAMMATE: POSITIVE FEEDBACK

Deborah M. Fairbanks

> ## Goals
>
> - To provide the participants with an opportunity to experience positive feedback.
> - To offer the participants an opportunity to practice giving specific positive feedback.
> - To offer the participants a method for improving their working climate.

Group Size

All members of an ongoing work group.

Time Required

Thirty minutes or less, depending on the size of the group.

Materials

- Several sheets of colored paper for each participant.
- Colored pens for each participant.
- A clipboard or other portable writing surface for each participant.
- A newsprint poster prepared in advance with the following information:
    - Take responsibility for the perception—use "I."
    - Make it personal—use "you" or the person's name.
    - Use the present tense.
    - Use positive, active verbs ("has," "can," "chooses," "deserves," "sees").
    - Focus on specific, concrete, observable behaviors, as opposed to general, abstract personality qualities that are inferred from behavior.
    - A copy of A Note to My Teammate Theory Sheet for the facilitator.

Physical Setting

Any room in which the group can meet comfortably.

Process

1. The facilitator explains that the participants will have an opportunity to write and to share positive phrases, to develop the habit of thinking positively, and to experience receiving positive feedback. He or she then presents a lecturette based on A Note to My Teammate Theory Sheet. (Ten minutes.)

2. The facilitator distributes paper, pencils, and portable writing surfaces to the participants and instructs each person to write his or her name on the paper.

3. The participants are asked to circulate, and each is asked to write a positive phrase on every person's paper. (Five to ten minutes.)

4. The facilitator leads a concluding discussion based on questions such as the following:

   ■ How do you feel about yourself right now?

   ■ What do you notice about the phrases that others use to describe you? What themes do you recognize? What does that tell you about yourself? What does that tell you about your contribution to the team?

   ■ How can you use positive feedback on yourself to help break a habit or overcome a limitation?

   ■ How might the group use this process during its work? How will this kind of experience aid the group in being more productive?

   (Fifteen minutes.)

Variations

■ This activity can be conducted during each meeting of the group, becoming a regular programming practice. It can be carried into the general work place, with coworkers writing phrases on posted sheets or on a community board.

■ The group can brainstorm a group or team phrase.

■ Rather than circulate the notes, each participant could write a separate note to every other team member. Each team member could be given a big envelope to serve as a mailbox.

A Note to My Teammate Theory Sheet

Throughout a person's personal and professional life, he or she gives and receives feedback. Some feedback comes from other people; other feedback can be self-feedback, based on one's own observations and evaluations of experiences. A person's feelings, thoughts, and behavior are shaped by this feedback, whether it be positive or negative.

Self-feedback influences behavior. For example, when a person makes a mistake, his or her self-feedback might take the form of "What a dunce I am! I can't seem to do anything right!" On the other hand, the self-feedback might sound more like "That didn't work the way that I wanted it to work. Next time I'll try something else." The phrasing of the self-feedback makes a difference in how this person will react to the experience of making the mistake.

Feedback from others also influences behavior. For instance, if another person sees the mistake and judges it to be the result of a lack of experience, he or she might say, "That's O.K. What works best for me is to do it this way." However, if that person perceives the mistake to be a careless one, he or she might say, "Why can't you be more careful? You must pay more attention to what you're doing!" Once again, the phrasing of the feedback from others makes a difference in how a person reacts to an experience.

A person's tendency to respond positively or negatively—constructively or destructively—is a pattern that can be modified. Positive feedback empowers, supports, and informs. It is a technique for managing one's thoughts and making conscious choices about how to respond to people and to situations. Learning to use positive feedback appropriately can alter a person's responses and can create a more positive and supportive environment.

One form for giving positive feedback is "I think/perceive/sense that you, (name), (general quality), because (specific description)." For example, a person might say, "I think that you, Chris, are a dedicated worker because I see the quality of the work you produce." Another example might be to say "I perceive that you, Robin, are a careful listener because I hear you ask insightful questions."

In summary, key characteristics of positive feedback include the following:

- Take responsibility for the perception—use "I."

- Make it personal—use "you" or the person's name.

- Use the present tense.
- Use positive, active verbs ("has," "can," "chooses," "deserves," "sees").
- Focus on specific, concrete, observable behaviors, as opposed to general, abstract personality qualities that are inferred from behavior.

CORNERSTONES: A MEASURE OF TRUST IN WORK RELATIONSHIPS

Amy M. Birtel, Valerie C. Nellen, and Susan B. Wilkes

Abstract: Trust between co-workers in the workplace has been demonstrated to be a key component of effective management, organizational commitment, and job satisfaction. The Cornerstones Trust Survey can be used to assess the level of trust between individuals in organizational life and in work relationships. It measures three dimensions of trust: *competence* (the person's perceived ability to do the work), *credibility* (the person's consistency and predictability), and *care* (the other person's valuing of the respondent's needs and concerns).

Respondents answer fifteen questions regarding their level of trust for an identified colleague. Composite scores are obtained on the three dimensions. Instructions are included for using this instrument as a basis for personal feedback and action planning.

Introduction

The Cornerstones Trust Survey is designed to assist the professional in assessing the level of interpersonal trust among respondents who work together. The reasons for wanting to measure interpersonal trust are many and are supported by research emphasizing the importance of trust between individuals in the workplace. McAllister (1995) suggests that it is especially important for managers to be able to build trust with employees, as much of their work function involves acting as a conduit between people and/or systems. Mishra and Morrissey's (1990) study of employee/employer relationships found six main advantages for an organization when workers trusted their leaders: improved communication; greater predictability, dependability, and confidence; a reduction in employee turnover; openness and willingness to listen and accept criticism nondefensively; repeat business; and a reduction of friction between employees. Posner and Kouzes (1988), two highly regarded scholars of leadership, cite research in which the degree to which employees trusted their management directly affected their organizational commitment, job satisfaction, role clarity, and perceptions of organizational effectiveness. It thus seems evident that the ability to inspire interpersonal trust is an invaluable asset in the workplace and that evaluating it and finding ways to improve it are important in today's organizations.

There is a great deal of research on the situational antecedents of trust, and many of the findings are similar or related. For purposes of this instrument, many of the researchers' suggested antecedents were subsumed into three major categories: *competence, credibility,* and *care.* A similar grouping is seen in the work of Mayer, Davis, and Schoorman (1995). *Competence* refers to the ability of the individual in question to perform the task or activity on which the assessment of trust is being based. For example, if a person is thinking about allowing a doctor to perform heart surgery on him or her, the person must trust in the doctor's skill as a cardiac surgeon. In the same way, an employee must trust his or her coworker or manager to carry out assigned duties in a highly effective way. *Credibility* is defined as a measure of the individual's consistency across situations. For example, one person's trust in another is strongly influenced by the degree to which that person's word matches his or her deeds, as well as by the predictability of the person's behaviors based on previous behaviors or statements. Finally, the construct of *care* provides an assessment of how much the individual in question has demonstrated a willingness to value the needs and concerns of the person who is thinking about trusting him or her. People are more likely to trust others if they have evidence to suggest that the others will consider their interests when taking actions that may affect them, especially important in employer/employee relationships.

DESCRIPTION OF THE INSTRUMENT

The Cornerstones Trust Survey is a self-scoring instrument with fifteen items, five on each of the three dimensions described above. Respondents use a seven-point Likert scale to rate the trust they hold in an identified colleague, co-worker, or supervisor. The instrument takes approximately five minutes to complete.

Respondents can calculate their own scores on this survey, using the Cornerstones Trust Survey Self-Scoring Sheet. After scores have been tabulated, they are plotted onto a grid provided on the scoring sheet. There are a number of potential uses for the results, described in the "Using the Results" section.

ADMINISTERING THE SURVEY

Explain to respondents that they will complete a brief survey to determine the level of trust they feel for an identified colleague. If the results will not be shared with the other person, assure the respondents that they do not need to write the person's name on the survey and that you will not be "sharing" their results with others or requiring them to do so. In this case, mention that some people do find it helpful to use the survey simply as a way to get in touch with their own feelings about another.

If the survey is being used as a feedback tool, remind them to be especially conscientious, as they will be sharing their answers with the persons they rated. Remind them that the purpose of the instrument is not only to help them learn about trust and its component parts but to provide feedback to their colleagues in order to improve their working relationships.

Distribute copies of the survey. Instruct participants to think of only one colleague and to use the full range of responses from 1 to 7 when answering each of the questions about that particular colleague. (It is possible to use this survey in a team-building workshop, in which case a small work group fills out surveys on each of their co-workers and their manager and then spends time sharing with one another one-to-one and in a facilitated group discussion.)

After respondents have finished filling out the survey, but prior to scoring it, give a brief explanation about the importance of interpersonal trust in the workplace. Explain the three components of trust that have been identified in the research and distribute a copy of the Cornerstones Trust Survey Handout to each respondent.

Explain that it is important for colleagues to build trust in order to work together effectively and to maximize job satisfaction and organizational commitment. Show the participants the key components of trust, as seen on the diagram on the handout; then read through the handout with them. *Competence* refers to the ability of the individual in question to perform the task or activity on which the assessment of trust is being based. For example, if a person is thinking about allowing a doctor to perform heart surgery on him or her, the person must trust in the doctor's skill as a cardiac surgeon. In the same way, an employee must trust his or her co-worker or manager to carry out assigned duties in a highly effective way. *Credibility* is defined as a measure of the individual's consistency across situations. For example, one person's trust in another is strongly influenced by the degree to which that person's word matches his or her deeds, as well as by the predictability of the person's behaviors based on previous behaviors or statements. Finally, the construct of *care* provides an assessment of how much the individual in question has demonstrated a willingness to value the needs and concerns of the person who is thinking about trusting him or her. People are more likely to trust others if they have evidence to suggest that the others will consider their interests when taking actions that may affect them, especially important in employer/employee relationships.

Scoring the Survey

Hand out copies of the Cornerstones Trust Survey Self-Scoring Sheet. Instruct respondents to transfer their answers to the scoring sheet and to follow the instructions for calculating their scores. Offer assistance to any participants who may need help.

Once respondents have scored their surveys, have them plot their scores to create a visual representation of the levels of trust experienced on the three dimensions using the diagram on the second page of the scoring sheet. The center of the triangle represents 0 and each point of the triangle represents a score of 35 on that dimension. After participants have plotted their scores, tell them to connect the three points to create a "trust triangle" that can be used as a basis for discussion, if desired. If the survey is being used as the focus of a team-building session, repeat the process for each member of the team before continuing.

INTERPRETING THE RESULTS

Next, help the respondents interpret their results. Draw a sample triangle on a piece of flip-chart paper with scores of 10, 23, and 15 on care, competence, and credibility, respectively. Note how, in this case, the respondent feels that the person is skilled, but the respondent is not confident that the individual being rated cares about him or her personally or would be truthful under all circumstances. On the other hand, if the scores were high on care, high on credibility, and low on competence, the interpretation might be that the respondent thinks the person is open, honest, and can be trusted, but that he or she needs to improve his or her overall competence in doing the work. Finally, tell respondents that the overall size of the triangle can be interpreted as a measure of general trust, with a small but balanced triangle suggesting that improving trust on all three dimensions might be useful. Suggest that examining individual items to detect particular areas of strength or weakness in their level of trust for the other person can also be beneficial. They should mark items that they want to discuss one-on-one.

USING THE RESULTS

Following are a number of ways that the Cornerstones Trust Survey can be used.

1. The survey can be included as an activity in a workshop module on trust, leadership, or team building. The focus would be on understanding the components of trust and on learning more about the implications of levels of trust in work relationships. Additional discussion topics might include ways of building trust in work relationships.

2. The survey can provide a basis for intervention in dyads offering one another one-on-one feedback. Participants can provide feedback to

one another in pairs, using their survey results. In some cases, it may be useful for this discussion to be facilitated by a skilled consultant. In preparation for giving one another feedback, the participants may want to review specific items with particularly high or low scores. As with any form of feedback, remind participants to provide examples and to focus on actual behavior rather than on personal characteristics or on supposition about another's motives.

3. The survey can be employed in 360-degree feedback sessions by aggregating a number of respondents' scores for one individual and providing the scores to that person with accompanying qualitative feedback.

4. The survey may be adopted on a team or organization-wide basis to assess general levels of trust within the organization by compiling a number of individual results.

In all of these cases, an action plan should be created to assist the individual(s) to apply what each has learned. Generally speaking, an action plan would include goals, specific action steps leading to the achievement of the goals, and a time frame for accomplishing each step.

PSYCHOMETRIC PROPERTIES OF THE INSTRUMENT

Demographics of the Sample

In order to test reliability of the instrument, 118 employees from a variety of organizations completed the Cornerstones Trust Survey. Of those completing the survey, 69.8 percent were female and 30.2 percent were male. The large majority of the respondents were working adults, 88.7 percent of whom were twenty-six or older (61.7 percent were thirty-six or older). Racial breakdowns were as follows: 82.8 percent Caucasian, 9.5 percent African-American, 3.4 percent Asian-American, 3.4 percent Latino, and .9 percent "other."

Reliability

Internal consistency for the overall scale and each of the three subscales was calculated using Cronbach's alpha for the full sample of 118 participants. The internal consistency score for the overall scale of fifteen items was very high, with an alpha of .96. Alpha coefficients for the subscales of competence, caring, and credibility were .95, .92, and .92, respectively.

Validity

Validity of the instrument as a measure of trust in a work relationship was assessed by examining the relationship between scores on the scales and a separate item about trust. The item was "This is a person I trust." Correlations between the item and the scales are noted in Table 1. All correlations were significant at the p<.01 level.

	General Trust Item
Competence Score	.617
Care Score	.860
Credibility Score	.853

Table 1.   Correlations for General Item

References

Mayer, R.C., Davis, J.H., & Schoorman, F.D. (1995). An integrative model of organizational trust. *Academy of Management Review, 20*(3), 709–734.

McAllister, D.J. (1995). Affect- and cognition-based trust as foundations for interpersonal cooperation in organization. *Academy of Management Journal, 38*(1), 24–59.

Mishra, J., & Morrisey, M.A. (1990). Trust in employee/employer relationships: A survey of West Michigan managers. *Public Personnel Management, 19*(4), 443–486.

Posner, B., & Kouzes, J. (1988). Relating leadership and credibility. *Psychological Reports, 63*(2), 527–530.

CORNERSTONES TRUST SURVEY

Amy M. Birtel, Valerie C. Nellen, and Susan B. Wilkes

Instructions: Think of the individual for whom you are filling out this survey and, using the seven-point scale below, respond to the following with only that person in mind. Circle the numbers that correspond to your level of agreement. If you will be sharing your feedback with this person, write his or her name at the top of the page.

1 = Very strongly disagree 2 = Strongly disagree 3 = Disagree 4 = Neutral 5 = Agree 6 = Strongly agree 7 = Very strongly agree

This is a person . . .

1. who effectively completes the tasks on which he or she works.　1　2　3　4　5　6　7

2. who tells me the truth.　1　2　3　4　5　6　7

3. who considers my needs and interests when making decisions that impact me.　1　2　3　4　5　6　7

4. to whom I would delegate important tasks, if I had the opportunity.　1　2　3　4　5　6　7

5. who keeps confidential any information that he or she has promised not to share.　1　2　3　4　5　6　7

6. who does things to help me out when I need help.　1　2　3　4　5　6　7

7. who demonstrates an appropriate level of skill in completing tasks.　1　2　3　4　5　6　7

8. who honors his or her commitments.　1　2　3　4　5　6　7

9. who demonstrates concern for my well-being.　1　2　3　4　5　6　7

10. who produces work that is useful to others.　1　2　3　4　5　6　7

11. who is honest about his or her own ability to get things done.　1　2　3　4　5　6　7

12. who has expectations of me that challenge me, but who provides the support
I need to live up to those expectations.   1   2   3   4   5   6   7

13. who demonstrates competence in
his or her work.   1   2   3   4   5   6   7

14. who makes statements that are credible.   1   2   3   4   5   6   7

15. who knows some personal details of
my life outside of work because I've felt
comfortable sharing that information.   1   2   3   4   5   6   7

CORNERSTONES TRUST SURVEY SELF-SCORING SHEET

Instructions: Transfer your responses for each question to this page. Add the numbers in each column to obtain a total score for each dimension of trust.

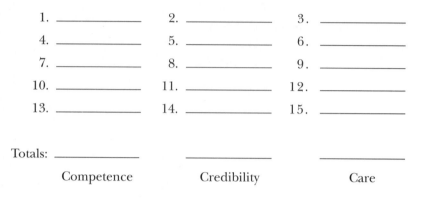

1. _____	2. _____	3. _____
4. _____	5. _____	6. _____
7. _____	8. _____	9. _____
10. _____	11. _____	12. _____
13. _____	14. _____	15. _____

Totals: _____   _____   _____

  Competence   Credibility   Care

What Your Scores Mean

29 through 35: You have a great deal of trust in this individual on this dimension.

20 through 28: You have a reasonable amount of trust in this individual on this dimension, but would like to feel more comfortable trusting the individual.

11 through 19: You are somewhat wary of this individual on this dimension, and your relationship would likely benefit from increased trust.

5 through 10: You have very little trust in this individual on this dimension, and it is imperative that this be improved in order for you to work well together.

Now, plot your scores on the following diagram, with the middle of the triangle representing a score of 0 and each end point representing a score of 35 on the dimension identified. Finally, connect the plotted points to create a "trust triangle" representing your overall level of trust in the identified individual.

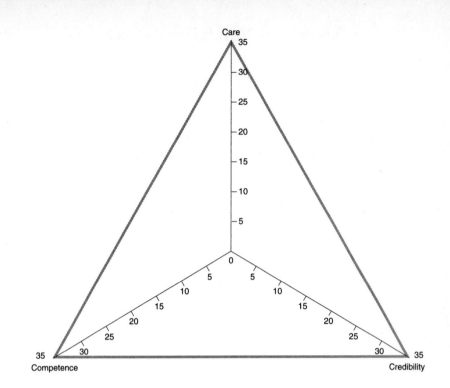

Care
35
30
25
20
15
10
5
0
5   5
10   10
15   15
20   20
25   25
30   30
35   35
Competence   Credibility

Cornerstones Trust Survey Handout

Competence refers to the ability of the individual in question to perform the task or activity on which the assessment of trust is being based. For example, if a person is thinking about allowing a doctor to perform heart surgery on him or her, the person must trust in the doctor's skill as a cardiac surgeon. In the same way, an employee must trust his or her co-worker or manager to carry out assigned duties in a highly effective way.

Credibility is defined as a measure of the individual's consistency across situations. For example, one person's trust in another is strongly influenced by the degree to which that person's word matches his or her deeds, as well as by the predictability of the person's behaviors based on previous behaviors or statements.

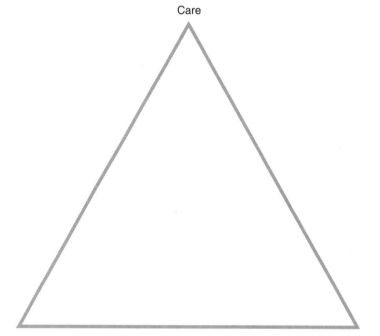

Finally, the construct of *care* provides an assessment of how much the individual in question has demonstrated a willingness to value the needs and concerns of the person who is thinking about trusting him or her. People are more likely to trust others if they have evidence to suggest that the other will consider their interests when taking actions that may affect them, especially important in employer/employee relationships.

11

Cooperative Relationships

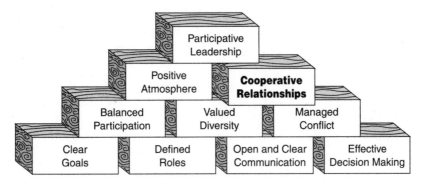

Copyright © 1999 ebb associates inc

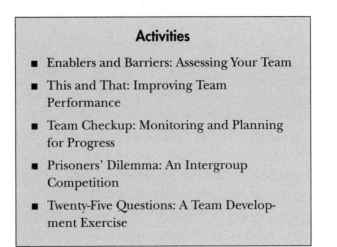

Activities

- Enablers and Barriers: Assessing Your Team

- This and That: Improving Team Performance

- Team Checkup: Monitoring and Planning for Progress

- Prisoners' Dilemma: An Intergroup Competition

- Twenty-Five Questions: A Team Development Exercise

Cooperative Relationships are the sign of a mature team. To build cooperative relationships on your teams, look for opportunities to recognize the value each team member brings. You can also look for ways that team members can evaluate themselves and the team as a whole to improve effectiveness. In addition, find ways to celebrate team accomplishments.

It was difficult to select only a few activities for this chapter. Each of the five activities presents a completely different tactic for building relationships. "Enablers and Barriers" uses force-field analysis to identify specific enablers and barriers that impact a team's effectiveness. "This and That" uses a process in which team members communicate their expectations of one another. "Team Checkup" gives teams a method to evaluate and monitor their progress. "Prisoners' Dilemma" is another classic that demonstrates effects of interpersonal competition and betrayal. "Twenty-Five Questions" is one of my all-time favorites. It is one of the best activities I've seen for opening communication and building relationships in a work group.

ENABLERS AND BARRIERS: ASSESSING YOUR TEAM

Karen Vander Linde

Goals

- To encourage a team to identify specific enablers and barriers that impact its effectiveness.

- To provide an opportunity for a team to recommend ways to increase its effectiveness.

Group Size

All members of a team, divided into subgroups of three to five participants each. If the team has fewer than six members, subgroups should not be formed.

Time Required

One and one-half to two and one-half hours. The time is dependent on the size of the team and the number of subgroups.

Materials

- A copy of the Enablers and Barriers Key-Factor Sheet for each participant.
- A copy of the Enablers and Barriers Force-Field Analysis Sheet for each participant.
- A pencil for each participant.
- An overhead transparency made from the Enablers and Barriers Key-Factor Sheet.
- An overhead transparency made from the Enablers and Barriers Force-Field Analysis Sheet.
- An overhead transparency made from the Enablers and Barriers Illustration of Forces.
- An overhead projector.

Physical Setting

A room large enough for the subgroups to work without disturbing one another. A table and chairs should be provided for each subgroup.

Process

1. After introducing the goals, the facilitator explains why the assessment is appropriate at this stage of the team's life:

   - If the team is just starting, the assessment will help members become aware of issues that need to be addressed.

   - If the team is mature, the assessment will help members become more effective.

   (Ten minutes.)

2. The facilitator provides an overview of the process.

3. The facilitator distributes copies of the Enablers and Barriers Key-Factor Sheet and pencils, displays the overhead transparency made from this sheet, defines the factors aloud, and answers any questions. (Five minutes.)

4. Participants are asked to select the key factor(s) they wish to examine. They may select all of them or one or more priority items. Unless the team has fewer than six members, the participants are asked to assemble into subgroups. Subgroups are assigned one or more of the key factors. (The number of factors examined by each subgroup is dependent on the number of subgroups and the number of factors selected by the group.) (Ten minutes.)

5. The facilitator distributes copies of the Enablers and Barriers Force-Field Analysis Sheet and displays the overhead transparency made from this sheet. The facilitator describes force-field analysis, explaining that, for each factor chosen, the subgroup members must identify both the forces working for the team (enablers) and those working against the team (barriers). The facilitator displays the Illustration of Forces transparency so that the participants can visualize the concept of the enablers and barriers that are pulling against each other. After ensuring that all participants understand the task, the facilitator asks the subgroups to begin. (Ten to fifteen minutes per key factor.)

6. Each subgroup brainstorms recommendations for action, building on the enablers and addressing the barriers they identified. (Five to ten minutes per key factor.)

7. The facilitator brings the group together and asks a spokesperson from each group to present its recommendations to the larger group. The large group is encouraged to add to the recommendations. (Up to one hour, depending on the size of the team, number of subgroups, and amount of discussion.)

8. After the final recommendations, the facilitator leads a concluding discussion by asking:

   ■ How easy was it to identify enablers? Why?

   ■ How easy was it to identify barriers? Why?

   ■ Which recommendations are you most looking forward to implementing?

   ■ How will you ensure that these recommendations will be implemented?

   (Fifteen minutes.)

Variations

■ The facilitator may wish to interview participants before the session begins (by telephone or face-to-face) to gather data about the enablers and barriers that impact the team's effectiveness. The data is categorized into the seven factors and provided to the subgroups.

■ The activity may be continued by creating an action plan to prioritize, assign, and implement the recommendations.

■ The activity may be used at the end of a team project to serve as an evaluation, identifying lessons learned.

ENABLERS AND BARRIERS KEY-FACTOR SHEET

Following are the key factors that impact team effectiveness:

- *Communication*: Do the right people receive the right information at the right time? Do people with whom the team interacts receive information in a timely manner? Where do communication breakdowns or errors occur?

- *Common Direction/Goals*: Does the team have a clear mission? Do all team members agree on the desired outcome? Do specific tasks exist and are they completed in a timely way? Are roles and responsibilities clear?

- *Rewards and Recognition*: What are the incentives for being a member of the team? How are team members' contributions recognized? Who is rewarded? Who rewards?

- *Trust*: What trust issues or concerns exist among team members? How do team members demonstrate trust? How does the team build trust? Do nonmembers trust the team?

- *Decision Making*: How does the team make decisions? Are the right people involved in making decisions? Does the team have appropriate levels of decision-making authority?

- *Perceptions*: Does the team represent an appropriate diversity of viewpoints? What are the team members' perceptions of one another? What are nonmembers' perceptions of the team?

- *Conflict*: How does the team manage conflict? What conflicts currently exist in the team? How could conflict be managed more productively?

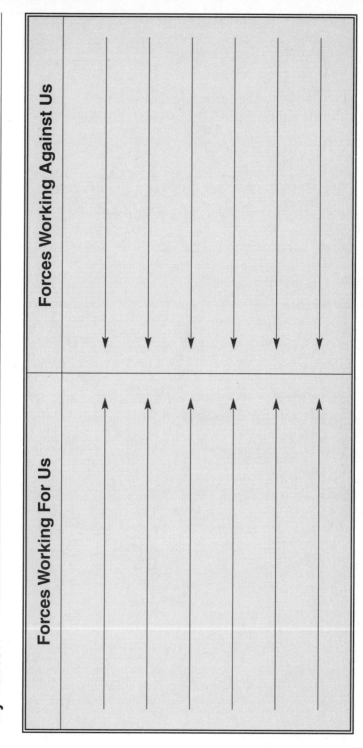

ENABLERS AND BARRIERS FORCE-FIELD ANALYSIS SHEET

Key Factor: _____

Forces Working For Us

Forces Working Against Us

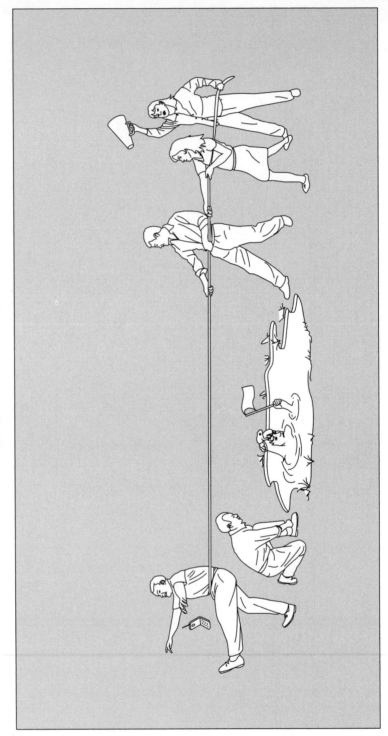

THIS AND THAT:
IMPROVING TEAM PERFORMANCE

James W. Kinneer

> ## Goals
>
> - To help team members identify opportunities for improvement in their team's performance.
> - To assist team members in establishing and communicating their expectations of one another.

Group Size

All members of an ongoing work team, divided into subgroups of three to four members each.

Time Required

Approximately one hour and ten minutes.

Materials

- A newsprint poster prepared in advance with the following statement: "A group does not instantly transform into an effective team. The transformation is a gradual, continual process that involves becoming more of <u>this</u> and less of <u>that</u>."
- A newsprint flip chart and a felt-tipped marker for each subgroup and for the facilitator.
- Masking tape for posting newsprint.

Physical Setting

A room large enough for each subgroup to work without disturbing the others. Movable chairs should be provided. Plenty of wall space must be available for posting newsprint.

Process

1. The facilitator announces the goals of the activity.

2. The newsprint poster is displayed and read aloud. The facilitator defines "this" as the *positive* behaviors necessary for effective teamwork and "that" as the *negative* behaviors that prevent effective teamwork.

3. The facilitator divides the team into subgroups of three to four members each. Each subgroup is given a newsprint flip chart, a felt-tipped marker, and masking tape for posting newsprint.

4. Each subgroup is asked to label a newsprint sheet (and any subsequent sheets used) with the heading "More of This." The facilitator explains that the subgroups are to brainstorm behaviors that the team needs to *increase* in order to improve its performance; that each subgroup should choose a recorder to write down the members' ideas; and that all filled sheets are to be posted. Then the subgroups are told to begin. While they are working, the facilitator monitors their progress. If they have difficulty getting started, the facilitator suggests that they consider issues such as communication, trust, commitment, goals, morale, quality of work, and procedures and processes. (Five to ten minutes.)

5. After the subgroups have finished brainstorming, the facilitator asks them to review their posted newsprint and to convert any attitudes or values into behaviors (actions that the team members can take). The facilitator also states that any unreadable newsprint sheets be recopied, the old sheets removed, and the new sheets posted. (Five minutes.)

6. Each subgroup is instructed to label another newsprint sheet (and any subsequent sheets needed) with the heading "Less of That," to brainstorm behaviors that the team needs to *decrease* in order to improve its performance, and to post all filled sheets. (Five minutes.)

7. After brainstorming, the subgroups review their posted newsprint; convert attitudes or values into behaviors; and, if necessary, recopy the final items onto new sheets of newsprint, remove the old sheets, and post the new ones. (Five minutes.)

8. After all the final lists have been posted, the facilitator asks the team members to walk around and review the work of other subgroups. (Five minutes.)

9. The facilitator draws a vertical line down the center of a sheet of newsprint and labels the left column "THIS" and the right column

The Pfeiffer Book of Successful Team-Building Tools

"THAT." Then the facilitator leads the team in identifying the items that consistently appeared on the subgroups' lists and writes these recurring items in the appropriate columns. Each filled sheet of newsprint is posted. (Ten minutes.)

10. The facilitator leads a discussion with questions such as the following:

   ■ Which column was easier to fill? Why?

   ■ What would be the result if the team demonstrated more of "this"? What would be the result if the team demonstrated less of "that"?

   ■ What personal changes do you need to make so that the team can demonstrate more of "this"? What changes do you need to make in order for the team to demonstrate less of "that"?

   ■ Which of the listed items are most important? Which need to be implemented first to ensure that the team's performance will improve?

   (Twenty minutes.)

11. A volunteer takes responsibility for:

   ■ Reproducing the newsprint lists of "THIS" and "THAT" completed in Step 9 and ensuring that each member receives a copy; and

   ■ Posting these lists in the team's regular meeting room.

   Arrangements are made to review the team's progress in a few weeks.

Variations

■ If the team has fewer than six members, the activity may be conducted without subgroups.

■ The final lists of "This" and "That" may be used for planning further team-building activities.

■ The participants may be asked to prioritize the items on the final lists.

■ The participants may develop a survey from items on the final lists. A Likert-type scale will help determine the extent to which the behaviors are exhibited by the team. Then the survey may be repeated after six months or a year and the results compared to those from this session.

■ The participants may be asked to develop specific performance standards for each item on the "This" list.

Team Checkup:
Monitoring and Planning for Progress

Michael L. Mazzarese

Goals

- To offer team members a way to evaluate and monitor the progress of their team.
- To encourage team members to devise priorities and action plans for improving their team.
- To encourage team members to execute action plans for team improvement.

Group Size

All members of an ongoing team.

Time Required

One hour and forty minutes to two and one-half hours (excluding pre-work), depending on the size of the team.

Materials

- A copy of the Team Checkup Questionnaire for each team member.
- Newsprint sheets listing the team members' responses to the questionnaire items (prepared in advance). A separate sheet (or sheets) should be created for each item.
- A newsprint flip chart and a felt-tipped marker.
- Masking tape for posting newsprint.

Physical Setting

A room in which the team members can work without interruption. Movable chairs should be provided, and plenty of wall space should be available for posting newsprint.

Process

1. *Prework 1:* The facilitator distributes copies of the Team Checkup Questionnaire and asks each team member to complete this questionnaire and return it to the facilitator at least twenty-four hours before the activity session. In explaining the activity, the facilitator states that undergoing a team "checkup" will help the members to form a picture of the team's present situation; then they can decide in which direction they want to move in the future. The facilitator says that he or she will be recording the team members' responses from the completed forms, but assures the members that those responses will remain anonymous. (Five minutes.)

2. *Prework 2:* Once all members' completed questionnaires have been collected (approximately a day before the activity session), the facilitator records on sheets of newsprint all responses to each individual item so that everyone's views can be displayed during the activity session. (A *minimum of one hour* to record data.)

3. At the beginning of the activity session, the facilitator posts all newsprint sheets with the members' recorded responses. The facilitator leads a discussion of each item, striving for understanding and consensus on each. (One to one and one-half hours.)

4. The facilitator instructs the team members to focus on suggestions for improvement (item 4 on the questionnaire) and asks if there are now additional improvement ideas. Any new ideas are recorded on newsprint and clarified as necessary. Then all improvement ideas are reviewed, and similar ideas are assembled into categories. The members may want to eliminate any plans for improvement that are already in motion or that are not within the team's control. From the remaining list the team members choose the top one to three priorities. (*Note:* The team should not work on too much at once; one to three improvement items are enough. After the initial items have been tried and modified as needed, other items may be tackled.) (Twenty minutes.)

5. The team members are assisted in devising action plans from the list of priorities. The four critical elements (*who* will commit to action, *what* will be done, *by when,* and *how you will know your actions are working*) are determined and recorded on newsprint. The facilitator keeps the newsprint action plans so that he or she can create a handout from them and distribute a copy to each team member. (Twenty to thirty minutes.)

The Pfeiffer Book of Successful Team-Building Tools

6. The facilitator leads a discussion of the activity based on questions such as the following:

- What did you learn about yourself as a team member?

- What did you learn about your fellow team members?

- What did you learn about working together as a team?

- How can you use what you learned to address team issues in the future?

(Ten minutes.)

7. The facilitator encourages the team members to meet every few months to fill out the questionnaire again, to review progress, and to modify goals as necessary.

Variations

- Instead of administering the questionnaire, the facilitator may interview each team member separately and record his or her responses to the items on the questionnaire form. The facilitator should clarify for everyone that responses will be shared but will remain anonymous. Subsequently, all responses to each item should be recorded on newsprint. The activity then begins at Step 3.

- The facilitator may, if appropriate, encourage the team members to own their responses during the discussion of the questionnaire items. (However, the members must not feel pressured to relinquish the anonymity of their responses.)

TEAM CHECKUP QUESTIONNAIRE

1. How would you describe the interactions when the members of your team get together to plan, solve problems, or make decisions?

   Have interactions improved or worsened in the past two or three months? What have you observed that tells you this?

2. How would you describe the team's relationships with outside groups (for example, other teams or units, other organizations, suppliers)?

   Have these relationships improved or worsened in the past several months? What have you observed that leads you to this conclusion?

The Pfeiffer Book of Successful Team-Building Tools

3. What are your team's greatest strengths?

How can you build on these strengths?

4. What two or three things does your team need to improve?

What are you as an individual doing to improve these things? What
is the team as a unit doing to improve these things?

What could you and the team do that you are *not* doing now?

5. How would improving the things identified in item 4 benefit your team's planning, problem solving, decision making, member interactions, or relationships with outside groups?

PRISONERS' DILEMMA: AN INTERGROUP COMPETITION

Editors

Goals

- To explore trust between group members and effects of betrayal of trust.
- To demonstrate effects of interpersonal competition.
- To dramatize the merit of a collaborative posture in intragroup and intergroup relations.

Group Size

Two teams of no more than eight members each.

Time Required

Approximately one hour. (Smaller teams take less time.)

Materials

- Copies of the Prisoners' Dilemma Tally Sheet for all participants.
- Pencils.

Physical Setting

Enough space for the two teams to meet separately without overhearing or disrupting each other. For step 7, two chairs for team representatives should be placed facing each other in the center of the room.

Process

1. The facilitator explains that the group is going to experience a "risk-taking" situation similar to that experienced by guilty prisoners being interrogated by the police. Before interrogating prisoners suspected

of working together, the questioner separates them and tells each one that the other has confessed and that, if they both confess, they will get off easier. The prisoners' dilemma or risk is that they may confess when they should not or they may fail to confess when they really should. (The facilitator carefully avoids discussing goals.)

2. Two teams are formed and named Red and Blue. The teams are seated apart from each other. They are instructed not to communicate with the other team in any way, verbally or nonverbally, except when told to do so by the facilitator.

3. Prisoners' Dilemma Tally Sheets are distributed to all participants. They are given time to study the directions. The facilitator then asks if there are any questions concerning the scoring.

4. Round 1 is begun. The facilitator tells the teams that they will have three minutes to make a team decision. He or she instructs them not to write their decisions until signaled that time is up, so that they will not make hasty decisions.

5. The choices of the two teams are announced for round 1. The scoring for that round is agreed upon and is entered on the scorecards.

6. Rounds 2 and 3 are conducted in the same way as round 1.

7. Round 4 is announced as a special round, for which the payoff points are doubled. Each team is instructed to send one representative to the chairs in the center of the room. After representatives have conferred for three minutes, they return to their teams. Teams then have three minutes, as before, in which to make their decisions. When recording their scores, they should be reminded that points indicated by the payoff schedule are doubled for this round only.

8. Rounds 5 through 8 are conducted in the same manner as the first three rounds.

9. Round 9 is announced as a special round, in which the payoff points are "squared" (multiplied by themselves: e.g., a score of 4 would be $4^2 + 16$). A minus sign should be retained: e.g., $(-3)^2 = -9$. Team representatives meet for three minutes; then the teams meet for five minutes. At the facilitator's signal, the teams write their choices; then the two choices are announced.

10. Round 10 is handled exactly as round 9 was. Payoff points are squared.

11. The entire group meets to process the experience. The point total for each team is announced, and the sum of the two team totals is calculated and compared to the maximum positive or negative out-

comes (+126 or –126 points). The facilitator may wish to lead a discussion about win-lose situations, zero-sum games, the relative merits of collaboration and competition, and the effects of high and low trust on interpersonal relations.

Variations

- The competition can be carried out using money instead of points.
- Process observers can be assigned to each team
- Teams can be placed in separate rooms, to minimize rule-breaking.
- The number of persons in each team can be varied.
- In round 10, each team can be directed to predict the choice of the other. These predictions can be posted before announcing the actual choices, as in the following diagram. (Actual choices are recorded in the circles after the predictions are announced.)

	Predicted Choice	
Predicting Team	Red Team	Blue Team
Red	◯	
Blue		◯

PRISONERS' DILEMMA TALLY SHEET

Instructions: For ten successive rounds, the Red team will choose either an A or a B and the Blue team will choose either an X or a Y. The score each team receives in a round is determined by the pattern made by the choices of both teams, according to the schedule below.

Payoff Schedule

AX	Both teams win 3 points.
AY	Red Team loses 6 points; Blue Team wins 6 points
BX	Red Team wins 6 points; Blue Team loses 6 points
BY	Both teams lose 3 points

Scorecard

		Choice		Cumulative Points	
Round	Minutes	Red Team	Blue Team	Red Team	Blue Team
1	3				
2	3				
3	3				
4*	3 (reps.) 3 (teams)				
5	3				
6	3				
7	3				
8	3				
9**	3 (reps.) 3 (teams)				
10**	3 (reps.) 3 (teams)				

*Payoff points are doubled for this round
**Payoff points are squared for this round. (Retain the minus sign.)

Twenty-Five Questions: A Team Development Exercise

John E. Jones

Goals

- To enhance the team members' relationships with one another.
- To stimulate a team discussion about work-related topics.
- To clarify assumptions that the team members make about one another.

Group Size

All members of an ongoing team.

Time Required

Approximately one and one-half hours.

Materials

A copy of the Twenty-Five Questions Form for each team member.

Physical Setting

A room with chairs arranged in a circle.

Process

1. The facilitator introduces the goals of the activity and briefly discusses the importance of being open in relationships with coworkers and of obtaining feedback on one's work style. (Five minutes.)

2. The facilitator distributes copies of the Twenty-Five Questions Form, explains the ground rules, and elicits and answers questions to ensure that each team member understands the procedure. (Five minutes.)

3. The facilitator asks the team members to volunteer to initiate questions. (The team members may need to be encouraged to confront one another. For example, each member may be asked to read the list of questions silently, to select one question, and to look around the circle and choose one person to become the focus of that question. Then the facilitator may solicit a volunteer to ask a question; after each question has been asked and answered, the facilitator may need to encourage others to volunteer. Also, some direction from the facilitator may be required for questioners to answer their own queries.)

4. The facilitator interrupts the question-and-answer procedure after about thirty minutes to assist the team members in discussing how the activity is progressing. Questions such as the following may be useful:

   - Who questions whom?
   - How open are we being?
   - What risks are present in this activity?
   - To what degree is trust being generated?
   - What are we learning about ourselves?
   - What are we learning about one another?
   - Whom might you want to do this with privately?
   - How might we improve the activity in the next round?

   (Fifteen minutes.)

5. The procedure is resumed, and the team members are urged to note any change that can be attributed to the processing intervention of the previous step.

6. After about twenty minutes, the procedure is stopped. The facilitator encourages the team members to respond to the question "If we were to quit right now and never do this again, what question would you regret not having asked someone?"

7. The entire activity is critiqued by the team members, and its implications for the team's continued development are discussed. The team members make plans to use the same questions in a follow-up session to be held in a few months.

Variations

- The team members may be paired in the initial phase to work through as many questions as they can during the time allotted. Then in the second round the risk taking may be increased by forming pairs on the basis of a variety of criteria (for example, leader and follower, people who know each other least well, and people who think that they are different from each other).

- The question form may be supplemented with items suggested by the team members.

- An entirely different question form may be generated from items suggested by the team members. For example, the team members may have a discussion of what they would need to talk about in order to increase openness and trust in their interpersonal relations. The resulting items may be duplicated later for use in a subsequent session.

- Each team member may be asked to write a name or names at the end of each of the twenty-five questions when the list is read for the first time. This approach may heighten the volunteering.

- In an extended session (two to three hours), the process may be interrupted several times so that the team members can rate themselves and the team on honesty and risk taking (see the continua that follow). Subsequently, the two scales are displayed on newsprint, and the members record their ratings independently on blank paper.

Dishonest, evasive			**ME**		Completely honest, open
0	1	2	3	4	5

THE TEAM

Playing it safe			**ME**		Taking many risks
0	1	2	3	4	5

THE TEAM

TWENTY-FIVE QUESTIONS FORM

Ground Rules: The list of questions below is designed to stimulate team discussion of work-related topics. The following ground rules should govern this discussion:

1. Take turns asking questions, either to specific individuals or to the team as a whole.

2. You must be willing to answer any question that you ask.

3. Any member may decline to answer any question that someone else asks.

4. Work with the person who is answering to make certain that effective two-way understanding takes place.

5. All answers remain confidential within the team.

Questions: (may be asked in any order)

1. How do you feel about yourself in your present job?

2. What do you see as the next step in your career development?

3. What personal characteristics do you have that get in the way of your work?

4. What are you doing best right now?

5. What are you trying to accomplish in your work?

6. Where do you see yourself ten years from now?

7. How are you perceiving me?

8. What would you predict to be my assessment of you?

9. What was your first impression of me?

10. How many different kinds of responsibilities do you have?

11. How do you typically behave when a deadline is approaching?

12. What kind of relationship do you want with me?

13. What things do you do best?

14. What factors in your job situation impede your goal accomplishment?

15. Which team member are you having the most difficulty with right now? (What is that person doing? What is your reaction?)

16. To whom are you closest in your work situation?

17. Where would you locate yourself on a ten-point scale of commitment to the goals of this team (1 = low, 10 = high)?

18. What part are you playing in this team?

19. How do you want to receive feedback?

20. What do you think I am up to?

21. What puzzles you about me?

22. How are you feeling right now?

23. What issue do you think we must face together?

24. What do you see going on in the team right now?

25. What personal-growth efforts are you making?

Participative
Leadership

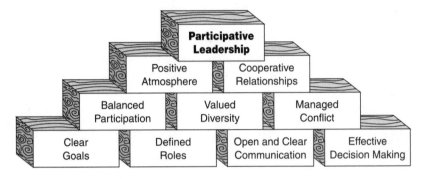

Copyright © 1999 ebb associates inc

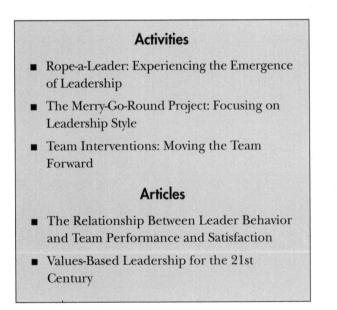

Activities

- Rope-a-Leader: Experiencing the Emergence of Leadership
- The Merry-Go-Round Project: Focusing on Leadership Style
- Team Interventions: Moving the Team Forward

Articles

- The Relationship Between Leader Behavior and Team Performance and Satisfaction
- Values-Based Leadership for the 21st Century

Participative Leadership is the block at the top of the model, not because it is most important, but because it is the ultimate goal of an effective, efficient team. The leader is not the most important member of a team. A good leader shares responsibility and glory, is supportive and fair, creates a climate of trust and openness, and is a good coach and teacher. Effective leadership is assumed in all the other blocks of the model. Yet the test of a truly good leader is that the team operates as smoothly whether the leader is present or absent.

This chapter presents three activities and two articles. "Rope-a-Leader" allows the team to explore emerging leadership. "Team Interventions" presents a model that can be used by team leaders to understand the needs of teams at various stages. This activity is steeped in the classic team stages as originally defined by Bruce W. Tuckman.* "The Merry-Go-Round Project" develops an awareness of the impact of various leadership styles.

The articles present two topics that team leaders should consider. "The Relationship Between Leader Behavior and Team Performance and Satisfaction" presents a summary of leader behaviors that help and behaviors that hinder the development of a high performing team. "Values-Based Leadership for the 21st Century" focuses on what a leader needs to believe and do in order to promote high performance. The reference list at the end of this article provides a list of some of the most important recent publications about leadership.

---

* See B.W. Tuckman, & M.S. Jensen (1977). "Stages of Small Group Development Revisited." *Group & Organization Studies, 2,* 419-427.

The Pfeiffer Book of Successful Team-Building Tools

ROPE-A-LEADER:
EXPERIENCING THE EMERGENCE OF LEADERSHIP

John W. Peterson and Sherry R. Mills

> ## Goals
>
> - To provide the participants with the opportunity to experience and observe the emergence of leadership within a group.
> - To discuss the emergence of leadership.

Group Size

Twenty to thirty-five participants in subgroups of five or seven.

Time Required

Forty minutes.

Materials

- Twenty-five feet of ¼-inch rope, twine, or macramé cord for each subgroup.

Physical Setting

Any area large enough so that all the subgroups can work on the floor without disturbing one another.

Process

1. Ask the participants to assemble in subgroups of five or seven. (Odd numbers work best.) Once subgroups have assembled, place a rope on the floor near each group. (*Note:* You may place ropes in several locations prior to beginning this activity.) (Five minutes.)

2. Explain that the task of each subgroup is to use the rope to form "an absolutely perfect" circle on the floor. When finished, the rope should

lie on the floor with no one touching it to hold it in place. Tell participants they may *not* talk to one another or to you during the activity and that you will be the final judge as to when they have accomplished the task. Tell them to begin, giving them no more than two or three minutes.

3. While subgroups are completing the task, walk around from subgroup to subgroup "judging" their work and being critical about the final shapes they have created.

4. After the circles have been completed, tell the subgroups to form a perfect square, then a triangle, a trapezoid, and an octagon. Remind the participants not to talk. (Ten minutes.)

5. After all of the shapes have been completed say, "On the count of 3, point to the leader of your subgroup. Ready? 1, 2, 3." Ask members of each subgroup, in turn, how they selected that particular leader.

6. Reconvene the large group and lead a discussion based on the following questions:

   ■ How did the leadership evolve in your group?

   ■ How did other members of the group acquiesce to the leadership?

   ■ Did conflict occur in any groups? Why or why not?

   ■ How does what happened here compare to what happens in a typical work setting at your organization?

   (Fifteen minutes.)

Variations

■ This activity can be used for team building.

■ At the end of the activity, the group can discuss what attributes of the leaders made the process work. List the attributes on a flip chart for a further discussion of leadership.

THE MERRY-GO-ROUND PROJECT: FOCUSING ON LEADERSHIP STYLE

Deborah Spring Laurel

Goals

- To provide a model for planning a team project.
- To develop the participants' awareness of the impact of different project leadership styles on project results.
- To test the effectiveness of project leadership behaviors in response to simulated real-job obstructions and challenges.

Group Size

Fourteen to thirty-five participants from the same organization or department in table groups of seven participants.

Time Required

Approximately ninety minutes.

Materials

- One Tinkertoy® Colossal construction sets (with 142 pieces) for each group of seven participants.
- A Merry-Go-Round Project Background Information sheet for the facilitator.
- A Merry-Go-Round Project Planning sheet for each participant.
- A Merry-Go-Round Project Construction Instructions sheet for each project leader.
- A Merry-Go-Round Project Observer Briefing sheet for each observer.
- One or two Merry-Go-Round Project Voice of Reality Briefing sheets for each subgroup.

- A Merry-Go-Round Project Summary sheet for each participant.
- Pencils or pens for all participants.

Physical Setting

A room large enough for two to five round or rectangular tables that each seat five participants, with five chairs at each table. (*Note:* The three to five participants involved in the actual construction of the merry-go-round will be seated at the table. The two volunteers serving as the Voice of Reality and the Observer will be standing.)

Facilitating Risk Rating

Moderate.

Process

1. Organize the participants into project teams, with five to seven participants at each table. Have them clear off the surface of the table so that they have plenty of space.

2. Place one Tinkertoy construction set on each table, with the instruction not to open the sets until given the go-ahead.

3. Introduce the Merry-Go-Round Project by reading through the Merry-Go-Round Project Background Information sheet. (Five minutes.)

4. Explain that only one person at each table will be the Project Leader. However, each participant should complete a Merry-Go-Round Project Planning sheet. Hand these sheets out at this point, along with pens or pencils. (Ten minutes.)

5. Ask the group: "Why should everyone complete the Project Planning sheet, even though only one person at each table grouping will be the actual Project Leader?" Ensure that they recognize the fact that all team members come to a project with their own ideas regarding how to organize and implement the project. Because of this, the Project Leader will need to obtain their buy-in to the Project Leader's vision and plan, which can be problematic. (Five minutes.)

6. Appoint a Project Leader at each table, handing that person the Merry-Go-Round Construction Instructions. Tell the Project Leaders that it will be left to their discretion to decide whether to show the diagram and instructions to their teams.

7. Ask for two volunteers from each group and ask them to join you in the hall for a briefing. Tell the remaining participants that, during your absence, they may dump out the contents of their Tinkertoy containers and organize the contents. However, they are not to begin with any discussion of the project until the other players have returned.

8. In the hall, hand out the Merry-Go-Round Project Observer Briefing sheet and the Merry-Go-Round Project Voice of Reality Briefing sheets to the volunteers, one of each for each group.

9. Explain the role of the Voice of Reality and read through the briefing sheet. Emphasize the importance of making the project interruptions as realistic and as frequent as possible. Indicate that they should feel free to be as creative as they like. However, caution the volunteers that they should ensure that their project groups are actually able to complete construction of their Merry-Go-Rounds within the allotted fifteen minutes. Warn them that the participants tend to become very stressed if they are denied the opportunity to reach closure with their construction project. Ask for and respond to any questions from the volunteers. (Two minutes.)

10. Explain the role of the Observer and read through that briefing sheet. Point out that the briefing sheet questions reflect the Project Planning sheet, so their job is to observe and assess the effectiveness of the Project Leader's project planning and leadership style. Remind them that they must stay silent throughout the activity, but they will be expected to provide a brief, non-judgmental summary of their observations. Say that humor is encouraged. Emphasize that their job is not to tear anyone down or to hurt anyone's feelings, but instead to provide objective, fact-based feedback. Ask for and respond to any questions. (Two minutes.)

11. Return to the room, ask the volunteers to join their groups, and give the go-ahead to start, reminding the groups that they have only fifteen minutes to complete their projects.

12. Observe the process, moving around the room to quietly encourage or acknowledge the activities of the Voices of Reality and the Observers. Serve as the timekeeper, alerting the groups when they have ten minutes left, five minutes left, and one minute left. Make sure that the Voices of Reality cease obstructing the construction process by the five-minute mark so that the groups can actually complete their merry-go-rounds. (Fifteen minutes.)

13. After stopping the process, hand out the Project Summary sheets and ask the participants who were involved in constructing the merry-go-rounds to complete them individually. (Three minutes.)

14. Ask the Observers to use this time to plan their brief feedback reports to the entire group.

15. Allow each Observer approximately three minutes to provide feedback, reminding them before they begin of their responsibility to provide helpful, non-judgmental feedback. (Ten to fifteen minutes.)

16. Bring closure by facilitating a directed large group discussion of the participants' responses to each of the questions on the Merry-Go-Round Project Summary sheet. Ask additional questions, as relevant:

   ■ To what degree did each team member's own idea of how to organize and implement the project either assist with or detract from the Project Leader's vision and plan?

   ■ What options and alternatives do teams have when faced with the obstacles, interruptions, and challenges that occur daily to impede their progress?

   ■ How important was the planning process to the effective completion of the project?

   ■ How often do we take the time to plan properly before we begin a project? How does that affect the result?

   ■ How often do we consider the importance of gaining the buy-in of the team members and actually take some action to achieve that buy-in?

   ■ How often are project teams thrown together without regard to background, experience, or capability to actually perform the project work? What can you do differently back on the job?

   ■ What key learning are you taking from this experience?

   (Thirty minutes.)

Variations

■ With groups of five or six per table, reduce the number of participants actually involved in the construction of the merry-go-round. Retain one Voice of Reality and one Observer for each table.

■ With table groups of more than seven, increase the number of participants actually involved in the construction of the merry-go-round and/or add one more Voice of Reality (who might impose obstructions created by a regulatory agency or some other entity).

- To increase complexity, incorporate specific personality traits, work habits, motivations, and behavioral issues that are typical to the participants' workplace into roles assigned to the participants involved in the construction of the merry-go-round.

MERRY-GO-ROUND PROJECT BACKGROUND INFORMATION

Situation

Organization X has successfully marketed a brand new product: a high quality, attractive, and affordable merry-go-round that is now small enough to be safely installed in urban parks, playgrounds, and even residential yards.

As a matter of fact, the marketing has been so successful that consumer demand has far exceeded the supply of available merry-go-rounds. Organization X needs to increase productivity to fill the current backorders.

However, since Organization X has sunk all of its available cash into marketing and inventory, it is not in a position to hire additional workers. Instead, the company has been forced to re-deploy workers from all of its other departments. None of these workers has ever worked on this merry-go-round project before.

Challenge

Your project team will be responsible for making a Tinkertoy merry-go-round that meets all engineering, quality, and OSHA requirements within fifteen minutes.

There are five participants on each team. In addition, there are two other individuals involved with each team with special roles.

They will be responsible, respectively, for making this activity as realistic as possible by posing the types of challenges that teams typically experience and for silently observing the process and then reporting to the entire group at the end of the activity.

MERRY-GO-ROUND PROJECT PLANNING

The Project Leader is responsible for ensuring that the project team constructs a functioning Tinkertoy merry-go-round within fifteen minutes despite the challenges that teams typically experience.

Assume that you will be the Project Leader and take ten minutes to plan out the project before it begins:

1. What are the specific tasks that need to be done?

2. How will the work be divided among the team members?

3. How will you obtain the team's commitment to the project?

4. What information does the team need so that this project will run smoothly?

5. How will you manage the project to ensure that the construction process is successful?

6. What will your involvement be in the actual construction process?

7. What are the most probable challenges that may affect project completion?

8. How will you handle these challenges so that the project can continue?

9. How will you ensure that the project is completed on time?

10. Is there any other information that you need?

MERRY-GO-ROUND PROJECT CONSTRUCTION INSTRUCTIONS

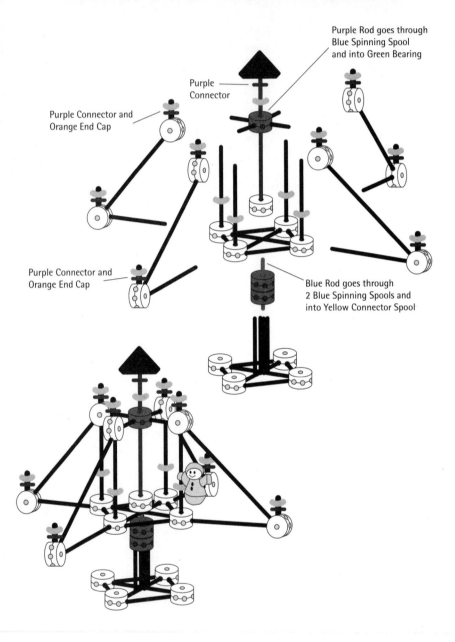

Purple Rod goes through
Blue Spinning Spool
and into Green Bearing

Purple
Connector

Purple Connector and
Orange End Cap

Purple Connector and
Orange End Cap

Blue Rod goes through
2 Blue Spinning Spools and
into Yellow Connector Spool

Merry-Go-Round Project Observer Briefing

You are expected to

- Quietly observe the project in progress;
- Answer the questions below; and
- Report your observations to the larger group in a *helpful, non-judgmental* manner.

1. How did the project leader obtain the team's commitment to the project?

2. What information did the project leader give the team so that this project would run smoothly?

3. How was the work divided among the team members?

4. What was the project leader's involvement in the actual construction process?

5. How did the project leader manage the project team?

6. How did the project leader maintain team commitment to the success of the project?

7. How did the team members work together to accomplish the goal?

8. How did the project leader handle interference?

9. How did the team members handle interference?

10. How did the project manager ensure that the project was completed on time?

11. How did the project team complete the task?

12. Did the team build the merry-go-round properly?

13. Does it function?

14. Would you purchase or ride on the merry-go-round?

15. Other observations or comments.

The Pfeiffer Book of Successful Team-Building Tools

MERRY-GO-ROUND PROJECT VOICE OF REALITY BRIEFING

You are responsible for making this activity as realistic as possible by posing the challenges that the teams in your organization typically experience. You will need to be creative. For example, consider the following distractions:

Lack of Staff

- Pull one member off the project for personal illness or a family emergency.

Policy Makers

- Tell them that they cannot use any green pieces. Then a couple of minutes later, tell them they can.

Standards

- Tell them that all of the connectors need to be washed, so they must remove them and wipe them down.

Lack of Resources

- Simply remove some pieces that they need. You can return them later, or not, as you wish.

Regulations

- Impose some restriction on them. For example, say, "Sorry, but you can only use your left hand to put on that kind of piece."

Miscommunication

- Give them misleading instructions. For example, say, "Two of you will need to work with your eyes closed" or "I'm sorry, but we'll need that completed in the next five minutes." You can correct your communication later, if you want.

Lack of Skill

- Find out who is spatially challenged and insist that this person be in charge of the more technical work.

Have fun with it, but try to keep your negative impact on the project realistic, relative to the fifteen-minute time frame. We will enroll you in a witness protection program after the exercise!

MERRY-GO-ROUND PROJECT SUMMARY

Instructions: Fill out the answers to the questions below in preparation for a group discussion.

1. How did this experience feel?

2. How realistic was this experience compared with your actual workplace?

3. What strategies or emotions did it raise in you?

4. What did the project leader do well?

5. What could the project leader have done differently?

6. What can you take from this experience to apply to a current workplace team?

TEAM INTERVENTIONS: MOVING THE TEAM FORWARD

Chuck Kormanski

Goals

- To present a team-development model for team leaders and supervisors.
- To provide an opportunity for participants to analyze team performance and assess team needs.
- To provide an opportunity for participants to suggest leader interventions that are based on stages of team development.

Group Size

Ten to thirty team leaders/supervisors in subgroups of five to seven members each.

Time Required

Two to two and one-half hours.

Materials

- A copy of the Team Development Summary Sheet for each participant.
- A copy of the Team Development Intervention Sheet for each participant.
- A copy of the Team Development Vignettes Sheet for each participant.
- A newsprint flip chart and felt-tipped markers for each team.
- Masking tape for each team.

Physical Setting

A room large enough for teams to work without disturbing one another. Movable chairs and tables are suggested.

Process

1. The facilitator presents the goals of the activity and forms subgroups ("teams") of five to seven members each. Each team is given a news-print flip chart, felt-tipped markers, and masking tape. (Five minutes.)

2. The team members are requested to get acquainted by sharing their names, job information, and two or three suggestions about how the group might work together as a team. (Five to ten minutes.)

3. The facilitator delivers a lecturette on stages of team development, then gives each participant a copy of the Team Development Summary Sheet and reviews the contents. (Ten to fifteen minutes.)

4. The facilitator explains that certain interventions by the team leader can assist the team in completing the outcomes for each stage of development and moving into the next. The facilitator gives each participant a copy of the Team Development Intervention Sheet and reviews the contents. (Five to ten minutes.)

5. The facilitator gives a copy of the Team Development Vignettes Sheet to each participant and reads the instructions aloud. Teams are advised to spend about ten minutes on each vignette and to list their interventions on newsprint. The facilitator makes ten-minute announcements and calls time. (Sixty minutes.)

6. Each team is requested to post its interventions so that all can see them. (Five minutes.)

7. The total group is reassembled. Posted interventions are compared with the Team Development Intervention Sheet in the following manner: all groups' strategies for vignette 11 are compared with the sheet; all groups' strategies for vignette 12 are compared with the sheet; and so on. Team vignette 11 represents stage 1; vignette 12 represents stage 2; vignette 13 represents stage 3, and so on. The facilitator leads an ongoing discussion relating interventions to team-development concepts. (Fifteen to twenty minutes.)

8. The facilitator engages the participants in a discussion of the activity. The following processing questions may be included:

   ■ What were your reactions as you progressed through this activity?

   ■ How did your team members interact while you were working on this task?

   ■ How did this reflect the team's stage of development?

   ■ What interventions were used to move your team along?

- What have you learned about the stages of team development?
- What, specifically, did you learn in this activity about what a team leader can do to affect the group's progress?
- How can you use the information from this activity in your jobs?

(Ten to fifteen minutes.)

Variations

- Teams can work on only one, two, or three of the vignettes, thus reducing the amount of time required for the activity.
- The facilitator can demonstrate effective leader behavior using one of the vignettes.
- Each team can write its own real-life vignette and then exchange with another team to get a different perspective on it. (A real-life vignette can be role played.)
- The Team Development Summary Sheets can be distributed prior to the activity.

TEAM DEVELOPMENT SUMMARY SHEET

Introduction

Like individuals, teams progress through different stages of development as they mature. Tuckman[1] identified five stages of team development: forming, storming, norming, performing, and adjourning.

In each stage, team members exhibit typical "task" and "relationship" behaviors, consistent with the basic theme of that particular stage of development. The relationship behaviors correlate with the development of the identity and functions of the group from the personal orientations of the members. The task behaviors correlate with the progress of the group in understanding and accomplishing its work. Issues and concerns must be resolved in each stage before the group can move on. The completion of each stage results in specific task outcomes as well as relationship outcomes that address member needs at that stage.

Both transactional leader skills (those that get the task completed) and transformational leader skills (those that influence and inspire people) can be used to move the team from one stage of development to the next. The leader skills listed for each stage of team development are translated into actions, or interventions, the leader can make in order to help the group to complete each stage's task.

Figure 1 summarizes the stages of group development, team building, and leadership skills.

GROUP DEVELOPMENT			
Tuckman Stage	General Theme	Task Behavior	Relationship Behavior
1. Forming	Awareness	Orientation	Dependence
2. Storming	Conflict	Resistance	Hostility
3. Norming	Cooperation	Communication	Cohesion
4. Performing	Productivity	Problem Solving	Interdependence
5. Adjourning	Separation	Termination	Disengagement

Figure 1.   Group Development, Team Building, and Leadership Skills

---

[1]B.W. Tuckman & M.A.C. Jensen (December, 1977), "Stages of Small-Group Development Revisited," in *Group & Organization Studies, 2*(4), 419–427.

TEAM BUILDING			
Tuckman Stage	**Task Outcome**	**Relationship Outcome**	**Individual Need**
1. Forming	Commitment	Acceptance	Security
2. Storming	Clarification	Belonging	Social
3. Norming	Involvement	Support	Recognition
4. Performing	Achievement	Pride	Achievement
5. Adjourning	Recognition	Satisfaction	Recognition

LEADERSHIP SKILLS		
Tuckman Stage	**Transactional Leader Skills**	**Transformational Leader Skills**
1. Forming	Getting Acquainted, Goal Setting, Organizing	Value Clarification, Visioning, Communicating Through Myth and Metaphor
2. Storming	Active Listening, Assertiveness, Conflict Management	Flexibility, Creativity, Kaleidoscopic Thinking
3. Norming	Communication, Feedback, Affirmation	Playfulness and Humor, Entrepreneuring, Networking
4. Performing	Decision Making, Problem Solving, Rewarding	Multicultural Awareness, Mentoring, Futuring
5. Adjourning	Evaluating, Reviewing	Celebrating, Bringing Closure

Based on C.L. Kormanski & A. Mozenter (1987), "A New Model of Team Building: A Technology for Today and Tomorrow," in J.W. Pfeiffer (Ed.), *The 1987 Annual: Developing Human Resources,* San Francisco, CA: Pfeiffer.

Figure 1.   Group Development, Team Building, and Leadership Skills,
(continued)

TEAM DEVELOPMENT INTERVENTION SHEET

Stage One: Forming. Theme: Awareness

- Allow time for members to get acquainted
- Provide essential information about content and process
- Emphasize new skills required
- Identify and relate key team values to current task
- Share stories of past accomplishments and celebrations
- Create a team vision of outcome
- Set goals to achieve outcome

Stage Two: Storming. Theme: Conflict

- Act assertively and set parameters for the team
- Listen attentively to all viewpoints
- Use mediation, negotiation, and arbitration
- Consider new perspectives and alternatives
- Suggest and solicit optional ways to view the problem

Stage Three: Norming. Theme: Cooperation

- Provide opportunity for involvement by all
- Provide opportunity for members to learn from and assist one another
- Model and encourage supportive behavior
- Open communication lines
- Provide positive and corrective task-related feedback
- Add some humor and fun to the work setting

Stage Four: Performing. Theme: Productivity

- Reward and recognize performance outcomes and positive work relationships
- Involve the team in group problem solving and futuring
- Share decision-making opportunities

The Pfeiffer Book of Successful Team-Building Tools

- Examine how implementation will affect the team and the rest of the organization
- Use delegation to foster professional development

Stage Five: Adjourning. Theme: Separation

- Provide evaluative performance feedback
- Review task and working relationships
- Create a celebration activity with emphasis on recognition and fun
- Conduct a closure ceremony to specify the project's conclusion

Team Development Vignettes Sheet

Instructions: Read each vignette and suggest some interventions that the team leader might make in order to improve team development.

Team Vignette #11

You are working with an old team on a new, very different, project. The task is challenging, and creative problem solving will be critical. In past efforts of the team, there were few choices and very little flexibility. Some talents that team members have but have not used recently will be needed on this project. You are concerned about increasing the motivational level of the team in addition to getting the project completed in a superior fashion.

Team Vignette #12

Team members disagree about the importance of the current project and, therefore, the time needed to complete it. One group of team members sees the task as helpful but not essential to the organization. They want to finish it adequately but quickly. A second set of team members wants to complete the task comprehensively, with the high quality characteristic of past team performance. A third group is trying to develop a compromise. A few members have not expressed opinions and are attempting to stay out of the debate. You would like to resolve the matter and get the team to reach agreement or, at least, consensus. Your personal preference is for a quality effort.

Team Vignette #13

The team has recently resolved a volatile disagreement regarding the appropriate strategy to use in the implementation of a major goal. You want to move forward as quickly as possible. The group appears somewhat hesitant and continues to look to you for direction. Members appear capable of continuing the task but are concerned about how much time will be required. Some work has been begun by individuals working independently and in pairs. Although you see some progress, you would like more of a unified effort.

Team Vignette #14

The team appears to be cohesive and unified regarding the current project. All members are competent to complete the task. The implementation and evaluation phase will be critical and will impact the total organization. Current goals are challenging but realistic. So far, quality standards have been maintained. You are eager to complete the project at this high level of performance.

Team Vignette #15

The team has just completed a major project. Although there were some difficulties getting started and some conflicts concerning the use of resources, compromises were used to move to completion. Each team member made a significant contribution, adding specific skills that were critical to the success of the project. The team views this accomplishment as a total team effort. However, all members of the team will not be needed for the next project, which is less complex. Some members will be assigned to other tasks. All assignments will be based on the skill requirements of the new projects.

THE RELATIONSHIP BETWEEN LEADER BEHAVIOR AND TEAM PERFORMANCE AND SATISFACTION

Mary Ann Burress

Abstract: The relationship between team leader behavior and team performance and satisfaction was investigated by field research that tested dimensions of leader behavior based on two theoretical models of team effectiveness: Hackman's (1992) "expert available coaching" and Cohen's (1994) "encouraging supervisory behaviors." The results indicated that leader behavior is a less important component of team effectiveness than expected.

The research determined some essential skills for managing high-performance teams, improving employee satisfaction, and creating an empowered environment. Managers in a team environment may need to develop new skills, such as building and developing the organization's business, creating in-depth relationships with customers, and establishing alliances and partnerships with other organizations. These new roles may lead to high performance, employee and manager job satisfaction, and increased managerial value to the organization.

An enormous body of literature suggests that leader behavior impacts the effectiveness of self-managing teams. Theoretical models of team leadership indicate leaders should be coaches and mentors, not supervisors or directive managers (Cohen, 1994; Hackman, 1992; Manz & Sims, 1987). Few empirical studies have tested these theories. Thus, there is a lack of knowledge about the appropriate managerial behaviors for leading self-managing individuals and teams.

A study was conducted to increase knowledge about the impact of managerial behavior on the performance of self-managing teams and the effect of encouraging supervisory behavior on employee satisfaction with the supervisor. The leader behavior measures used in the study were developed from the Manz and Sims theory of team leadership. The following were key focal areas:

- Specific leader skills that are critical for managing high-performance teams;

- The relationship between leader behaviors and employee satisfaction with supervision; and

- Leader behaviors that are most strongly associated with customer satisfaction.

METHODOLOGY

Forty-three first-level customer service field managers and one hundred seventy-five work group members participated in the study. Managers were primarily white males between the ages of forty and forty-nine with sixteen to thirty years' tenure. Work group members were primarily white males thirty to forty-nine years old with six to twenty-five years' tenure.

The study was conducted in Xerox's U.S. Customer Services Organization (USCO). The USCO Division maintains and repairs office equipment. At the time of the study, USCO employed approximately sixteen thousand people in sixty-eight districts across the United States. Each district is divided geographically and/or by the type of machine serviced. Field managers are responsible for the approximately twenty to thirty customer service technicians who report to them. The service technicians are organized into work groups and repair office equipment in customer locations. Xerox's field employees have worked in empowered work groups since 1988.

MEASURES

The Team Leader Survey

Leading self-directed teams requires different skills from leading traditional teams or individuals. The Team Leader Survey collects behavioral data that leaders and teams can use to improve the way they work together. The survey allows leaders to receive behavioral feedback from their managers, their peers, and their teams. This 360-degree feedback provides information about the managers' unique strengths and developmental needs. The purpose of the survey is to promote the development of effective leadership skills. Its emphasis on strengths helps leaders build on their successes.

The Team Leader Survey has six scales; the scales and reliability coefficients are: Influence (.85), Interpersonal Skills (.87), Administration (.83), Communication (.81), Thinking (.81), and Flexibility (.89).

- Influence is defined as influencing, encouraging, and developing people.
- Interpersonal skills include valuing diversity and input from everyone on the team, and addressing the group rather than the individual.
- Administration includes coordination, process improvement, juggling priorities, scheduling, and resource acquisition.
- Communication comprises listening, sharing information, presenting ideas, and giving feedback.
- Thinking skills include analytical and anticipatory problem solving, attending to nonverbal cues, and exploring multiple sides of an issue.
- Flexibility is defined as responding to unanticipated change, coping with uncertainty, and deviating from an initial strategy when new contradictory information is available.

The survey focuses on abilities found most important for effective team leadership. It is a research-based tool suitable for team leader training and development programs (Burress, 1992, 1993, 1995).

Employee Satisfaction

Every year, USCO monitors its employees' satisfaction with the company and their immediate managers. The Immediate Manager Index (IMI), a twelve-item subscale from the employee satisfaction survey, indicates the satisfaction level of employees on topics that are within a local manager's control. Employee responses on the IMI are part of a manager's performance evaluation process.

The IMI asks employees about their work, company expectations regarding performance, and how well managers communicate and share information. Employees are asked whether cooperation exists in their department, whether opportunities exist for their professional growth and development, and whether they receive recognition for their performance. These data were obtained from company archival records.

Customer Satisfaction

Archival records provided performance data for the six months prior to and six months after data collection. Performance criteria included parts expense, response time, repair time, machine reliability, and customer satisfaction, the performance measure most relevant to this study. Customer satisfaction data were obtained from periodic customer surveys. These indicate the customers' satisfaction with their machines and service. Based on the survey responses, customers are coded as either satisfied or as dissatisfied with Xerox's performance. Group performance is measured by the percent of the group's customers who describe themselves as "satisfied" or "very satisfied."

FINDINGS

This section is composed of three primary topics: major findings, the implications of these findings for leadership development, and implications for organizational design.

Major Findings

The study investigated the overall contribution of leader behavior to team effectiveness and satisfaction.

- Not surprisingly, high-performing teams are more likely to satisfy customers and are more satisfied with their managers than low-performing teams.

- Surprisingly, in light of the team-performance literature, flexibility on the part of the manager had a negative correlation to high team performance and employee satisfaction. The flexibility scale differentiated managers of high and low performing teams more than any other.

- Managerial interpersonal skills were associated with high team performance, while leadership was associated with high team performance and employee satisfaction.

- The relationship between leader behaviors and customer satisfaction was not linear; the sample size was a likely limitation.

Wageman (1997) tested Hackman's theoretical model for leading self-managing teams. Wageman found that coaching influenced team member satisfaction and group process and that performance was more strongly influenced by organizational design conditions and self-management. The most important organizational design conditions were (1) a clear direction and (2) tasks and rewards designed for teams and not individuals. Wageman determined that leader behavior accounted for approximately 20 percent of the variance between high-performing and low-performing teams.

Wageman's findings are consistent with the current study. Both studies concluded that leader behavior is a less important component of team effectiveness than initially expected, accounting for only 10 percent of the variance between high-performing and low-performing teams.

Leader Behaviors That Help

The findings indicate that interpersonal skills and leadership are associated with high-performing teams and that administration and coordination activities by the manager nurture employee satisfaction.

Interpersonal Skills. High levels of interpersonal skills by managers predicted high team performance. Interpersonal skills include how well the manager encourages collaboration, fosters smooth team interaction, and works through conflicts. Capitalizing on diversity and valuing input from everyone on the team are also important leader skills. Encouraging the team to address interpersonal problems as a group is another key manager skill. Establishing personal growth opportunities for team members also was found to be important.

These positive managerial behaviors are consistent with the team effectiveness literature and the research of Manz and Sims (1987). The conclusions also support Bass's (1981) recommendation that today's managers must balance technical, conceptual, and interpersonal skills.

Influence. High-performing team leaders encourage responsibility, accountability, and the team's monitoring of their own performance goals. These leader skills encourage teamwork and foster an environment in which the team coordinates its own work. The leader who exhibits these skills places decision-making authority with the team, based on team member knowledge and skills. Such leadership fosters team member learning and provides opportunities for teams to acquire and apply new skills. The leader also challenges the status quo and demonstrates willingness to change.

Coaching leaders who encourage, influence, and provide developmental opportunities are more likely to have high-performing teams and satisfied employees. Treating job openings in their departments as developmental opportunities for employees also helps to increase employee satisfaction. The findings also suggest that high-performing employees receive a sense of personal accomplishment at work and are satisfied with their workload and how they are recognized for their performance.

The positive relationship between employee satisfaction and managers' providing developmental opportunities also supports Miles and Snow's (1994) managerial philosophy of human investment, which assumes that employees are trustworthy and have the potential to develop new skills and increase their business understanding. Providing development opportunities is the manager's basic task. Employee acquisition of new skills builds the organization's adaptive capacity and ensures its future.

Administration. Leaders who coordinate activities between teams, implement process improvements, and handle scheduling requirements create environments that support their teams. Other important leader skills include the ability to acquire resources and attention to detail. The positive relationship between manager administrative activities and employee satisfaction was expected. These findings suggest employees welcome inter-team coordination and assistance with process improvements. They also imply that designing organizational processes is an important managerial role.

Another important managerial role is establishing and coordinating relationships within and between other organizations. The work of Miles and Snow (1994) on new organizational forms supports this, which is especially important because many companies are creating inter-organizational alliances and new network structures and are using contract employees and other outsourcing arrangements.

Leader Behaviors That Hinder

Several findings of the study are inconsistent with the team leadership and team effectiveness literature. A negative relationship was found between leader skill flexibility and high team performance and satisfaction. Communication skills and thinking skills both had marginally negative relationships with high team performance.

Flexibility. Flexibility refers to the leader's ability to respond to unanticipated changes and cope with uncertainty. Although flexibility was the skill that most differentiated managers of high-performing and low-performing teams, the relationship between leader behavior and team performance and customer satisfaction was negative. This means that managers of low-performing teams demonstrated more flexible behavior than managers of high-performing teams.

Taking advantage of opportunities and deviating from an initial strategy in the face of new information have been considered important leader skills. Generating options and presenting alternative ideas for team consideration and handling multiple assignments are also regarded as important for team leadership. All these skills seem critical for organizations adapting to changing environments and increasing competition. So, why were these skills negatively related to team performance and customer satisfaction? A discussion with employees and internal organization development experts offered some explanations for this apparent inconsistency.

The team members in the study were technicians who repair office equipment and copy machines. The work is procedurally oriented, held to rigid codes with low tolerance for error and precise measurements on machines. Machines are taken apart and put back together systematically and are then expected to run. The technical part of the work is highly structured, and it is performed by individuals who value sameness and consistency.

There is much potential variety in the human element of the work, as each customer call is different. The technician initiates customer interactions in a negative environment, that is, the customer's equipment is not working properly. Repairing the machine usually satisfies the customer and changes this environment. Each customer call is different because of the problem, the human element, and the service issue.

It is likely that managers give high-performing teams more autonomy in their work. It is also likely that high-performing teams have better problem-solving and technical skills, so do not need their managers' intervention or input as much.

Task intervention by managers of low-performing teams is mentioned by other researchers as a negative leader behavior (Wageman, 1997). Managers of low-performing teams may focus on how the work gets done, become more involved in day-to-day operations, and monitor the team members' problem solving and customer interactions more closely. The coaching behavior "present alternative ideas to team members" may be an attempt to stimulate team member thinking and resolution of customer issues. Their higher flexibility scores could reflect managers' frustration with low performance and their attempts to increase performance by using many different coaching skills, rather than directive behavior, because that is what the literature recommends.

The organizational design context also is an important predictor of high performance (Wageman, 1997). Wageman found that clear direction and tasks and rewards designed for teams, rather than individuals, contributed most to high team performance. Managers may need organizational design skills as well as coaching skills.

It also is possible that the managers of low-performing work groups did not anticipate environmental and organizational changes. These findings suggest questions for further study.

Communication. Contrary to what the literature indicates, the relationship between managerial communication skills and team performance was negative. Communication skills are defined as how clearly the manager presents ideas and how proficient the leader is in giving constructive feedback, which allows team members to build on their successes and correct any deficits. By definition, a leader with good communication skills shares customer and company information, fosters an atmosphere in which team members express ideas and opinions freely, and is adept at listening and reflecting back what people say to ensure understanding and the feeling of being heard. Sharing company and customer information has long been considered an important managerial role. In fact, managers are the information conduits in most organizations. So why was the relationship between communication and performance negative?

One possible explanation is that self-directed teams at USCO receive performance data and management information directly from headquarters and not from their managers. High-performing teams were more autonomous and did not interact so much with their managers.

Perhaps it does not matter where or in what form company and customer information originates. Maybe teams do not need communication and information to come from a manager. Integrated databases with all customer information and virtual office environments worked just as well in this company. This indicates that integrated data bases that permit a free flow of customer information throughout an organization should become essential supportive mechanisms for high-performance teams. A more effective role for managers in organizations with virtual offices is interpreting reports and other organizational information.

However, the communication skills defined above were positively associated with customer satisfaction. Managers of high-performing teams were more likely to express ideas, share information, and give feedback about customers.

These findings suggest that managers and high-performing teams should communicate about the results that need to be produced, rather than about how the work gets done.

Thinking. Anticipating, identifying, and solving team problems are leader behaviors that reduce employee satisfaction and have no effect on team performance. These finding are consistent with the literature, which states that effective teams are responsible for solving their own problems. Wageman (1997) and Manz and Sims (1987) also found that manager intervention undermines work satisfaction.

CUSTOMER SATISFACTION

Customer satisfaction is a measure of team performance used by many organizations. Organization development experts at USCO think that customer satisfaction is the most important predictor of corporate profitability. Managers are indirectly responsible for customer satisfaction and spend approximately 25 percent of their time addressing customer issues. Solving customer problems was the focus for the work groups.

There were two important findings in the study regarding customer satisfaction and leader behavior. First, there was a significant difference between high-performing and low-performing teams on customer satisfaction. Second, the overall relationship between leader behavior and customer satisfaction was positive. The number of participants in the study limited further conclusions about customer satisfaction.

IMPLICATIONS FOR LEADERSHIP DEVELOPMENT

The findings in this study resolved some issues about the leader behaviors appropriate for self-directed teams and raised additional questions for leadership development.

Manager-Subordinate Interaction

That managers intervene more with low-performing teams than with high-performing teams is not surprising. Perhaps accountability for performance outcomes increases managerial intervention. The questions raised by the results of this study are whether knowledge of organizational design concepts would help managers to identify the causes of low performance and whether managerial intervention or the lack of team-member skills, experience, or motivation cause low performance. The leadership literature offers some potential answers.

Graen et al. (1975) found that managers give better assignments and more influence and autonomy to "in-group" members. Subordinate performance and positive personal interaction were significant predictors of this leader-employee interaction. Green and Mitchell (1979) suggest that leaders interpret employee performance information and respond with interactions based on attributions, the thought processes we use to determine the cause of our own or others' behavior. A manager will try to change a situation when it is attributed to an external or environmental cause. However, if the cause is attributed to an internal trait in the employee, the manager will provide detailed instruction, coach and monitor the subordinate more closely, or set easier goals and deadlines.

Educating managers about their attributions and the potential effects on their employees would be invaluable for a couple of reasons. It is possible that internal attributions would set in place a negative downward spiral, that is, closely monitoring subordinates, giving more detailed instruction for how to do the work, and setting easier goals and deadlines.

Wageman (1997) found the organizational design context the most significant predictor of performance. This indicates that managers should evaluate the environments and create appropriate contexts rather than provide close supervision.

These findings also reflect Wolford's (1982) emphasis on the macro level influences of the situation. The leader increases performance and motivation with incentives, participation, job redesign, and high expectations. The leader uses diagnostic behavior to assess deficiencies and take corrective action by changing the context, modifying the technology, removing physical constraints, and providing resources. Hackman (1992) also indicates that manager actions should include diagnosing the organizational context and taking action where necessary. In this way managers can ensure that problems are solved without undermining the team.

There are fundamental differences between traditionally structured organizations and team-based systems. In a team-based design, employees are not as dependent on the leader. Years of nontheoretical leadership research found that the more subordinates are dependent on the leader for things they need, the higher will be the relationship between leader consideration and structure and subordinate satisfaction and performance. This relationship is based on subordinate dependence on the leader and the amount the leader can deliver. Team-based organizations reduce subordinate dependence on the leader, and systems thinking indicates that changing this dependence relationship will require other changes. This is obviously a question for further research.

Organizational Design

The fact that leader behavior accounts for a small percentage of the difference between high and low performance indicates that other factors matter more. Wageman (1997) determined that a clear, engaging direction was the most important organizational predictor of high performance. A clear direction reflects corporate strategy and directs employee activities. Clear objectives imply knowledge of the organization's key markets, the application of products and services to each market, and customer requirements.

Consistent goals and objectives are only possible with cross-functional collaboration (Mohrman, Mohrman, & Cohen, 1994). Understanding the customers' business means that managers should have broad industry knowledge, understand the opportunities and challenges within each sector, and have knowledge about the productivity drivers for each industry. Thus, scanning the environment and knowing what is going on in the marketplace are increasingly important responsibilities for managers. Getting managers in the marketplace, making external alliances, and building the company's business are expanding roles. Creating inter-organizational alliances, joint ventures, and other network arrangements are key future management activities. Entrepreneurial skills that include business development, revenue generation, and investment management will be required. Learning how to negotiate and create "win-win" situations will be critical in ensuring trust and long-term alliances and relationships.

For example, at USCO, in-depth customer relationships are a prerequisite to offering document solutions. Resolutions of customer problems are necessary to maintain good customer relationships. Managers must work in collaborative, cross-functional ways with customers. This means that developing general managers with cross-functional perspectives will be useful in the future. Managers also will need the ability to establish inter-organizational trust and set a clear, engaging direction for the work.

Mohrman, Mohrman, & Cohen (1994) suggest that changes in corporate systems (that is, rewards, performance evaluation, information, and communication) are necessary for a successful and sustained implementation of teamwork. Wageman (1997) determined that tasks and rewards designed for teams are key enabling conditions and predictors of high performance. Designing corporate systems suitable for high-performance teams should be a primary obligation of managers. Managers need to have diagnostic and design capabilities in order to determine the systems that are appropriate for their organizational situations. Managers should ensure that teams are necessary to accomplish the work, and that the work is designed for interdependence if teams are necessary. Ensuring that other corporate support systems are designed to support the team is another component of this organizational design role. In addition, teaching managers the diagnostic skills necessary to evaluate the impact of their designs on the team is critical. Diagnosing and taking action regarding the organizational context for each team will likely enhance high performance (Hackman, 1992). Organizational design skills should become a significant component of leader development programs.

Assessment of Leader Behavior

Although leader behavior accounts for a small percentage of the difference between high and low team performance, knowledge of what that behavior is and its impact on the team is important. Behavioral assessment and feedback can establish strengths and developmental opportunities while opening communication between the manager and team.

All managers need to understand the effects of various aspects of their behavior on team performance, employee satisfaction, and customer satisfaction. Managers need to move away from managing individuals and concentrate on leading and interacting with the team.

To improve performance, leaders should have high interpersonal skills, which means that they encourage collaboration, help to smooth team interchanges and resolve conflict, appreciate diversity, and value input from everyone. This also means that growth opportunities are made available to everyone in the organization.

Holding teams responsible and accountable for work outcomes changes who has the authority and responsibility for results. If high employee satisfaction is a desired outcome, the manager's role is keeping the organization and teams focused on the results that need to be produced. Managers should set strategic direction, create a vision for the organization, and let the team determine how the work is done. This framework gives the team room to operate within a defined structure and with definite expectations. Appropriate leadership skills include influencing and encouraging responsibility, accountability, and self-management by team members. Such leadership fosters team learning, provides developmental opportunities, teaches appropriate decision making, and encourages teamwork. The leader gives people the information, knowledge, and skills to make intelligent decisions and then steps aside. The team members solve their own problems and determine how they do their work. Team members should generate options for solving customer problems and identify different ways to accomplish goals. The team should shift priorities to juggle assignments, obligations, and change with the circumstances. This is only possible if the team has the knowledge, skills, and authority to make effective decisions. The manager should provide a consistent message about direction and expectations and ensure that the team has the requisite knowledge, skills, abilities, and resources to perform. In today's competitive, global environment, leaders need high-performance teams that are partners in building the business.

Leaders who coordinate between teams and establish processes that support their teams' work are likely to achieve high performance. Establishing inter-organizational alliances that encourage collaboration is a key leader role. Letting teams interact directly with external customers and suppliers encourages high performance and resolution of problems.

Managers also must anticipate environmental and organizational changes. Appropriate customer and market research can help managers to determine a consistent strategic direction for the organization's products and services which, in turn, can be used to present employees with guidelines for decisions and actions. Such a focus would result in higher performance and customer satisfaction.

LIMITATIONS OF THE STUDY

The small sample was the most pronounced limitation of the study. Work groups in the study were nominated based on either high or low performance, which caused statistical problems. Differences between high-performing and low-performing groups were easily identified, however, which created a trade-off.

Because a single firm was used in the study, generalizing the findings to other organizations requires caution.

The findings of this study regarding communication and customer satisfaction are inconsistent with literature on team effectiveness, thus raising questions for further research. The results imply that high-performance teams communicate less with their managers and that the nature of the communication is different than with low-performing teams. The type of communication appropriate for high performance or where the information originates (that is, manager or database), however, is not clear. An important question for future research is determining whether the flexibility scale really measures what it is intended to measure. Determining the construct validity of the instrument, and in particular the flexibility scale, would help answer some the psychometric questions.

Future answers to questions about communication, flexibility, and customer satisfaction can broaden our understanding of the requirements for high-performance work systems.

References

Bass, B.M. (1981). *Handbook of leadership: Revised and expanded edition.* New York: New York Press.

Burress, M.A. (1992). *Development of a model of leadership for self-managed teams in a greenfield environment.* (MicS 160 no. 6788).

Burress, M.A. (1993). *Leader behaviors for self-managing teams.* Unpublished manuscript.

Burress, M.A. (1995). *A reliability study and factor analysis of the team leader survey.* Unpublished manuscript.

Cohen, S. (1994). Designing effective self-managing work teams. In M. Beyerlein and D. Johnson (Eds.), *Advances in interdisciplinary studies of work teams.* (pp. 67–102). Greenwich, CT: JAI Press.

Graen, D.F., Graen, G.B., et al. (1975, February). A vertical dyad linage approach to leadership within formal organizations. *Organizational Behavior and Human Performance, 31*(1), 46–78.

Graen, G.B., Scandura, T.A., & Graen, M.R. (1986). A field experimental test of the moderating effects of growth need strength on productivity. *Journal of Applied Psychology, 71*(3), 484–491.

Green, S.G., & Mitchell, T.R. (1979). Attributional processes of leaders in leader-member interactions. *Organizational Behavior and Human Performance, 23,* 429–458.

Hackman, J.R. (1987). The design of work teams. In J.W. Lorsch (Ed.), *Handbook of organizational behavior* (pp. 315–342). Englewood Cliffs, NJ: Prentice Hall.

Hackman, J.R. (1992). The psychology of self-management in organizations. In R. Glaser (Ed.), *Classic readings in self-managing teamwork* (pp. 143–193). King of Prussia, PA: Organization Design and Development.

Manz, C.C., & Sims, H.P., Jr. (1987). Leading workers to lead themselves. *Administrative Science Quarterly, 32*(1), 106–128.

Miles, R.E., & Snow, C.C. (1994). *Fit, failure, & the hall of fame.* New York: The Free Press.

Mohrman, S.A., Mohrman, A.M., Jr. & Cohen, S.G. (1995). *Designing team-based organizations.* San Francisco, CA: Jossey-Bass.

Wageman, R. (1993). *Fostering productive interdependence at work: The interactive effects of task design, reward strategy, and individual preference for autonomy.* Unpublished doctoral dissertation, Harvard University, Boston, MA.

Wageman, R. (1997, Summer). Critical success factors for creating superb self-managing teams. *Organizational Dynamics, 25*(1), 49 (13).

Wolford, J.C. (1982). An integrative theory of leadership. *Journal of Management, 8,* 27–47.

Values-Based Leadership for the 21st Century

Robert C. Preziosi

Abstract: In this article the author concentrates on what a leader need to *believe* and *do* in order to promote the high performance that will be required for organizational success in the 21st Century. His premise is that leader values are the guiding principles that determine leader behavior, which, in turn motivates and inspires follower behavior. The author describes twenty attitudes and associated behaviors that the effective leader needs to exhibit. In addition, he presents an example of how a leader might generate behavioral options stemming from one of the essential values.

Management in the 21st Century will focus on the well-documented values-based theory of leadership (DePree, 1992; Tichy & Sherman, 1993). The companies that DePree and Tichy and Sherman have written about offer powerful examples of the practical impact of this new theory: Leader values are the guiding principles that determine leader behavior, which, in turn, motivates and inspires follower behavior. The end result is the high performance required for an organization to achieve competitive advantage and future success.

THE CONNECTION BETWEEN LEADER VALUES AND HIGH PERFORMANCE

Several authors have helped to identify the specific leader values and associated behaviors that foster high follower performance: Covey, 1991; Garfield, 1986, 1991; and Leonard, 1991. What I have learned from these authors is consistent with my own experience with high-performance organizations.

There is no magic involved in promoting high performance, although the phenomenal success of some organizations might lead others to wonder if there is. Instead, the same kind of performance is within the reach of virtually any organization.

What exactly does a leader need to *believe* and *do* in order to promote high performance?

1. *Attend intently.* Regardless of the setting, the situation, and the characters involved, the leader needs to demonstrate the same totality of focus—physical, mental, and emotional—until closure is achieved.

2. *Build on success.* All successful leadership situations share certain elements. The leader needs to identify those elements and consciously repeat them as a foundation for building increasingly better leadership performance.

3. *Champion the shared vision.* The assumption underlying this point is that the leader has worked with followers to develop such a vision. Then the leader's responsibility is to serve as the energizing force behind that vision—so much so that every follower acts in support of the vision.

4. *Generate renewal.* The organizational world of the 21st Century will be characterized by continual, rapid change. Constantly adapting to changing organizational circumstances requires that the leader not only be creative, but also encourage creativity on the part of followers. It is the leader's example of creative behavior that allows the organization to renew itself continually and flourish, regardless of the stage of organizational development involved.

5. *Embrace diversity.* Increasing diversity within organizations will lead to an important opportunity for organizational redefinition. The successful leader will honor many different sets of values in order to take advantage of this opportunity.

6. *Energize oneself.* With so many responsibilities, a leader may forgo tasks that he or she feels passionately about in order to take care of more pressing matters. It is important to note, though, that leaders maintain high levels of physical and emotional energy by including activities they love in their daily schedules.

7. *Learn from others.* Heroes, mentors, and instructors all provide opportunities for learning. Regardless of success in past performance, the effective leader is always ready, willing, and able to learn and to apply that learning.

8. *Listen to internal prompts.* Often a leader is placed in a situation involving conflicting information or conflicting interpretations of that information. Although the successful leader carefully considers and compares all positions, he or she is most influenced by internal directives.

9. *Honor the environment.* The old cliché about the environment is still true: "It's the only one we have." The successful leader knows how important it is to replenish a resource before it is entirely depleted.

10. *Measure all activities.* The leader must know the state of everything in the organization, and the only way to stay informed is to measure all human activity.

11. *Offer learning resources.* Every person in an organization must be as self-renewing as the organization itself. As self-renewal is dependent on learning, the leader must develop and implement a total learning system consisting of accessible resources. With such a system, each person can learn whatever needs to be learned, whenever it needs to be learned, in the most effective way.[1]

12. *Acknowledge everyone's value.* Superior service, quality, and productivity are dependent on employees' self-esteem. The leader must first

---

[1]For more information about organizational learning, see *The Faster Learning Organization: Gain and Sustain the Competitive Edge* by Bob Guns, 1996, San Francisco, CA: Pfeiffer.

recognize people's value. Then he or she must exhibit and promote behaviors that build esteem and must work to rid the organization of behaviors that destroy esteem.

13. *Practice effective leadership behavior.* Leadership, like other behavior, is learned. The leader's responsibility in learning a new, effective leadership behavior is to practice that behavior until it becomes habit.

14. *Provide opportunities for people to succeed.* The leader's task is to create opportunities so that each person will be limited only by his or her own behavior and not by the fact that opportunities do not exist.

15. *Put followers first.* This is perhaps the most difficult of the leader values and behaviors; it asks that the leader subjugate personal objectives. But the leader's foremost responsibility is to provide followers with the resources they need—at his or her own expense, if necessary.

16. *See the "big picture."* The leader must be able to see how all organizational elements interconnect in a single entity. This entity must be viewed in past, present, and future terms.

17. *Extend the boundaries.* The leader is obligated to take the organization and its members beyond the current boundaries of performance. Consequently, the successful leader is always inspiring people by painting new pictures of the organization's desired state. Higher and higher levels of performance are the result.

18. *Encourage team development.* Teams are becoming a natural part of the organizational landscape. Employees at all levels are finding that collaboration is preferable to conflict and frequently even to individual effort. The effective leader encourages team development and uses it as a force for greater productivity and quality.

19. *Exercise mental agility.* Organizational functioning leads to a lot of surprises. Responding appropriately requires that the leader be able to switch gears, see a surprise as an opportunity, and act quickly on that opportunity. This ability is dependent on mental agility and flexibility.

20. *Use mental rehearsal.* Sports champions are not the only ones who mentally rehearse activities in order to enhance performance; many successful leaders do, too. In effect, the leader creates a mental video for replay in a real situation in the future. The shorter the time between rehearsal and actual performance, the greater the impact of the rehearsal.

How to Use Values

The role of a value is to trigger behavioral options, and in choosing options the leader develops a personal behavior system. The leader may act alone in response to his or her own values or may consult others—

followers, for instance—and lead them in a brainstorming session to increase the number of options.

For example, "generate renewal," a value/behavior discussed in the previous section, might lead to a group-brainstormed list of options like the following:

1. Develop and conduct a three-day training session on creativity for all employees;

2. Design a program for recognizing and rewarding individual and group creativity;

3. Hire a creativity consultant to identify which organizational activities suffer from a lack of creativity;

4. Hold an annual creativity fair at which organizational members present the products of their creativity;

5. Train all employees in stress-management techniques so that they feel free to release their creativity;

6. Start a creativity newsletter to provide organizational members with tools and techniques for enhancing creativity;

7. Stop all normal organizational activity for two hours once a week so that people can concentrate on unleashing their creativity;

8. Require every member of senior management to develop an annual creativity plan for his or her part of the organization;

9. Build a library of books and tapes for all employees to use;

10. Place posters about creativity in every room in the building;

11. Attend a creativity conference for senior executives;

12. Purchase computer software that assists the creative process and have it installed in every PC;

13. Have each member of the organization develop a personal creativity plan with a checklist to measure conformance to the standards of the plan; and

14. Incorporate a requirement of one new product (or service) per quarter for each business unit.

Choosing from these options will depend on the following variables:

- The requirements of the work unit;

- The participative process that is used to determine choices;

- The results desired;
- The leader's ability; and
- The organization's capacity.

There may be other variables that come into play, depending on the leader, the organization, and the specific group members involved. The important thing is to be aware of which variables to consider.

Conclusion

Values-based leadership has a significant impact on an organization. Each organization needs to decide which leadership values will drive its functioning. Once these values have been established, specific behavioral options present themselves. After options have been taken, the results can be measured to determine whether the organization is headed in the direction it desires.

References

Covey, S.R. (1991). *The seven habits of highly effective leaders.* New York: Simon & Schuster.

DePree, M. (1992). *Leadership jazz.* New York: Doubleday.

Garfield, C. (1986). *Peak performers.* New York: William Morrow.

Garfield, C. (1991). *Second to none.* Burr Ridge, IL: Irwin.

Leonard, G. (1991). *Mastery.* New York: Dutton.

Tichy, N.M., & Sherman, S. (1993). *Control your destiny or someone else will.* New York: Doubleday.

13

General
Team-Building Tools

Introductory Activities, Icebreakers, Warm Ups, and Energizers for Teams

- Take Note of Yourself: A Team-Development Activity
- I Have an Opinion: Opening an Event
- Thumbs Up, Thumbs Down: A Conflict-Management Icebreaker
- That's Me: Getting to Know Your Team Members
- Group Savings Bank: An Introductory Experience

Team Questionnaires and Surveys

- The Team Effectiveness Critique
- The Team Orientation and Behavior Inventory (TOBI)

General Team-Building Articles

- What If We Took Teamwork Seriously?
- Team Building
- What to Look for in Groups: An Observation Guide

This chapter ties the team-building experience into a neat package, providing answers to questions you may still have, such as:

- How can I open the team-building session and still use my time wisely?
- How can I gather information about the team to know where to begin to build the team? or
- How can I explain the team-building process to the team?

The chapter presents team-building tools and information of a general nature. It includes activities to introduce your team-building session, including icebreakers like "Thumbs Up, Thumbs Down," warm-ups such as "Group Savings Bank," and introductory activities including "That's Me" and "Take Note of Yourself." You may wish to use some of these, such as "I Have an Opinion," as energizers as well.

You will also find two questionnaires, "The Team Effectiveness Critique" and "The Team Orientation and Behavior Inventory" to use with your teams. They will help you identify where each team needs to improve.

And finally, you will find three articles that will provide you with a basis for your team-building activities, "What If We Took Teamwork Seriously?" "Team Building" and "What to Look for in Groups."

TAKE NOTE OF YOURSELF: A TEAM-DEVELOPMENT ACTIVITY

Michael P. Bochenek

Goals

- To become better acquainted with individuals in a group or team.
- To identify and discuss differences among members of a team.
- To have an opportunity to discuss how differences may affect the team in the future.

Group Size

Eight to twenty members of a team who are not yet well acquainted.

Time Required

Forty to fifty minutes.

Materials

- Post-it® Notes, at least six per participant.
- A pen, pencil, or marker for each participant.
- A flip chart and felt-tipped markers for the facilitator.

Physical Setting

A room that is large enough for participants to move around and plenty of wall space for posting Post-it® Notes.

Process

1. Distribute six Post-it® Notes to each participant. Ask the participants to write adjectives or phrases that describe one of their physical features, interests, characteristics, or attitudes on five of the notes, one descriptive word or phrase per note. Participants should sign their initials on each note. (Five minutes.)

2. Ask the participants to write a quality or feature that is *not commonly known* about them on the sixth note. Participants should *not* add their initials to this note. (One minute.)

3. When the participants have finished, ask them to post their notes on the wall. Designate a specific place for the notes with no initials, separate from the notes with initials.

4. After all notes have been posted, have the participants walk around, read one another's notes, and then select several initialed notes that interest them. Tell them to take the notes, approach other participants at random, and ask if each note could apply to them or is actually the person's note. If they find the individual who wrote a note, they are to ask the person to explain why he or she selected this particular adjective or phrase to describe himself or herself. If the person approached did not write that particular note, participants are to inquire whether the phrase is like or unlike the person and why. Each participant should speak with at least three others. (Fifteen to twenty minutes.)

5. Monitor the activity to observe the level and type of interactions. Ask everyone to be seated.

6. To summarize the activity, ask the following questions, posting answers on the flip chart:

   ■ What criteria did you use to select the notes you did?

   ■ Why did you approach the individuals you did?

   ■ How comfortable were you when approaching people you did not know well or discussing notes you were interested in?

   ■ What differences did you discover among individuals?

   ■ How might those differences influence how you work together as a team?

   (Fifteen to twenty minutes.)

7. Ask one or two individuals to collect and read the unsigned notes aloud. Ask the participants what each statement might mean and

what implications it may have for the person when working with a group. (Fifteen minutes.)

8. Conclude the activity by summarizing some of the statements from the flip chart. State that the future success of any team will be, to some extent, dependent on knowing the strengths and preferences of each team member. Encourage participants to continue to learn more about individuals on their team and to consider what they have learned when working with any team in the future.

Variations

■ After everyone has met several new people, form subgroups. Post the questions from Step 6 and have the subgroups explore the questions before reconvening the larger group.

■ Form subgroups to identify the authors of the unsigned notes. Award a token prize for the subgroup with the highest number of correct matches.

■ Have the group select distinctive notes based on criteria such as most unusual, humorous, or intriguing description.

I HAVE AN OPINION: OPENING AN EVENT

Gail Rae-Davis

Goals

- To generate immediate involvement and open discussion for a training event.

- To assess participant attitudes about the training without engaging in methods that the participants might find invasive or stressful, such as administering a written questionnaire.

- To offer participants an opportunity to experience the diversity of one another's attitudes about the training.

- To help participants get to know one another.

Group Size

Ten to fifty participants.

Time Required

About forty-five minutes.

Materials

- Five large signs (at least 12" × 24") posted around the room, each indicating a level of agreement:

  - Absolutely

  - Agree

  - Don't Know

  - Disagree

  - No Way

- A separate overhead transparency for each of four or five predetermined statements that relate to important points to be covered in the training. Each statement should be phrased so that it generates an emotional response, should be complex enough to be arguable, and should be ambiguous enough to rely on underlying assumptions for evaluation. For example, the statements for a team-building seminar might read:

  1. Open criticism is necessary to establish trust.

  2. You can't survive in this world if you don't look out for "Number 1."

  3. It is the responsibility of the team leader to generate enthusiasm.

  4. People who aren't strongly opinionated are boring.

  5. Let's face it—some people have better ideas than others.

- An overhead projector.

Physical Setting

A room large enough for all participants to move safely and easily from sign to sign at the same time.

Process

1. The facilitator introduces the activity by stating that every participant arrived with a set of personal views, including opinions about the training topic. The facilitator explains that during this activity the participants will share their views on statements related to the training goals and that this process will enable them to get to know one another better.

2. The facilitator points out the five posted signs, explaining that these signs indicate levels of agreement and participants should think of them as a five-point scale to rate their opinions. The facilitator goes on to explain that after each of several overhead transparency statements is read, participants will determine their level of agreement with the statement and will stand next to the sign that matches that level.

3. The facilitator displays and reads the first statement and asks participants to stand next to the signs that best represent their opinions. (If the participants ask for more specificity, the facilitator asks them to base their choices on their own assumptions and states that group discussion will follow each statement.)

4. The facilitator asks one or two members of each subgroup to explain to the group why they chose as they did. (Approximately five minutes.)

5. The facilitator repeats steps 3 and 4 for each statement. (Approximately twenty minutes.)

6. After the final statement has been discussed, the facilitator reconvenes the total group and concludes the activity by asking these questions:

   ■ How easy was it to select your personal level of agreement with each of the statements? Why was it easy or difficult?

   ■ How were your opinions affected by hearing and seeing others' opinions?

   ■ What were you most looking forward to learning in this training event?

   (Ten minutes.)

Variations

■ If time is limited, in step 4 the facilitator may ask only people from the "extreme" subgroups, Absolutely and No Way, why they chose as they did.

■ The strengths of this activity are its adaptability to topics and its potential to initiate individual involvement. To take this involvement one level higher and to emphasize the diversity of opinions, the facilitator may wish to conduct controlled mini-debates. Each subgroup would be asked to defend its view based on experience and/or knowledge.

■ This activity may serve as a baseline for attitude change. The facilitator would use the levels of agreement for each statement as an informal survey. The statements would also be reviewed after the training event to determine whether an attitude shift had occurred. For example, for a training on prevention of sexual harassment, one statement might be, "Women should take more responsibility for what they wear." After the training, participants would be asked to reassess their opinions and share any changes.

THUMBS UP, THUMBS DOWN: A CONFLICT-MANAGEMENT ICEBREAKER

Roger Gaetani

Goals

- To open a session or a training event on conflict management.
- To illustrate the fact that people sometimes erroneously assume that conflict or competition is necessary to resolve a problem or situation.

Group Size

Six to fifty participants.

Time Required

Approximately fifteen minutes.

Physical Setting

A room in which the participants can sit beside or close to one another. Movable chairs are desirable but not essential.

Process

1. The facilitator starts the activity by saying, "Let's do a quick experiment. Turn to the person sitting next to you and take that person's hand like this." The facilitator approaches one of the participants and takes his or her hand in the posture shown in Figure 1. However, *the facilitator is careful not to use the term "thumb wrestling" and gives no further instructions or clues*. If the participants ask questions, the facilitator repeats, "Take your partner's hand like this."

2. Once the partners have positioned their hands properly, the facilitator announces the objective: "Each of you is to get your partner's thumb down, like this." To demonstrate, the facilitator releases the

Figure 1. Illustration of Hand Positioning for Step 1

participant's hand and models the position alone by moving the thumb down from its upright position so that it rests on top of the index finger. *The facilitator must not use his or her other hand to push the thumb down.* (By this time most participants will assume that they will be thumb wrestling and that the objective can only be accomplished through that form of conflict.)

3. The facilitator asks the participants to reposition their hands as they did during Step 1 and then says, "Begin." (If there is an odd number of participants, the facilitator should work with the remaining participant and follow that person's lead.)

4. After one person from each pair has triumphed, the facilitator says, "Winners?," and pauses, waiting for a show of hands. Similarly, the facilitator says, "Losers?," and waits for a show of hands. *Note:* If both people in a partnership raise their hands, the facilitator asks them to explain how they both won. The ensuing explanation will eliminate the need for Step 5.

5. The facilitator then says, "Watch me," and goes back to the participant who had helped him or her model the posture in Step 1. They reassume the Step 1 positioning of hands, and the facilitator says to the partner, "Let's try putting both of our thumbs down together." Then each puts his or her thumb down on the forefinger so that no conflict is involved.

6. The facilitator processes the activity briefly with the following questions:

   ■ What did you assume that you were supposed to do in this activity? How does your assumption differ from what you just saw?

   ■ How did you feel when you and your partner were trying to meet the objective? How did you feel immediately after you finished?

   ■ What did you think or feel after you witnessed the cooperative approach to meeting the objective?

- What does this activity tell you about conflict? About your assumptions regarding conflict?

- What have you learned that will help you the next time you approach a conflict?

(Ten minutes.)

Variations

- This activity may be used when learning is blocked through the interference of other dynamics in the group. For example, it may be used as an intervention with an ongoing team when the members are experiencing interpersonal conflict or are battling one another instead of the team problem.

- The participants may be assembled into two groups, one based on competition and the other based on cooperation. The facilitator then addresses the differences in processing.

- The activity may be used as an icebreaker in a team-building session when the team members are having difficulty cooperating with one another.

THAT'S ME:
GETTING TO KNOW YOUR TEAM MEMBERS

Debbie Seid

Goals

- To kick off a team-building session for an intact work team.

- To encourage team members to learn more about one another.

- To uncover interesting information about one another that can be used and referred to throughout the team-building session.

Group Size

All members of an intact work team.

Time Required

Approximately thirty-five to fifty minutes.

Materials

- A copy of the That's Me Work Sheet for each participant.
- A copy of the That's Me Score Sheet for each participant.
- A pencil and a portable writing surface for each participant.
- A stopwatch for the facilitator's use.

Physical Setting

A room large enough for participants to work independently.

Process

1. The facilitator makes the following introductory remarks:

   "The activity you are about to participate in is called 'That's Me.' It is intended to provide you with an opportunity to find out how well you really know one another."

2. The facilitator distributes the That's Me Work Sheet, pencils, and portable writing surfaces to the participants and explains:

   "You have five minutes to complete the four questions on the That's Me Work Sheet. Please do not let anyone see your responses. This is not a test—just have fun with it. When you are finished, turn your work sheets over and I will collect them from you. Then we will all try to identify the person by his or her answers."

   (Five minutes.)

3. The facilitator collects the work sheets and numbers them sequentially. He or she then distributes copies of the That's Me Score Sheet to each participant with the following instructions:

   "I will read the work sheets for each participant, one at a time. Your job will be to guess who the person is. You will have only fifteen seconds to make your decision and to write down the person's name. You cannot change the name once it is written down. When I call time at the end of fifteen seconds, your pen must be down on the table or you lose one point. If you don't know who the person is, you are better off to guess. Wrong answers will not be penalized. However, only correct answers will receive points. There will be one point awarded for each correct name. The person with the most points wins. Any questions before we start?"

   (Five minutes.)

4. The facilitator reads the first work sheet and then asks each participant group to identify the person and write the appropriate name in the first space. This continues until the facilitator reads all work sheets. (Five to ten minutes.)

5. After the facilitator finishes reading all work sheets, he or she re-reads the first one and asks the group to name the person. The facilitator then asks the person who wrote those answers to say "That's me!" The participants who guessed correctly are instructed to circle the answer; those who did not answer correctly are instructed to cross it out. The facilitator continues through the remaining work sheets in the same manner. (Five to ten minutes.)

6. The facilitator leads a concluding discussion based on the following questions:

- How did you feel about completing the work sheet?

- What level of risk did you take with your answers and why? How do you think that compares with the risks that your team members took? What do you wish you had done differently?

- How do you feel about the number of correct answers you had? How do you account for that? What would you like to do differently?

- What answers surprised you about your coworkers? What did you learn about what your coworkers have in common? What strengths about your team have you discovered?

- How can this information help you in working as a team?

(Ten to fifteen minutes.)

Variations

- The questions can be changed to focus on work-related items, such as expectations, concerns, positive aspects of job, favorite customers, motto for team, and so on.

- At the end of Step 4, team members can be asked to predict how many names they have identified correctly.

- The element of competition can be introduced by announcing a "winner" (the person with the most correct answers in Step 5).

- The activity can be extended by pairing up people who did not guess each other correctly and having them complete an additional activity, such as "Work Dialogue: Building Team Relationships" in *The 1995 Annual: Volume 1, Training.*

THAT'S ME WORK SHEET

Instructions: Answer each of these questions about yourself. You may respond at whatever level of risk you choose, but avoid answers that might mislead your coworkers.

1. The one thing that nobody in this room realizes about me is . . .

2. My favorite leisure activity is . . .

3. A perfect day for me would be to . . .

4. The actor or actress who should portray me in the movie of my life is . . .

THAT'S ME SCORE SHEET

Instructions: The facilitator will read each work sheet and give each one a number. Write the name of the person whom you believe gave those answers next to the corresponding number.

1. _____

2. _____

3. _____

4. _____

5. _____

6. _____

7. _____

8. _____

9. _____

10. _____

11. _____

12. _____

13. _____

14. _____

15. _____

16. _____

Total correct _____

GROUP SAVINGS BANK: AN INTRODUCTORY EXPERIENCE

Debera Libkind and Dennis M. Dennis

Goals

- To help the participants to become acquainted with one another.
- To develop the participants' readiness for involvement at the beginning of a group session.
- To provide the participants with an opportunity to experiment with abandoning old behaviors and/or adopting new behaviors.

Group Size

A maximum of ten trios.

Time Required

Approximately forty-five minutes.

Materials

- Three large signs designated as Sign 1, Sign 2, and Sign 3, respectively, and printed with copy as follows:
  - *Sign* 1: Welcome. You are to work on your own to complete the first phase of this group session. Start now with Sign 2.
  - *Sign* 2: Think for a moment about two services offered by banks: the use of a safe-deposit box and the provision of loans.
  - *Sign* 3: This is the newly formed Group Savings Bank, which offers unique safe-deposit and loan services that will be of use to you. Pick up a copy of the handout entitled "Group Savings Bank Procedures" and follow the instructions provided.
- A copy of the Group Savings Bank Procedures for each participant.

- Masking tape.

- A pencil for each participant.

- An envelope for each participant.

- A number of index cards equivalent to approximately ten times the number of participants.

- A shoe box.

Physical Setting

A room large enough to accommodate all participants as they complete their individual banking activities. Movable chairs should be provided for the participants. Sign 1 should be placed at the entrance to the room, Sign 2 farther into the room, and Sign 3 on the wall above a table holding the pencils, envelopes, index cards, and shoe box.

Process

1. As each participant arrives, he or she follows the written directions on the three signs and the procedures handout. The facilitator monitors and observes this process and answers questions as necessary. (Fifteen minutes.)

2. After all of the participants have arrived and completed the introductory banking activities, the facilitator assembles the participants into trios and instructs the members of each trio to share the contents of their deposits, loans, and grants. (Ten minutes.)

3. New trios are formed, and the members of each trio again share the results of their banking transactions. (Ten minutes.)

4. New trios are formed again, and step 3 is repeated. (Ten minutes.)

5. The facilitator directs the participants' attention to the content of the rest of the activity.

Variations

- Between steps 4 and 5, the facilitator may ask the participants to form subgroups on the basis of similar desired qualities or behaviors. Within these subgroups the participants contract for new behaviors.

- This activity may be used at the beginning of an extended workshop. In this case the procedures handout should be altered to include the following paragraph:

The bank will remain open during the entire workshop. If, at any time, you find it necessary either to make a withdrawal from your safe-deposit box or to take out a loan or grant in order to use a specific quality or behavior, you are welcome to return to the bank to do so. Similarly, you may make a deposit whenever you wish.

The facilitator may also want to lead a total group discussion between steps 4 and 5 by asking the following questions:

- How did you feel when you deposited some of your characteristic qualities and behaviors? How did you feel when you assumed loans or grants?

- From what you have heard about the qualities and behaviors deposited and assumed, what is your sense of the members of this group?

- How can you help yourself to retain the qualities and behaviors that you desire for this workshop? How can you obtain help from the other members in this regard?

Intermittently throughout the workshop and at the closing, the participants share feedback with one another regarding their success at abandoning and adopting specific behaviors.

GROUP SAVINGS BANK PROCEDURES

The bank materials on this table include pencils, envelopes, index cards, and a shoe box. Write your name on the outside of one of the envelopes, which will serve as your safe-deposit box. It is to be stored at the bank in the shoe box.

Next think of several different qualities or behaviors that you see as characteristic of yourself. If you would like to abandon one of these qualities or behaviors from time to time, write it on an index card and place it in your safe-deposit box. Use as many cards as you need for this purpose.

In addition, the bank will provide qualities or behaviors that you desire but do not already possess. Such a provision can be either a short-term loan or a permanent grant. To make use of this service, designate on an index card whether you want a loan or a grant and write the quality or behavior that you wish to assume; then keep the card. Again, use as many cards as you need for this purpose.

If you have any questions regarding bank services, direct them to your facilitator. After you have completed the tasks described in this handout, wait until the facilitator instructs you further.

The Team Effectiveness Critique

Mark Alexander

Abstract: A team's effectiveness is measured by its ability to achieve its objectives and to satisfy the needs of the team's members. A periodic review of how a team functions is a practical process to determine both of these. The instrument presented here measures a team's effectiveness by examining nine specific functions of a team. This nine-question critique can be used as a training and development tool by the team itself, or conducted by a facilitator. The facilitator could use it as an observation guide or as the basis of an activity with team-member involvement. Descriptions of the nine functions are included and can be used as a lecturette if necessary.

Most groups exist and persist because (a) the purpose of the group cannot be accomplished by individuals working on their own, and (b) certain needs of individual members can be satisfied by belonging to the group. Of course, the mere existence of a group does not ensure that it will operate effectively; a group is effective only to the degree to which it is able to use its individual and collective resources. The measure of the group's effectiveness is its ability to achieve its objectives and satisfy the needs of the individuals in the group.

An organization is a collection of groups. The success of an organization depends on the ability of the groups within it to work together to attain commonly held objectives. Because organizations are becoming increasingly more complex, their leaders must be concerned with developing more cohesive and cooperative relationships between individuals and groups. Similarly, the development of effective groups or teams within the organization will determine, to a large extent, the ability of the organization to attain its goals.

Factors Contributing to Team Development and Effectiveness

Team development is based on the assumption that any group is able to work more effectively if its members are prepared to confront questions such as: How can this collection of individuals work together more effectively as a team? How can we better use the resources we represent? How can we communicate with one another more effectively to make better decisions? What is impeding our performance?

The answers to these questions may be found by examining the factors that lead to team development and effectiveness. These factors can be measured, or inventoried, by team members with the use of the Team Effectiveness Critique. Before the critique form is administered, however, all team members should understand the terminology used to describe the nine factors. The following descriptions can be presented in a lecturette format to the team members prior to completion of the critique.

1. Shared Goals and Objectives

In order for a team to operate effectively, it must have stated goals and objectives. These goals are not a simple understanding of the immediate task, but an overall understanding of the role of the group in the total organization, its responsibilities, and the things the team wants to accomplish. In addition, the members of the team must be committed to the goals. Such commitment comes from involving all team members in defining the goals and relating the goals to specific problems that are relevant to team members. The time spent on goal definition in the initial stages of a team's life results in less time needed later to resolve problems and misunderstandings.

2. Utilization of Resources

The ultimate purpose of a team is to do things effectively. In order to accomplish this, the team must use effectively all the resources at its disposal. This means establishing an environment that allows individual resources to be used. Team effectiveness is enhanced when every member has the opportunity to contribute and when all opinions are heard and considered. It is the team's responsibility to create an atmosphere in which individuals can state their opinions without fear of ridicule or reprisal. It is each individual's responsibility to contribute information and ideas and to be prepared to support them with rational arguments. Maximum utilization of team members requires full participation and self-regulation.

3. Trust and Conflict Resolution

In any team situation, disagreement is likely to occur. The ability to openly recognize conflict and seek to resolve it through discussion is critical to the team's success. People do not automatically work well together just because they happen to belong to the same work group or share the same job function. For a team to become effective, it must deal with the emotional problems and needs of its members and the interpersonal problems that arise in order to build working relationships that are characterized by openness and trust. The creation of a feeling of mutual trust, respect, and understanding and the ability of the team to deal with the inevitable conflicts that occur in any group situation are key factors in team development.

4. Shared Leadership

Individuals will not function as a team if they are brought together simply to endorse decisions made by their leader or others not in the group. The development and cohesion of a team occurs only when there is a feeling of shared leadership among all team members. This means that all members accept some responsibility for task functions(those things necessary to do the job(and maintenance functions(those things necessary to keep the group together and interacting effectively. Task functions include: initiating discussions or actions, clarifying issues and goals, summarizing points, testing for consensus or agreement, and seeking or giving information. Task leadership helps the group to establish its direction and assists the group in moving toward its goals. Maintenance functions include encouraging involvement and participation, sensing and expressing group feelings, harmonizing and facilitating reconciliation of disagreements, setting standards for the group, and "gatekeeping" or bringing people into discussions. No one person can be expected to perform all these required leadership functions effectively all the time. Groups perform better when all members perform both task and maintenance functions.

5. Control and Procedures

A group needs to establish procedures that can be used to guide or regulate its activities. For example, a meeting agenda serves to guide group activities during a meeting. Schedules of when specific actions will be taken also regulate team activities. Team development and team-member commitment is facilitated through maximum involvement in the establishment of agendas, schedules, and other procedures. Of course, the team should determine how it wishes to maintain control. In meeting situations, control most often is achieved through the appointment of a chairperson whose responsibility is to facilitate the procedure established by the team. Some teams find that they do not need a formal leader; each member regulates his or her own contributions and behavior as well as those of others.

6. Effective Interpersonal Communications

Effective team development depends on the ability of team members to communicate with one another in an open and honest manner. Effective interpersonal communications are apparent when team members listen to one another and attempt to build on one another's contributions. Effective interpersonal communications are achieved through self-regulation by team members, so that everyone in the group has an equal opportunity to participate in discussions.

7. Approach to Problem Solving and Decision Making

Solving problems and making decisions are two critical team functions. If a group is going to improve its ability to function as a team, recognized methods for solving problems and making decisions should be studied and adopted. The lack of agreed-on approaches to problem solving and decision making can result in wasted time, misunderstandings, frustration, and (more importantly) "bad" decisions.

A generally accepted, step-by-step procedure for problem solving and decision making is as follows:

1. Identify the problem (being careful to differentiate between the real problem and symptoms of the problem).

2. Develop criteria (or goals).

3. Gather relevant data.

4. Identify all feasible, alternative solutions or courses of action.

5. Evaluate the alternatives in light of the data and the objectives of the team.

6. Reach a decision.

7. Implement the decision.

Needless to say, there are variations of this procedure. However, whatever method is used, an effective team will have an agreed-on approach to problem solving and decision making that is shared and supported by all members.

8. Experimentation/Creativity

Just as it is important for a team to have certain structured procedures, it also is important that the team be prepared occasionally to move beyond the boundaries of established procedures and processes in order to experiment with new ways of doing things. Techniques such as "brainstorming" as a means of increasing creativity should be tried periodically to generate new ways to increase the team's effectiveness. An experimental attitude should be adopted in order to allow the team greater flexibility in dealing with problems and decision-making situations.

9. Evaluation

The team periodically should examine its group processes from both task and maintenance aspects. This examination or "critique" requires the team to stop and look at how well it is doing and what, if anything, may be hindering its operation. Problems may result from procedures or methods, or may be caused by individual team members. Such problems should be resolved through discussion before the team attempts further task accomplishment. Effective self-evaluation is probably one of the most critical factors leading to team development.

Ultimately, the strength and degree of a team's development will be measured in two ways: first, in its ability to get things done (its effectiveness) and second, in terms of its cohesiveness—the sense of belonging that individual members have and the degree of their commitment to one another and the goals of the team.

USE OF THE TEAM EFFECTIVENESS CRITIQUE

The periodic review of a team's operating practices in light of the factors leading to team development is a simple and useful method for improving a team's effectiveness. The Team Effectiveness Critique can be used as an observational tool by an independent observer or as an intervention device for the entire team. In this case, the critique should be completed by each individual team member, who will then share his or her assessment with the entire team. This sharing can be expanded to a consensus activity by asking team members to reach a common assessment for each of the nine factors. (This use of the critique would be most appropriate with ongoing organizational teams.) Agreement about areas in which improvements could be made would then lead to team action planning.

The critique also can be used as an experiential training device. Participants would be asked to complete a group task on a simulation basis and would then assess their teamwork using the critique form. Again, the group members would discuss their assessments with one another, focusing on generally recognized weaknesses.

The Team Effectiveness Critique is intended to be used as a training and team-development tool; it is not intended to be used for statistical or research purposes. Therefore, the face validity of the form and its usefulness in team work speak for themselves. No statistical validity has been established.

THE TEAM EFFECTIVENESS CRITIQUE

Instructions: Indicate on the scales that follow your assessment of your team and the way it functions by circling the number on each scale that you feel is most descriptive of your team.

1. **Goals and Objectives**

   There is a lack of commonly understood goals and objectives.

   Team members understand and agree on goals and objectives.

   1   2   3   4   5   6   7

2. **Utilization of Resources**

   All member resources are not recognized and/or utilized.

   Member resources are fully recognized and utilized.

   1   2   3   4   5   6   7

3. **Trust and Conflict**

   There is little trust among members, and conflict is evident.

   There is high degree of trust among members, and conflict is dealt with openly and worked through.

   1   2   3   4   5   6   7

4. **Leadership**

   One person dominates, and leadership roles are not carried out or shared.

   There is full participation in leadership; leadership roles are shared by members.

   1   2   3   4   5   6   7

5. **Control and Procedures**

   There is little control, and there is a lack of procedures to guide team functioning.

   There are effective procedures to guide team functioning; team members support these procedures and regulate themselves.

   1   2   3   4   5   6   7

6. Interpersonal Communications

Communications between members are closed and guarded.

Communications between members are open and participative.

```
1       2       3       4       5       6       7
```

7. Problem Solving/Decision Making

The team has no agreed-on approaches to problem solving and decision making.

The team has well-established and agreed-on approaches to problem solving and decision making.

```
1       2       3       4       5       6       7
```

8. Experimentation/Creativity

The team is rigid and does not experiment with how things are done.

The team experiments with different ways of doing things and is creative in this approach.

```
1       2       3       4       5       6       7
```

9. Evaluation

The group never evaluates its functioning and process.

The group often evaluates its functioning or process.

```
1       2       3       4       5       6       7
```

THE TEAM ORIENTATION AND BEHAVIOR INVENTORY (TOBI)

Leonard D. Goodstein, Phyliss Cooke, and Jeanette Goodstein

Abstract: No single theoretically based definition of team building exists. This article presents several atheoretical approaches and develops a theoretically based definition of team building for your consideration. It also includes an instrument for assessing both the need for and an approach to team building in work groups. The Team Orientation and Behavior Inventory (TOBI) was developed to help consultants distinguish issues of values from issues of skills in teams. It is based on task and maintenance roles required for effective team functioning. It assesses how much improvement is needed in values and skills as well as the task and maintenance areas to achieve a fully functioning team.

One of the most important strategies of organization development (OD) (perhaps the most important) is team building. Effective and productive teams, at both the worker and managerial level, are the desired end product of most OD interventions. As organizations become more complex in their structures, team work, through task forces, committees, staffs, and so on, will become even more important—and thus the importance of team building.

Surprisingly, there is no theoretically based approach to team building with the exception of the Tavistock model of group functioning (Rioch, 1975). The Tavistock approach, based on psychoanalytic theory, places primary emphasis on issues of authority and power in small groups. Clarifying how the group copes with the leadership issue is the major developmental focus or purpose of the group.

More generally, team-building efforts tend to be atheoretical. Beckhard (1972) saw four major purposes of team building:

1. To set goals or priorities.

2. To analyze or allocate the way work is performed according to team members' roles and responsibilities.

3. To examine the way the team is working (norms, decision making, conflict management, etc.)

4. To examine relationships among team members.

Similarly, Dyer (1977), in his classic book on team building, supplied three checklists to examine the need for team building in a work group. Reilly and Jones (1974) defined team building as providing the opportunity for a work group "to assess its strengths, as well as those areas that need improvement and growth." Solomon (1979) defines team building as "the introduction of a systematic, long-range plan for the improvement of interpersonal relationships among those workers who are functionally interdependent." All these definitions are fairly clear and can readily be used, but no theoretical basis for team building has been presented.

The purposes of this article are to generate a theoretically based definition of team building and then to present a rational-theoretical

(Lanyon & Goodstein, 1982) instrument for assessing both the need for and an approach to team building in work groups.

A Theoretically Based Definition of Team Building

The primary work group is the most important element or subsystem of any organization, and the team leader or manager is the linking pin between that primary group and the rest of the organization (Likert, 1967). As Burke (1982) noted, work groups provide both the setting and opportunity for: (1) meeting the primary social relationship and support needs for all members of the work group; (2) providing work group members a view of the organization, its structure and goals; and (3) allowing work group members to connect with other organizational segments as well as the organization as a whole. Given these important functions, the degree to which work groups operate effectively is a critical determinant of the overall effectiveness of the organization.

Based on work by Bales (1950), Benne and Sheets (1948) found that group members assume social roles in order to influence the behavior of other group members. They identified three major classes of roles: those necessary to accomplish a task, those necessary to increase the supportive climate and cohesion of the group, and those necessary to satisfy their personal needs. Benne and Sheets labeled these three general classes as group task roles, group maintenance roles, and individual roles and said that effective team functioning requires a balance of the first two roles and a minimization of the last.

Their analysis provides the background for the following definition of team development or team building: Team development is the analysis of the relative strength of group task and maintenance roles in functionally interdependent teams for the purpose of establishing, restoring, or maintaining an adequate balance between these two roles in order for the team to function at its maximum potential.

The distinction between task and maintenance is scarcely a new one. The Ohio State Leadership Studies (Stogdill, 1974) clearly supported the notion of initiation of structure (task) and consideration for people (maintenance) as the two principal, independent axes for understanding leadership behavior. The extension of these dimensions to team work is natural.

Following the work of Blake and Mouton (1964), the two dimensions can be plotted on a grid, with maintenance orientation on the horizontal axis and task orientation on the vertical axis. An additional element, the distinction between attitudes or values on the one hand

and skill on the other, appears to be pertinent. One can hold a strong value toward task accomplishment but lack the specific skills for effective group work, such as agenda setting, summarizing, or integrating. Or a person may place a low value on group work, believing that groups and meetings are primarily a waste of time. Such a person might develop strong task skills, but these skills are typically acquired by people who set about to make groups and teams operate more effectively.

Similarly, a distinction can be made between values and skill in team members' maintenance orientation. Team members either value the support and cohesion that groups provide or they do not, and they either have the skills to enhance maintenance functions, like gatekeeping or checking on feelings, or they do not. It is more likely that a person will value maintenance but lack maintenance skills than that a person will not value maintenance but possess the skills. A fully functioning team can be characterized as having members with a high value commitment to both task and maintenance and with high skills in both areas. Such a team profile is illustrated in Figure 1. This profile of a fully functioning team should be the goal of team-development activities.

Trainers and consultants frequently fail because they approach the problem as a lack of skills and do not work with the lack of appropriate values on the part of team members. This Lone Ranger profile is illustrated in Figure 2. The task is first to clarify values related to the use of teams, the synergy that teams can produce, when it is appropriate to use teams, and so on, then to concentrate on skill development.

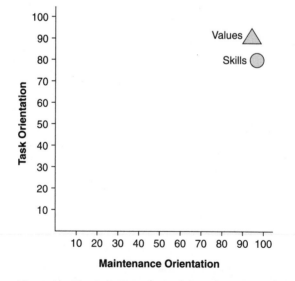

Figure 1.   The Fully Functioning Team Member Profile:
High Skills and High Values on Both Dimensions

The Pfeiffer Book of Successful Team-Building Tools

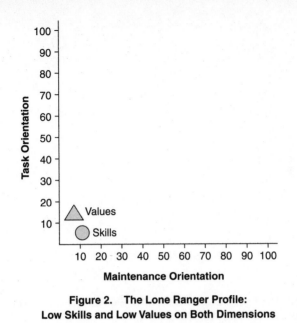

Figure 2. The Lone Ranger Profile:
Low Skills and Low Values on Both Dimensions

Skills training is accomplished readily with group members who have high values but low skills, the Educably Retarded profile shown in Figure 3. In this situation, the group member values both task and maintenance, but has only good task skills, or has low task and low maintenance skills. The trainer must concentrate on increasing both sets of skills.

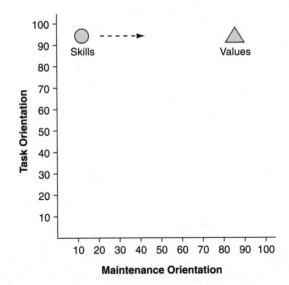

Figure 3. The Educably Retarded Profile:
Weak Maintenance Skills with High(er) Maintenance Values

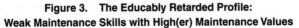

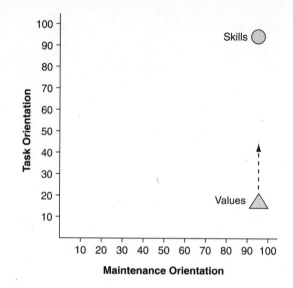

Figure 4.   The Trainer/Consultant Profile: High Skills for Both Task and Maintenance but Higher Values for Maintenance than for Task Activities

There are also some group members who have adequate skills in both task and maintenance but who tend to prize the maintenance functions so highly that little attention is paid to the task requirements. Such persons see groups as an opportunity to feel included, to practice their maintenance skills, and to feel good about themselves. This profile is often found among trainers and consultants and is shown in Figure 4 as the Trainer/Consultant profile. Such an orientation is appropriate for T-groups and personal-growth encounters, but not appropriate for work groups. Members with such an orientation are often a target of derision in work groups, and their lack of productivity is often the focus of management concern. Value clarification rather than skill development is necessary here.

Description of the Instrument

The Team Orientation and Behavior Inventory (TOBI) was developed to help the trainer distinguish issues of values from issues of skills. It provides a yardstick for assessing how much needs to be done on each dimension to achieve a fully functioning team. Fifty-six self-report items were developed from the descriptions of task and maintenance originally developed by Benne and Sheets (1948) and more recently described by Hanson (1981). Half of the items (28) are concerned with task orientation, half of these (14) with task values and half (14) with task skills. The other half (28) are concerned with maintenance orientation, half (14) with maintenance values and half (14) with maintenance skills. In each of the fourteen subsets, four items are worded in the negative direction in order to reduce any positive response set.

All items are on a seven-point Likert-type response format with a score of 7 indicating that the respondent strongly agreed with the item or that the item is strongly descriptive of him or her. The scoring on the negatively worded items is reversed on the TOBI Scoring Sheet. The instrument yields four separate scores: task values; task skills; maintenance values; and maintenance skills. Scores on each scale potentially range from 14 to 98, with the higher scores indicating a higher self-reported value or skill in that area.

Reliability

The reliability estimates, expressed in alpha coefficients, are presented in Table 1. The reported values indicate that the four scales are reliable, that is, the obtained scores can be regarded as reasonably stable or reproducible.

Validity

Early validity data on the TOBI indicate that ongoing work teams that are given high ratings by independent observers for effectiveness tend to produce scores in the high 70s and low 80s on all four scales. These fully functioning teams show very little difference in the four scores, and the intercept for both task and maintenance orientations is in the upper-right quadrant of the graph (see Figure 1). Teams rated as moderately effective yielded scores in the high 60s, again with little difference in their four scores, except for occasional scores of 50–55 on the maintenance-orientation scales.

Table 1.   Reliability of Scale Score (Alpha Coefficients)

Task Orientation		Maintenance Orientation	
Values	Skills	Values	Skills
.74	.79	.81	.83

Uses of the Instrument

Administration

Although the instrument is self-administered, the trainer should read the instructions with the participants to make certain that they have no questions. The TOBI Scoring Sheet should not be distributed to the participants until after the instrument is completed. Rather than having participants score their own instruments, the trainer can collect the materials and score the items for the participants. Individual scores should be plotted on the TOBI Profiles Sheet, and a group profile should be constructed by averaging the group scores on each of the four scales.

For best use of the TOBI, the trainer should follow the recommended procedure from Pfeiffer & Ballew (1988). They recommend:

1. Administering the instrument;

2. Presenting the underlying theory to the group;

3. Helping participants to understand the instrument and to predict their scores;

4. Scoring the instrument;

5. Discussing the results;

6. Posting the results, openly or anonymously; and

7. Interpreting the results and discussing the implications of these results.

With Work Groups

Several potential uses for the TOBI can be found in team development with ongoing work groups: (1) the instrument can be used to assess the task and maintenance commitment and skills of a team and of the individuals on the team; (2) differences across teams can be assessed and compared; (3) posting of individual or team results provides a strong data base for assessing actual team development before and after team-building efforts; (4) the items also provide a starting point for team building by identifying desired attitudes and behavior; and (5) it provides a convenient research instrument for examining group profiles in various work settings.

References

Bales, R.F. (1950). *Interaction process analysis.* Reading, MA: Addison-Wesley.

Beckhard, R. (1972). Optimizing team-building efforts. *Journal of Contemporary Business, 1*(3), 23-32.

Benne, K.D., & Sheets, P. (1948). Functional roles of group members. *Journal of Social Issues, 4*(2), 41-49.

Blake, R.R., & Mouton, J.S. (1964). *The Managerial Grid.* Houston, TX: Gulf.

Burke, W.W. (1982). *Organization development: Principles and practices.* Boston: Little, Brown.

Dyer, W. (1977). *Team building: Issues and alternatives.* Reading, MA: Addison-Wesley.

Hanson, P.G. (1981). *Learning through groups: A trainer's basic guide.* San Francisco, CA: Pfeiffer.

Lanyon, R.I., & Goodstein, L.D. (1982). *Personality assessment* (2nd ed.). New York: John Wiley & Sons.

Likert, R. (1967). *The human organization.* New York: McGraw-Hill.

Pfeiffer, J.W., & Ballew, A.C. (1988). *Using instruments in human resource development* (Vol. 2 in UATT set). San Francisco, CA: Pfeiffer.

Reilly, A.J., & Jones, J.E. (1974). Team building. In J.W. Pfeiffer & J.E. Jones (Eds.), *The 1974 annual handbook for group facilitators.* San Francisco, CA: Pfeiffer.

Rioch, M.J. (1973). Group relations: Rationale and technique. In A.D. Colman & W.H. Bexton (Eds.), *Group relations reader.* Washington, DC: A.K. Rice Institute.

Solomon, L.N. (1977). Team development: A training approach. In J.E. Jones & J.W. Pfeiffer (Eds.), *The 1977 annual handbook for group facilitators.* San Francisco, CA: Pfeiffer.

Stogdill, R.M. (1974). *Handbook of leadership: A survey of theory and research.* Riverside, NJ: The Free Press.

THE TEAM ORIENTATION AND BEHAVIOR INVENTORY (TOBI)

Instructions: Taking this instrument will help you to learn more about your attitudes toward teams and work groups as well as your behaviors in such groups. There are no right or wrong answers. You will learn more about yourself if you respond to each item as candidly as possible. Do not spend too much time deciding on an answer; use your first reaction. Circle one of the numbers next to each statement to indicate the degree to which that statement is true for you (or the degree to which that statement is descriptive of you).

1 = Strongly Disagree (very unlike me)
2 = Disagree (unlike me)
3 = Slightly Disagree (somewhat unlike me)
4 = Neither Agree nor Disagree (neither like nor unlike me)

5 = Slightly Agree (somewhat like me)
6 = Agree (like me)
7 = Strongly Agree (very like me)

1. I am often at a loss when attempting to reach a compromise among members of my group. 1 2 3 4 5 6 7

2. I am effective in ensuring that relevant data are used to make decisions in my group. 1 2 3 4 5 6 7

3. I find it difficult to summarize ideas expressed by members of the team. 1 2 3 4 5 6 7

4. I believe that the existence of positive feelings among team members is critical to the team's efforts. 1 2 3 4 5 6 7

5. It often is important in my group to summarize the ideas and issues that are raised. 1 2 3 4 5 6 7

6. I think that, to be effective, the members of a team must be aware of what is occurring in the group. 1 2 3 4 5 6 7

7. I am able to convey my interest in and support for the other members of my team. 1 2 3 4 5 6 7

1 = Strongly Disagree (very unlike me)
2 = Disagree (unlike me)
3 = Slightly Disagree (somewhat unlike me)
4 = Neither Agree nor Disagree (neither like nor unlike me)

5 = Slightly Agree (somewhat like me)
6 = Agree (like me)
7 = Strongly Agree (very like me)

8. In my opinion, it is very important that team members be sources of support and encouragement for one another.

1   2   3   4   5   6   7

9. I am effective in establishing an agenda and in reminding the other members of it.

1   2   3   4   5   6   7

10. I am particularly adept in observing the behaviors of other members.

1   2   3   4   5   6   7

11. When the group becomes bogged down, it often is helpful if someone clarifies its goal or purpose.

1   2   3   4   5   6   7

12. I frequently keep the group focused on the task at hand.

1   2   3   4   5   6   7

13. I think that testing for members' commitment is one of the most important components of group decision making.

1   2   3   4   5   6   7

14. In my opinion, summarizing what has occurred in the group usually is unnecessary.

1   2   3   4   5   6   7

15. One of the things that I contribute to the team is my ability to support and encourage others.

1   2   3   4   5   6   7

16. I think that examining the assumptions that underlie the group's decisions is not necessary in terms of the group's functioning.

1   2   3   4   5   6   7

1 = Strongly Disagree (very unlike me)
2 = Disagree (unlike me)
3 = Slightly Disagree (somewhat unlike me)
4 = Neither Agree nor Disagree (neither like nor unlike me)

5 = Slightly Agree (somewhat like me)
6 = Agree (like me)
7 = Strongly Agree (very like me)

17. It is difficult for me to assess how well our team is doing.

    1   2   3   4   5   6   7

18. In my opinion, work groups are most productive if they restrict their discussions to task-related items.

    1   2   3   4   5   6   7

19. I believe that for the team to regularly evaluate and critique its work is a waste of time.

    1   2   3   4   5   6   7

20. In my opinion, it is very important that team members agree, before they begin to work, on the procedural rules to be followed.

    1   2   3   4   5   6   7

21. I think that, to be effective, a group member simultaneously must participate in the group and be aware of emerging group processes.

    1   2   3   4   5   6   7

22. It is really difficult for me to articulate where I think other members stand on issues.

    1   2   3   4   5   6   7

23. I am effective in helping to ensure that all members of the group have an opportunity to express their opinions before a final decision is made.

    1   2   3   4   5   6   7

24. I believe that one's feelings about how well the group is working are best kept to oneself.

    1   2   3   4   5   6   7

25. I am skillful in helping other group members to share their feelings about what is happening.

    1   2   3   4   5   6   7

1 = Strongly Disagree (very unlike me)
2 = Disagree (unlike me)
3 = Slightly Disagree (somewhat unlike me)
4 = Neither Agree nor Disagree (neither like nor unlike me)

5 = Slightly Agree (somewhat like me)
6 = Agree (like me)
7 = Strongly Agree (very like me)

26. I usually am able to help the group to examine the feasibility of a proposal.

1   2   3   4   5   6   7

27. I believe that it is a waste of time to settle differences of opinion in the group.

1   2   3   4   5   6   7

28. I often am unaware of existing group dynamics.

1   2   3   4   5   6   7

29. I do not think that the participation of all members is important as long as final agreement is achieved.

1   2   3   4   5   6   7

30. I am skillful in organizing groups and teams to work effectively.

1   2   3   4   5   6   7

31. I feel that, to be effective, group members must openly share their feelings about how well the group is doing.

1   2   3   4   5   6   7

32. In my judgment, sharing feelings about how the group is doing is a waste of the members' time.

1   2   3   4   5   6   7

33. When the group gets off the subject, I usually remind the other members of the task.

1   2   3   4   5   6   7

34. One of the things that I do well is to solicit facts and opinions from the group members.

1   2   3   4   5   6   7

35. Ascertaining the other members' points of view is something that I do particularly well.

1   2   3   4   5   6   7

1 = Strongly Disagree (very unlike me)
2 = Disagree (unlike me)
3 = Slightly Disagree (somewhat unlike me)
4 = Neither Agree nor Disagree (neither like nor unlike me)

5 = Slightly Agree (somewhat like me)
6 = Agree (like me)
7 = Strongly Agree (very like me)

36. I think that it is important that my group stick to its agenda.

   1   2   3   4   5   6   7

37. In my opinion, an inability to clear up confusion among members can cause a team to fail.

   1   2   3   4   5   6   7

38. I feel that it is important to elicit the opinions of all members of the team.

   1   2   3   4   5   6   7

39. It is not easy for me to summarize the opinions of the other members of the team.

   1   2   3   4   5   6   7

40. A contribution that I make to the group is to help the other members to build on one another's ideas.

   1   2   3   4   5   6   7

41. I believe that the group can waste time in an excessive attempt to organize itself.

   1   2   3   4   5   6   7

42. I believe that it is very important to reach a compromise when differences cannot be resolved in the group.

   1   2   3   4   5   6   7

43. I am effective in helping to reach constructive settlement of disagreements among group members.

   1   2   3   4   5   6   7

44. I am effective in establishing orderly procedures by which the team can work.

   1   2   3   4   5   6   7

45. I think that effective teamwork results only if the team remains focused on the task at hand.

   1   2   3   4   5   6   7

1 = Strongly Disagree (very unlike me)
2 = Disagree (unlike me)
3 = Slightly Disagree (somewhat unlike me)
4 = Neither Agree nor Disagree (neither like nor unlike me)

5 = Slightly Agree (somewhat like me)
6 = Agree (like me)
7 = Strongly Agree (very like me)

46. I am particularly effective in helping my group to evaluate the quality of its work.

    1   2   3   4   5   6   7

47. In my opinion, it is important that the team establish methods by which it can evaluate the quality of its work.

    1   2   3   4   5   6   7

48. I find it easy to express ideas and information to the other members of my group.

    1   2   3   4   5   6   7

49. In my judgment, searching for ideas and opinions is one of the criteria of an effective team.

    1   2   3   4   5   6   7

50. I believe that it is critical to settle disagreements among group members constructively.

    1   2   3   4   5   6   7

51. I believe that it is important that the members of the team understand one another's points of view.

    1   2   3   4   5   6   7

52. I am adept in making sure that reticent members have an opportunity to speak during the team's meetings.

    1   2   3   4   5   6   7

53. I think that the synergy that occurs among group members is one of the most important components of group problem solving.

    1   2   3   4   5   6   7

54. I rarely volunteer to state how I feel about the group while it is meeting.

    1   2   3   4   5   6   7

1 = Strongly Disagree (very unlike me)
2 = Disagree (unlike me)
3 = Slightly Disagree (somewhat unlike me)
4 = Neither Agree nor Disagree (neither like
  nor unlike me)

5 = Slightly Agree (somewhat like me)
6 = Agree (like me)
7 = Strongly Agree (very like me)

55. When my group wanders from the task at hand, it is difficult for me to interrupt the members and attempt to refocus them.

1   2   3   4   5   6   7

56. I am able to restate clearly the ideas that are expressed in my group.

1   2   3   4   5   6   7

TOBI Scoring Sheet

Name _____ Date _____

Instructions: Transfer your scores from the response sheets directly onto this scoring sheet.

Task Orientation		Maintenance Orientation	
Values	*Skills*	*Values*	*Skills*
Item Your No. Score	Item Your No. Score	Item Your No. Score	Item Your No. Score
5. _____	3. _____*	4. _____	1. _____*
11. _____	9. _____	6. _____	2. _____
14. _____*	12. _____	8. _____	7. _____
18. _____	17. _____*	13. _____*	10. _____
19. _____*	30. _____	16. _____	15. _____
20. _____	33. _____	21. _____	22. _____*
32. _____*	34. _____	24. _____*	23. _____
36. _____	39. _____*	27. _____*	25. _____
38. _____	40. _____	29. _____*	26. _____
41. _____*	44. _____	31. _____	28. _____*
45. _____	46. _____	37. _____	35. _____
47. _____	48. _____	42. _____	43. _____
49. _____	55. _____*	50. _____	52. _____
53. _____	56. _____	51. _____	54. _____*
Total _____	**Total** _____	**Total** _____	**Total** _____

*Reverse score item. Change your score as follows:

1 = 7	3 = 5	5 = 3	7 = 1
	2 = 6	4 = 4	6 = 2

TOBI PROFILE SHEET

Name _____ Date _____

Instructions: Plot your values score by finding the place on the graph where your total scores on the task-values scale and on the maintenance-values scale intersect. For example, if your task-values score is 40 and your maintenance-values score is 35, find where 40 on the vertical axis and 35 on the horizontal axis intersect. Mark that spot with a small triangle.

Now plot your skills score by finding the place on the graph where your scores on the task-skills scale and on the maintenance-skills scale intersect. Mark that spot with a small circle.

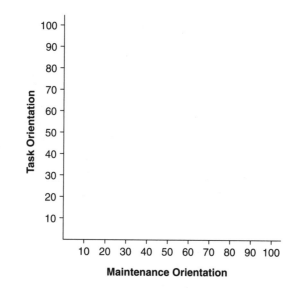

Interpretation Suggestions:

Individual: Compare your two points. Are they more or less at the same level? Which of the four profiles described earlier does your profile resemble? How strong is your personal commitment to your values? Do you need skills enhancement? What are your action steps?

Group: Compare your scores with the scores of the rest of your team. How do these scores help in understanding how your team conducts its business? Which team members are most committed to task? To maintenance? Who has the highest task-skill scores? The highest maintenance-skill scores? How do these compare with the group's perception? How can the team use its resources to improve its functioning?

WHAT IF WE TOOK TEAMWORK SERIOUSLY?

W. Warner Burke

Abstract: A great deal of time is spent talking about the importance of teams and teamwork. Yet it appears that little occurs or, if it does, the effects are not long-lasting. This article addresses why teamwork is less than 100 percent effective and what must be taken into consideration in order for it to be more effective.

Recently I witnessed something rare, an exceptional event. Six ad hoc teams in an organization presented the results of their work. For six months, each team of seven people had labored diligently on a significant problem or issue for its company. A final off-site event (two previous training and progress-report type off-site meetings had occurred) was held to hear each team's report and to make decisions regarding its recommendations. While there was some variance in the results of performance across these six teams, on the whole their work was impressive and rare compared with most such activities in organizations. They had accomplished much in spite of the fact that all team members had to maintain their regular, normal responsibilities during the six-month period; that is, the teams' work was in addition to each person's daily job responsibilities.

TYPICAL TEAMS

No doubt all of us have seen if not been a part of a task force with similar responsibilities over a similar period of time. What made this event exceptional?

Before considering the exceptions, however, a brief word about what was not special about these teams. First, each team was given the task of studying a company-wide problem or issue that had been in existence for quite some time; that is, it had been a lingering problem but had never really been addressed. It was time, if not past time, for something to be done. Each team tackled a different problem/issue; thus, there were six different tasks. There is nothing special about these team assignments. Organizational executives often compose task forces to take on such assignments.

Second, the teams were composed of individuals from different functions and business centers within the company. Composing task forces representing a cross section of the organization is common. Third, the team size of seven members was about right for the types of tasks. Again, nothing new here; task forces and similar groups are often about seven, plus or minus two members.

EXCEPTIONAL TEAMS

What, then, was special and exceptional regarding the work of these teams?

First, each and every team member at the end stated publicly what he or she had learned. In most cases, each person said something about being challenged, stretched. Yes, there was overlap among some forty statements, yet there was a sufficient number of unique expressions to make these statements ring with credibility.

Second, as stated above, the quality did vary somewhat from team to team, but the lowest performing team among the six would make most executives in most organizations happy.

Third, the teams were diverse, not only representing a cross section of the company but with a mix of genders and ethnicities in each group as well. We preach diversity, and should in my opinion, yet a diverse mix of people who achieve high performance is no small accomplishment.

EXCEPTIONAL OUTCOMES

Why was this a special event, an exceptional outcome?

The most important reason was the fact that each team had a highly challenging and compelling goal. The outcome of each team's work would potentially have a significant impact on the future of the company. Katzenbach and Smith (1993) claim that high-performing teams are rare. Moreover, what they argue is that a challenging goal is an absolute necessity for high performance.

A second reason was the immediate feedback and impact of the work. After each team had presented, all others answered a brief questionnaire rating, among other things, the feasibility of the team's recommendations. Then the team met in private with the CEO to discuss its recommendations. Next, the CEO met in the main room with two representatives from the presenting team and with his key executives in a "fishbowl" setting to decide on the recommendations. In other words, immediate action, one way or the other, was taken on each team's recommendations.

Another reason for this exceptional work in teams was the fact that these events were part of and integral to a larger change effort for the entire organization. The teamwork, even though ad hoc, was not an isolated set of events.

And, finally, there was pressure to perform well. Each group presented to members of the other five teams—their peers—as well as to the top executives of the company.

Effective Teamwork

We talk and talk about the value of teams and teamwork, but little real, effective teamwork occurs or, in any case, if achieved at all only lasts for a brief period (Burke, 1995). Why is this so? Among myriad reasons, here are a few that stand out:

1. We have seen and experienced such mediocrity, why bother?
2. Working as a member of an ad hoc team means attending yet another series of boring meetings.
3. Teamwork takes time, and we have so much individually to do that team participation requires such a sacrifice.
4. While there may be a chairperson for the team, real leadership is often lacking, with a consequence being a lack of clarity, unresolved conflicts, and eventual feelings of imposition and resentment.
5. And perhaps most important of all, who cares anyway? The team may work hard to produce good results, but the likelihood is that insufficient attention will be paid to its work.

To increase the effectiveness of teams, we must take teamwork seriously, that is, we must pay careful attention to such matters as:

- Goals: making certain they are challenging.
- The context within which the team's work will occur: ensuring it is part of some larger effort tied directly to organizational mission and strategy rather than an isolated event.
- Team composition: making certain the teams have the unique talent required for the task; the proper mix of people, i.e., experience and personality; and the right number of members, which, of course, should be a function of the nature and complexity of the task.
- Results: how the team's outcomes will be considered and treated, particularly with respect to decision making for the organization.
- Recognition: how the team's work will be evaluated and recognized by management, especially the CEO.

These five considerations are not exhaustive by any means but represent some of the most important matters to address to increase the odds in favor of team effectiveness.

References

Burke, W.W. (1995). Organization change: What we know, what we need to know. *Journal of Management Inquiry,* 4(2), 158-171.

Katzenbach, J.R., & Smith, D.K. (1993). *The wisdom of teams.* Boston: Harvard Business School Press.

TEAM BUILDING

Anthony J. Reilly and John E. Jones

Abstract: Are you facing your first team-building session? Are you wondering what you will do? How to start? This article provides the answers. Team-building is an organization development intervention that provides teams an opportunity to pause in their daily work to examine what's working and what could be improved. The consultant's role in team building is one of process guide, not content expert. This article provides insight into that role. It helps the consultant understand the goals of team building and how it differs from team training. It addresses when a consultant might use activities and simulations and summarizes the issues a consultant might face. The article is a guide for how to plan the session, as well as what to expect during the session. A must-read before you venture into team building.

If a creature came from another planet to study earth civilization and returned to give a report, a "fair witness" about us would be "They do almost everything in groups. They grow up in groups, learn in groups, play in groups, live in groups, and work in groups." Facilitators working in organizations understand that the basic building blocks of human systems are interdependent groups of people, or teams.

Some of the most exciting things about organization development (OD) are the many different, potentially useful activities and interventions that are available in this field. Many of these are oriented toward the individual working in the organization: career planning, one-to-one coaching and counseling, job enrichments, life planning. In this focus, individuals look at themselves in relation to their organization.

Another class of interventions, however—equally significant to an organization's growth—focuses on groups within the organization. This direction includes such activities as problem solving at the group level, confrontation meetings, diagnostic meetings, and goal-setting sessions.

A TEAM EFFORT

Team building—another type of intervention at the group level—is an activity that appeals particularly to group facilitators because of their intensive growth-group background and also because it generates considerable excitement among team members.

We, along with a number of other writers in the human relations field, contend that team-building activities represent the most important single class of OD interventions.

This paper considers team building in depth: what it is, its goals, how it differs from other OD activities, the steps that have to be taken to assure that it is done well, and specifics about conducting team-building sessions.

"Team," as it is used here, pertains to various kinds of groups. Most typically, it refers to intact, relatively permanent work groups, composed of peers and their immediate supervisor. But there are other kinds of teams, which may be more temporary in nature, whose charter is to come together for the purpose of accomplishing a particular task. Committees, task forces, "start-up" groups—each of these may be a team. For a group to function effectively as a team, several important elements must be present. (1) The group must have a charter or reason for working together; (2) members of the group must be interdependent—they need each other's experience, abilities, and commitment in order to arrive at mutual goals; (3) group members must be committed to the idea that working together as a group leads to more effective decisions than working in isolation; and (4) the group must be accountable as a functioning unit within a larger organizational context.

In this light, team building is seen as a vital part of an OD effort. It affords a work group the opportunity to assess its strengths, as well as those areas that need improvement and growth. A group's team-building effort has definite implications for the total effectiveness of the entire organization.

Team-Building Goals

Certain task and interpersonal issues impede a team's functioning. Team building aims at improving the problem-solving ability among team members by working through these issues. This major goal includes a number of subgoals:

1. A better understanding of each team member's role in the work group;

2. A better understanding of the team's charter—its purpose and role in the total functioning of the organization;

3. Increased communication among team members about issues that affect the efficiency of the group;

4. Greater support among group members;

5. A clearer understanding of group process—the behavior and dynamics of any group that works closely together;

6. More effective ways of working through problems inherent to the team—at both task and interpersonal levels;

7. The ability to use conflict in a positive rather than a destructive way;

8. Greater collaboration among team members and the reduction of competition that is costly to individual, group, and organization;

9. A group's increased ability to work with other work groups in the organization; and

10. A sense of interdependence among group members.

The final aim of team building, then, is a more cohesive, mutually supportive, and trusting group that will have high expectations for task accomplishment and will, at the same time, respect individual differences in values, personalities, skills, and idiosyncratic behavior. Successful team building should nurture individual potential.

Team Building vs. Training and Skill Building

The activities and norms developed in team-building sessions are different but complementary to those characteristic of management-training and skill-building sessions. Concepts such as leadership styles, decision making, communication patterns, motivation, competition, and morale are all relevant to the process of team development.

However, management training may encourage sameness rather than difference in the individuals' approaches to work and the organization. Instilling company values and philosophy into an individual's work personality does promote company loyalty. Nevertheless, we contend that such an approach can reach the point of diminishing returns; if it neglects the development of the individual employee, it will ultimately become costly to the organization (Reilly, 1973).

The Consultant's Role

The consultant working with a group in a team-building effort has a key task: "responsibility"—the skill of responding to the group and of intervening in the group's life in such a way as to facilitate its problem-solving capability. Thus the consultant's allegiance is to the entire group, not to the supervisor or to a particular clique within the team. This must be clear before the team-building venture begins. Of course, the consultant does not ignore the person in charge! Indeed, this person may need special counsel from the consultant outside the formal team-building session. But, in order to function in the best way possible, the consultant must be his or her own person, free to respond equally to each team member.

We see the consultant's role in team building as a "process" consultant rather than an "expert" consultant. It is the consultant's responsibility to develop the process awareness by which the team can take a meaningful look at itself, its functions, its method of working, and its goals for change.

The process consultant in team building should help the group solve its own problems by making it aware of its own group process and the way that process affects the quality of the team's work. In other words, the consultant's aim is to work himself or herself out of a job.

With this approach, the strength of the facilitator's influence in team building is not obvious to himself or herself or to members of the team. Yet we find that the consultant's skills and values generally carry considerable weight in the work group's opinion. It is the consultant's responsibility to be aware of his or her own impact on the group.

The Role of Games and Simulations

Since the focus of team building centers on real-life issues and concerns that the work group faces on a day-to-day basis, inventories, simulations, or structured experiences generally play a minor role in team-building sessions. They are best used when there is a need to generate data that the team uses to get a clearer understanding of its own process. Inventories such as FIRO-B, for example, may serve as excellent interventions to focus on behaviors of group members. Or a structured experience aimed at discerning group-leadership functions may prove very helpful in uniting the group.

We find that an activity or inventory can be especially useful in team-building sessions for the following purposes:

1. To help team members diagnose where they are as a group—what they do well or poorly;

2. To aid in the understanding of group members' communication patterns, decision-making approaches, and leadership styles;

3. To surface latent or hidden issues;

4. To focus an issue which the team understands but seems unable to investigate deeply; and

5. To demonstrate specific techniques that group members can use to improve the quality of their time together.

However, using activities and simulations in team-building sessions can have potential pitfalls. A group may spend valuable time working on issues unrelated to its day-to-day work as a group; or a facilitator may get caught up in the excitement that comes as a result of participating in simulations and inventories of an introspective type, even though such learnings are not the main objectives of team building. The facilitator must be able to balance both the concerns of team building and the learning needs of team members.

Issues

A number of issues are important in beginning a team-building effort. Since many facilitators approach team development from T-group and/ or clinical backgrounds, it is worthwhile to consider some special concerns about working with intact groups.

Climate Setting. Expectations about the differences in a group's way of working together at the completion of a team-building endeavor should be explored with the manager or supervisor of a group. In team building, the overall objective is to improve the team's performance and satisfaction through looking at its process and resolving conflicting situations. The kind of climate or atmosphere established in the group is affected by the group's new behaviors: communicating candidly, confronting and dealing with issues, and utilizing each group member's resourcefulness. Once a climate is created, it is important that it be supported and nourished.

It is critical that the consultant help the group leader understand the implications of the group's climate. For example, the supervisor may be accustomed to interacting with subordinates in an authoritarian manner. As a result, team members may harbor resentment toward him or her and also feel that they are underutilized in the group. If a norm of openness becomes established as the team building progresses, chances are that the supervisor will get this feedback. Therefore, it is vital to the success of the sessions that the supervisor enter the activity with a good understanding of the implications of opening up communications within the group.

Establishing Expectations. By devoting special time to examining its own workings, a group generally raises its expectation of improvement. This is usually realistic. However, it is easy for group members to develop unrealistic expectations. They may assume that as a result of a three- or four-day meeting, their group will be cured of all its ills. Such a notion, if not dealt with, can lead to considerable strain for the consultant and can frustrate team members so that they lose confidence in the team-building process.

It is the consultant's job to help the group set realistic and attainable objectives for its session. At the end of the meetings, participants should be able to evaluate the extent to which they have accomplished their aims. It is important that group members take responsibility for what they accomplish as well as for what they fail to accomplish in their team-building session.

At the same time, the consultant must be aware of the degree of responsibility he or she is willing to assume for the group's working through its issues. It is foolish for a consultant to guarantee that a group's problems will be solved. Rather, the facilitator's contract is to help develop a process which gives members the potential to work through their own problems.

The self-fulfilling prophecy is apparent here: If the consultant and group members set high but realistic expectations for themselves, they often accomplish their goals; on the other hand, if they expect to accomplish little, chances are they will accomplish little.

One-Shot Efforts. Ideally, team building is not a one-time experience. It can help a group develop to a higher level of functioning by strengthening group members' functional behaviors and deleting dysfunctional ones.

The effectiveness of most team-building efforts is increased if there is some follow-through after the initial sessions. This may be done formally by way of additional sessions or less formally by continuing to build on norms developed during the initial session. In either case, the consultant should stress the need for continuity in the team—that together the group is involved in an ongoing process. Such follow-up helps to ensure that action steps are implemented to resolve the issues focused during the session. Also the group is able to reassess where it is and exactly how it is functioning differently as a result of its earlier experience.

As an isolated event, then, team building decreases the learning potential for the group. It is most effectively carried out as part of a well-planned OD effort.

Systemic Effects. It is safe to assume that an intact group does not function independently of other work groups. What is done to one group more often than not affects the affairs of other groups. Team building often has systemic effects. For example, to go into an organization and work with one district within a region is likely to affect the entire region. People who have experienced successful team building are apt to want to share their enthusiasm with colleagues from other districts. By establishing new norms of working together more effectively, a particular work group can have quite a significant impact on the lives of other groups. Similarly, if a group has an unsuccessful experience, the negative fallout may affect the entire system.

Inherent in team building is a potential for change in specified areas. It is assumed that one team cannot change without affecting, at least indirectly, the functioning of other teams.

The consultant must be aware of the impact of the intervention on the immediate group with whom he or she works as well as on related groups in the organization. Such awareness can mean the difference between success and failure.

Task vs. Interpersonal Focus. Just as it is important for a consultant to have an understanding of the climate of the groups with which he or she works, so in team-building sessions it is vitally important for the consultant and the client groups to agree on the kinds of issues around which the group focuses its efforts. Identifying needs and designing effective interventions through which the group can meet its needs are the consultant's prime tasks.

It is difficult, but extremely important, to consider the balance between task and interpersonal concerns prior to the team-building session. The consultant's job is to state his or her own biases and help the group define workable boundaries.

Some teams consciously decide not to work at an interpersonal level during a team-building session, while other teams decide to invest considerable energy at this level.

We have found it helpful to work those interpersonal conflicts that interfere with the group's accomplishment of its task goals. It may be desirable to negotiate a contract with the group to determine what data will be considered out of bounds. A group whose members have had intensive growth-group experience may profitably wrestle with issues concerning their feeling reactions to each other's behavior.

Touchy-Feely. Most individuals become members of work groups to meet goals other than intrapersonal or interpersonal development. Therefore, it is usually inappropriate for the facilitator to advocate such growth in a team-building session. It is particularly unwise, in our judgment, to use techniques commonly associated with "sensitivity training" with people who must work together on a day-to-day basis.

Effective Problem Solving

Process awareness is, to our mind, the essence of team building. When it understands and monitors its own process, a group is better able to accomplish its tasks and to utilize the talents of its group members. Each process dimension—such as sharing ideas in the group, making decisions, the feeling tone of the group, and its morale—needs to be focused on as the opportunity arises in the group.

Norms of Trust and Openness. As a result of their increased ability to confront what develops in a group, members often grow toward a greater sense of trust and openness with one another. "Trust" and "openness" are two of the softest terms used in all of human relations training—and two of the hardest dimensions to cultivate in a group of individuals who work closely together. But it is our contention that greater trust and openness provide a greater potential for group task accomplishment as well as for personal satisfaction.

Trust and openness also lead to a climate in which conflicts are seen as healthy and productive. Dealing with conflict in a direct and forthright manner energizes groups. People say what they want to other individuals and expect other individuals on the team to do the same.

Feedback. Effective team building leads to more effective feedback to group members about their contributions to the work group. Individuals learn the value of being willing to give, solicit, and utilize feedback from their colleagues. This can lead not only to increased overall effectiveness for the group, but also to personal development and growth for team members.

Prelude to Intergroup Problem Solving

Before two groups meet jointly to improve their "interface," it is vitally important that each team first experience team building as an intact work group. Each group should have its own house in order before attempting to join other groups to explore mutual problems. This is not to say that a group should be functioning "perfectly." Rather, it means that group members should be able to listen effectively to one another and to approach problems straightforwardly.

Some of the variables that help pave the way for successful intergroup exchanges include being able to identify problems, to engage in feedback processes in a relatively nondefensive manner, and to be authentic and not play the game of one-upmanship.

One of the most helpful and effective interventions in getting groups prepared for an inter-group meeting is an activity commonly referred to as an organization mirror, or image exchange. Briefly, it is an activity whereby each group writes down adjectives or phrases that describe its perceptions of itself and of the other group. Group members also predict the other group's perceptions of them as a group. These lists are generated by the two groups separately. The consultant may help each group prepare to accept and react to the feedback or exchange perceptions it is about to receive.

In our experience, Group A generally predicts that Group B sees it much more negatively than Group B actually does. Furthermore, Group B often sees Group A more positively than Group A sees itself. Such discoveries quickly dispel a lot of ogres and nonproductive anxiety.

Preparing for the Meeting

It is important for the consultant to prepare participants for what will happen during the session. The sensing interview—which will be covered in more depth later in this paper—provides an opportunity for expectations to be clarified. The consultant can describe in general what the meeting will be about. Expectation gaps can be checked out and worked through if they exist. Participants usually want to know exactly what kind of interactions they can anticipate in the meeting. For the consultant to withhold responses to such legitimate inquiries can generate nonproductive anxiety.

Planning the Team-Building Session

Another relevant concern has to do with the physical environment surrounding the team-building session. At least two days of uninterrupted time away from the day-to-day work distractions are essential. Being away from the telephone and office interruptions can generate or free significant energy. It is also imperative that participants commit themselves to the entire team-building session. For several people to come and go over the course of the event spells potential disaster for the experience. It almost goes without saying, of course, that the team leader must be present for the entire session.

Sensing

One of the best ways for a consultant to make certain that he or she at least partially understands an intact work group is to talk with each member before the team-building session. Face-to-face interviews or "sensing" enables the facilitator to do a number of specific things in preparation for the team-building session (Jones, 1973).

First, sensing enables the consultant to gather diagnostic information about the group in its members' own words, information that is quite subjective, since it represents personal opinions. Secondly, sensing enables the consultant to clarify his or her own perceptions of how the team functions collectively. It serves as a supplement to other available sources of information about the group. And thirdly, sensing increases the psychological ownership of the information used in the team session, because it is generated by the actual group members.

We find the following guidelines helpful in conducting sensing interviews:

1. Sensing interviews should remain anonymous but not confidential. Since it is a frustrating experience for a consultant to receive confidential data that cannot be discussed in the session, we prefer to set an expectation of nonconfidentiality. Whatever information a team member shares with the interviewer becomes legitimate information for the session. We do, however, maintain anonymity. Thus, a team member can discuss a concern without his or her name being attached to it.

2. Only information that might realistically be dealt with over the course of the team-building session should be generated. To collect more data than can be processed may lead to false expectations and frustration.

3. Sensing is a rapport-building opportunity for the consultant. He or she has to make contact with each team member and vice versa.

4. During the interview the consultant should be quite open about answering questions about the session, its objectives, format, flavor—whatever may be of importance to the individual participants.

5. It is vital that sensing data not be shared with participants before the session begins, even though it is sometimes tempting to confirm what one person has said through probing with another.

6. Taking notes during the interviews is helpful. By writing down verbatim a group member's response to a question, individual quotes can be used to substantiate general points during the session. Doing this increases ownership of the data for the team members.

7. It is important that people being interviewed be told how the information that they share with the consultant is to be used. They may not ask directly, but they do want to know.

Sensing interviews are usually far more desirable than questionnaire-type surveys. The personal contact between consultant and participants can pave the way for an effective team-building session. The two approaches, sensing interviews and surveys, can be used together to good effect.

Preparing Data Feedback

Once sensing interviews are completed, it is the consultant's job to make some sense out of the data collected. He or she may note common themes, which become major categories for feedback to the group.

We find it useful to make a series of posters depicting the general themes of the data, including specific quotes, to make the data come alive. Posters may be made representing different categories of feedback: feedback for each team member; team members' perceptions of how the group makes decisions; and goal statements for the session. The exact nature of the posters depends on the consultant's judgment of the group's level of readiness for working at a particular level. This reality should be kept in mind when designing the feedback session.

Coaching the Team Leader

Of all the individuals participating in the team-building session, it is the supervisor (boss, chairman, leader, etc.) who probably has the most, potentially, to gain or to lose from the experience. Often it is he or she who suggests team building. Making the proposal for a session is a significant intervention in a group's life. It is bound to cause group members to react, varying from enthusiastic support to indifference to overt resistance.

It is crucial that the supervisor be adequately prepared for the session, since it is he or she who is most likely to be a target of feedback in the team-building session. To help make this a growth experience for both the supervisor and subordinates, the consultant should attend to several dimensions during the planning phase.

One guideline we firmly adhere to is that the consultant should never surprise the boss. Nothing can destroy trust faster than for the consultant to make a big intervention for which the supervisor is completely unprepared. For example, if the leader expects nothing but positive and supportive feedback in the session—however unrealistic this expectation may be—and the consultant confronts him or her with heavily negative feedback, one can well imagine the probable outcomes: hurt, defensiveness, disbelief, the feeling of being betrayed. To safeguard against this result, the consultant is wise to prepare the supervisor for the meeting.

However, the leader must not conclude, from this function of the consultant, that the consultant's role is to protect him or her from the feedback of the team members. Rather, the consultant's job is to work for the entire group, not to be partial to any one individual or to any subgroup. The client is the team, not the supervisor. In an OD effort, the real client is the organization of which the team is a part.

The method used to prepare the supervisor depends on who actually takes charge of and conducts the session, the supervisor or the consultant. Some consultants prefer for the supervisor to run the meeting. In this case, the supervisor must be given the results from the sensing interviews in enough detail to present data to the group. The consultant, then, generally will serve as a process observer, encouraging the group to take a look at its methods of working during the session.

Another option is for the consultant to conduct the majority of the session. In this case, it is of utmost importance that he or she know exactly what is going on with the group and exactly what outcome he or she wants the group to reach at the end of the session. If the consultant does not have this background or knowledge, it is better for him or her to concentrate on functioning as a reactive observer to the group's behavior.

Our own preference takes both options into account. That is, we prefer that the supervisor conduct the staff meeting while we observe the process and assist the group in studying its own process. But we also structure into the session specific activities, aimed at clarifying problems and working through to solutions.

Regardless of the format followed, the supervisor should be encouraged to be open to feedback and not to be defensive. Group members pay close attention to his or her receptivity, and his or her behavior is powerful in setting expectations. It is necessary, too, that the supervisor be authentic, that he or she not fake, for example, being receptive when actually feeling defensive. The norm should be one of strategic openness (Pfeiffer & Jones, 1972).

THE MEETING ITSELF

Expectations

It is helpful to begin the opening session by talking about what is actually going to take place. There should be no big surprises for anyone. One effective way to begin is to have both group members and the consultant specify their expectations for the meeting. In this way expectation gaps can be dealt with early.

One strategy is to have members list specifically what they want to happen and what they do not want to happen. The consultant may ask, "What is the best thing that could happen here, and what is the worst thing?"

Publishing the Sensing Data

After obtaining expectations, the data gained from the sensing interviews should be published in some form. During the presentation it is important that the team not begin to process the data. Team members should, however, be encouraged to ask for clarification so that everybody understands what the data say.

Agenda Setting

The group's next task is to set its agenda, focusing on the data at hand. This should be done within the time constraints of the meeting. If the group members commit themselves to a five-day agenda for a two-day meeting, the result can only be a frustrating experience.

Setting Priorities

Having an agenda to work on, the group should then prioritize the problem areas. It is important that the group (especially if it is undergoing its first team-building experience) be encouraged to start with a problem that can be solved. Members can then experience a feeling of success and begin to feel that they are a part of a team that is pulling together.

Problem Solving

We consider problem solving to be a pervasive and cyclical phenomenon that occurs throughout the team-building process. To assure its effectiveness, we find two techniques, used between cycles, to be helpful. One is to have the group critique (or process) its own style in working each problem on the list of priorities. That is, the group works one round, processes its functioning, and then takes on another problem. Such an approach provides an opportunity for the group to improve its problem-solving effectiveness over the course of a work session. Members can reinforce one another for their helpful behaviors and work through or lessen their dysfunctional behaviors.

Another technique is to post charts. These may include points of view about a problem, solutions, and action decisions. Such an approach enables the group to monitor its own progress or lack thereof. The chart serves as public "minutes" of the meeting, including problem statements, solutions, deadlines, and people responsible for implementing solutions.

Planning Follow-Up

The purpose of this phase of team building is to assure that the work begun by the group does not die once the group ends its formal team-building session.

It is helpful to have the group summarize the work accomplished during the team-building session: to take stock of decisions made during the session, and to reiterate which people are responsible for implementing which decisions within specific time parameters.

Within a month following the session a follow-up meeting should be held so that group members can assess the degree to which they have carried out expectations and commitments made during the team session.

DYSFUNCTIONAL BEHAVIORS

During a team-building session it is likely that a consultant will have to assist a team in confronting dysfunctional team behaviors. Listed below are the commonly observed behaviors that tend to obstruct team development, including ways of coping with and working the behaviors in a productive way.

Sabotage

A person who commits "sabotage" engages in behaviors designed to destroy or significantly impair the progress made by the team. Examples: "I got you" (trying to catch people in the act of making mistakes), "Wait until J.B. sees what you're up to," "Yes, but . . .," and "This will never work!"

Sniping

A person who takes cheap shots at group members (whether they are present or not) by throwing verbal or nonverbal "barbs" is likely to lessen the productivity of the group. For example, the sniper might say, "When we were talking about plant expansion, old J.B. (who always ignores such issues) made several points, all of which were roundly refuted."

Assisting Trainer

A team member who wants to demonstrate his or her awareness of group process may make interventions in order to "make points" with the consultant. He or she may make procedural suggestions to the point of being obnoxious. One of this person's favorite interventions is, "Don't tell me what you think; tell me how you feel!"

Denying

The denier plays the "Who, me?" game. When confronted, he or she backs off immediately. The denier may also ask many questions to mask his or her statements or points of view and generally refuses to take a strong stand on a problem.

Too Quiet

Members may be quiet for innumerable reasons. It has been remarked about silence: "It is never misquoted, but it is often misinterpreted."

Anxiety

The anxious member may engage in such counter-productive behaviors as smoothing over conflict, avoiding confrontation, doodling, "red-crossing" other members, and protecting the leader.

Dominating

Some team members simply take up too much air time. By talking too much, they control the group through their verbosity.

Side Tracking

The side tracker siphons off the group's energy by bringing up new concerns ("deflecting") rather than staying with the problem being worked on. Under his or her influence, groups can rapidly generate an enormous list of superfluous issues and concerns and become oblivious to the problem at hand. The game the side tracker plays is generally something like, "Oh, yeah, and another thing . . ."

Hand Clasping

Legitimacy and safety can be borrowed by agreeing with other people. For example, this person says, "I go along with Tom when he says . . ."

Polarizing

A person who points out differences among team members rather than helping the team members see sameness in the ownership of group problems can prevent the development of group cohesion. This is a person likely to have a predisposition toward seeing mutually exclusive points of view.

Attention Seeking

This behavior is designed to cover the group member's anxiety by excessive joking, horsing around, and drawing attention to himself or herself. He or she may do this very subtly by using the personal pronoun "I" often. The attention seeker may also be a person who describes many of his or her own experiences in an attempt to look good to other group members.

Clowning

This person engages in disruptive behavior of a loud, boisterous type. He or she may set a tone of play rather than of problem solving.

CONFRONTING DYSFUNCTIONAL BEHAVIORS

The characters described briefly above have one common theme: Each inhibits and distracts the group from working at an optimal level.

In dealing with such dysfunctional roles, the consultant will find it helpful to follow three general steps.

1. Draw attention to the dysfunctional behavior itself but avoid the trap of labeling or classifying the person as, for example, a "sniper" or a "hand clasper." Such evaluative labeling only elicits defensiveness from the individual. Instead, the behavior that is getting in the group's way should be described.

2. Spell out what appear to be the specific dysfunctional effects of the behavior. This should not be done in a punitive fashion, but in a supportive, confrontive manner. Often the person distracting the group is unaware of the negative impact of his or her behavior. Sometimes the person really wants to be making a contribution and does not know how to be an effective team member.

3. Suggest alternative behaviors that will lead to a more productive and satisfying climate for the disruptive person and his or her colleagues.

FACILITATOR INTERVENTIONS

Process Interventions

Centering around the ongoing work of the group as it engages in problem-solving activities, process interventions include ones aimed at improving the team's task accomplishment as well as helping to build the group into a more cohesive unit.

Process interventions to heighten task accomplishment include the following examples:

- Having the group translate an issue into a problem statement;

- Observing that the group is attending to several problems simultaneously rather than sticking to one problem at a time;

- Observing that a decision was made out of a "hearing-no-objections" norm and having the group deal with this posture;

- Inviting the group to develop action plans related to a problem solution;

- Suggesting that the group summarize what has been covered within a given problem-solving period;

- Helping the group to monitor its own style, using its resources; and

- Using instruments, questionnaires, and ratings to assess the group's position on a particular topic.

Process interventions aimed at group maintenance or group building include the following examples:

- Pointing out dysfunctional behaviors that keep the group from achieving a cohesive climate;

- Encouraging group members to express feelings about decisions the group makes;

- Encouraging group members to respond to one another's ideas and opinions verbally, whether in terms of agreement or disagreement;

- Confronting behaviors that lead to defensiveness and lack of trust among group members, e.g., evaluative feedback and hidden agendas; and

- Verbally reinforcing group-building behaviors such as harmonizing and gatekeeping.

Structural Interventions

Another class of interventions is termed structural because it deals with the way group members are arranged physically as a group. Structural interventions include the following:

- Having group members work privately—making notes to themselves, for example, before they discuss the topic jointly as a total group;

- Having members pair off to interview each other about the problem;

- Forming subgroups to explore the different aspects of the problem and then share their work with the remainder of the group; and

- Forming a group-on-group design, to enable an inner group to work independently of an outer group, which, in turn, gives process feedback to inner-group members.

FACILITATOR EFFECTIVENESS

The technology behind effective team building is vitally important. Of greater importance, however, is the facilitator's own personal uniqueness. To become more complete as a facilitator means to become more complete as a person.

Managing one's own personal growth is an important precondition to effectiveness in facilitating team-building sessions. If a facilitator is aware of his or her own needs, biases, and fears, he or she is less likely to project these onto the groups with which he or she works. Consequently, the facilitator is able to concentrate on the needs of the group.

A consultant can increase his or her team-building skills by working with different kinds of groups. Seeking out experiences in various organizations, with different types of clients, can be a creative challenge for the facilitator.

It is important that, whenever feasible, two people co-facilitate team-building sessions. Doing so serves as a source of perception checks for each facilitator. It also gives each the opportunity to support and enrich the personal and professional growth of the other.

Team building is an exciting activity for the facilitator. Intervening in the life of work groups affords both challenges and opportunities for direct application of behavioral science concepts.

References

Jones, J.E. (1973). The sensing interview. In J.E. Jones & J.W. Pfeiffer (Eds.), *The 1973 annual handbook for group facilitators*. San Francisco, CA: Pfeiffer.

Pfeiffer, J.W., & Jones, J.E. (1972). Openness, collusion and feedback. In J.W. Pfeiffer & J.E. Jones (Eds.), *The 1972 annual handbook for group facilitators*. San Francisco, CA: Pfeiffer.

Reilly, A. (1973). Three approaches to organizational learning. In J.E. Jones & J.W. Pfeiffer (Eds.), *The 1973 annual handbook for group facilitators*. San Francisco, CA: Pfeiffer.

WHAT TO LOOK FOR IN GROUPS: AN OBSERVATION GUIDE

Philip G. Hanson

Abstract: Group dynamics address "how" individuals in a group interact. Facilitators who conduct team-building sessions must be aware of the dynamics in a group to better understand the problems, their causes, and how to resolve them. This classic article addresses several critical processes that can be observed to better understand what is happening in a team and why it may be occurring. Questions are posed for each process to focus on what might be causing individual behavior and the team dynamics. These same questions offer clues toward what could change to improve the functioning of the group.

I n all human interactions there are two major ingredients—content and process. The first deals with the subject matter or the task on which the group is working. In most interactions, the focus of attention of all persons is on the content. The second ingredient, process, is concerned with what is happening between and to group members while the group is working.

Group process, or dynamics, deals with such items as morale, feeling tone, atmosphere, influence, participation, styles of influence, leadership struggles, conflict, competition, cooperation, etc. In most interactions, very little attention is paid to process, even when it is the major cause of ineffective group action. Sensitivity to group process will better enable one to diagnose group problems early and deal with them more effectively. Because these processes are present in all groups, awareness of them will enhance a person's worth to a group and enable him or her to be a more effective group participant.

Following are some observation guidelines to help one analyze group process behavior.

1. Participation

One indication of involvement is verbal participation. Look for differences in the amount of participation among members.

- Who are the high participators?
- Who are the low participators?
- Do you see any shift in participation, e.g., highs become quiet; lows suddenly become talkative. Do you see any possible reason for this in the group's interaction?
- How are the silent people treated? How is their silence interpreted? Consent? Disagreement? Lack of interest? Fear? etc.
- Who talks to whom? Do you see any reason for this communication pattern in the group's interactions?
- Who keeps the ball rolling? Why? Do you see any reason for this in the group's interactions?

2. Influence

Influence and participation are not the same. Some people may speak very little, yet they capture the attention of the whole group. Others may talk a lot but are generally not listened to by other members.

- Which members are high in influence (that is, when they talk others seem to listen)?

- Which members are low in influence? Others do not listen to or follow them. Is there any shifting in influence? Who shifts?

- Do you see any rivalry in the group? Is there a struggle for leadership? What effect does it have on other group members?

3. Styles of Influence

Influence can take many forms. It can be positive or negative; it can enlist the support or cooperation of others or alienate them. How a person attempts to influence another may be the crucial factor in determining how open or closed the other will be toward being influenced. The following items are suggestive of four styles that frequently emerge in groups.

- *Autocratic:* Does anyone attempt to impose his or her will or values on other group members or try to push them to support his or her decisions? Who evaluates or passes judgment on other group members? Do any members block action when it is not moving in the direction they desire? Who pushes to "get the group organized"?

- *Peacemaker:* Who eagerly supports other group members' decisions? Does anyone consistently try to avoid conflict or unpleasant feelings from being expressed by "pouring oil on the troubled waters"? Is any member typically deferential toward other group members—gives them power? Do any members appear to avoid giving negative feedback, i.e., being honest only when they have positive feedback to give?

- *Laissez faire:* Are any group members getting attention by their apparent lack of involvement in the group? Does any group member go along with group decisions without seeming to commit himself or herself one way or the other? Who seems to be withdrawn and uninvolved; who does not initiate activity, participates mechanically and only in response to another member's question?

- *Democratic:* Does anyone try to include everyone in a group decision or discussion? Who expresses his or her feelings and opinions openly and directly without evaluating or judging others? Who appears to be open to feedback and criticisms from others? When feelings run high and tension mounts, which members attempt to deal with the conflict in a problem-solving way?

4. Decision-Making Procedures

Many kinds of decisions are made in groups without considering the effects of these decisions on other members. Some people try to impose their own decisions on the group, while others want all members to participate or share in the decisions that are made.

- Does anyone make a decision and carry it out without checking with other group members (self-authorized)? For example, the group member decides on the topic to be discussed and immediately begins to talk about it. What effect does this have on other group members?

- Does the group drift from topic to topic? Who topic-jumps? Do you see any reason for this in the group's interactions?

- Who supports other members' suggestions or decisions? Does this support result in the two members deciding the topic or activity for the group (handclasp)? How does this affect other group members?

- Is there any evidence of a majority pushing a decision through over other members' objections? Do they call for a vote (majority support)?

- Is there any attempt to get all members participating in a decision (consensus)? What effect does this seem to have on the group?

- Does anyone make any contributions that do not receive any kind of response or recognition (plop)? What effect does this have on the member making the contribution?

5. Task Functions

These functions illustrate behaviors that are concerned with getting the job done, or accomplishing the task that the group has before it.

- Does anyone ask for or make suggestions as to the best way to proceed or to tackle a problem?

- Does anyone attempt to summarize what has been covered or what has been going on in the group?

- Is there any giving or asking for facts, ideas, opinions, feelings, feedback, or searching for alternatives?

- Who keeps the group on target? Who prevents topic-jumping or going off on tangents?

6. Maintenance Functions

These functions are important to the morale of the group. They maintain good and harmonious working relationships among the members and create a group atmosphere, which enables each member to contribute maximally. They ensure smooth and effective teamwork within the group.

- Who helps others get into the discussion (gate openers)?

- Who cuts off others or interrupts them (gate closers)?

- How well are members getting their ideas across? Are some members preoccupied and not listening? Are there any attempts by group members to help others clarify their ideas?

- How are ideas rejected? How do members react when their ideas are not accepted? Do members attempt to support others when they reject their ideas?

7. Group Atmosphere

Something about the way a group works creates an atmosphere which in turn is revealed in a general impression. In addition, people may differ in the kind of atmosphere they like in a group. Insight can be gained into the atmosphere characteristic of a group by finding words that describe the general impressions held by group members.

- Who seems to prefer a friendly congenial atmosphere? Is there any attempt to suppress conflict or unpleasant feelings?

- Who seems to prefer an atmosphere of conflict and disagreement? Do any members provoke or annoy others?

- Do people seem involved and interested? Is the atmosphere one of work, play, satisfaction, taking flight, sluggishness, etc.?

8. Membership

A major concern for group members is the degree of acceptance or inclusion in the group. Different patterns of interaction may develop in the group that give clues to the degree and kind of membership.

- Is there any subgrouping? Sometimes two or three members may consistently agree and support one another or consistently disagree and oppose one another.

- Do some people seem to be "outside" the group? Do some members seem to be "in"? How are those "outside" treated?

- Do some members move in and out of the group, e.g., lean forward or backward in their chairs or move their chairs in and out? Under what conditions do they come in or move out?

9. Feelings

During any group discussion, feelings are frequently generated by the interactions among members. These feelings, however, are seldom talked about. Observers may have to make guesses based on tone of voice, facial expressions, gestures, and many other forms of nonverbal cues.

- What signs of feelings do you observe in group members: anger, irritation, frustration, warmth, affection, excitement, boredom, defensiveness, competitiveness, etc.?

- Do you see any attempts by group members to block the expression of feelings, particularly negative feelings? How is this done? Does anyone do this consistently?

10. Norms

Standards or ground rules may develop in a group, which control the behavior of its members. Norms usually express the beliefs or desires of the majority of the group members as to what behaviors should or should not take place in the group. These norms may be clear to all members (explicit), known or sensed by only a few (implicit), or operating completely below the level of awareness of any group members. Some norms facilitate group progress and some hinder it.

- Are certain areas avoided in the group (e.g., sex, religion, talk about present feelings in group, discussing the leader's behavior, etc.)? Who seems to reinforce this avoidance? How do they do it?

- Are group members overly nice or polite to each other? Are only positive feelings expressed? Do members agree with each other too readily? What happens when members disagree?

- Do you see norms operating about participation or the kinds of questions that are allowed (e.g., "If I talk, you must talk"; "If I tell my problems you have to tell your problems")? Do members feel free to probe one another about their feelings? Do questions tend to be restricted to intellectual topics or events outside of the group?

OPPORTUNITY TO PUBLISH YOUR MATERIALS

Would you like to see some of your own material in one of our publications? How about submitting some of your good work to the Pfeiffer Consulting or Training *Annuals*? Possible topics for submissions include group and team building, organization development, leadership, problem solving, presentation and communication skills, consulting and facilitation, and training-the-trainer. Contributions may be in one of the following three formats:

1. Experiential Learning Activities or Structured Experiences
2. Inventories, Questionnaires, or Surveys
3. Presentations and Articles

Just contact me to have a submission packet emailed (or snail-mailed) to you. The submission packet will help you determine format, language, and style to use. It also explains the submission requirements. You can reach us at *pfeifferannual@aol.com* or by calling 757/588.3939.

Elaine Biech

Elaine Biech
Consulting Editor

Reading List

All Together Now!: A Seriously Fun Collection of Training Games and Activities by Lorraine L. Ukens

Cross-Functional Teams: Working with Allies, Enemies and Other Strangers by Glenn M. Parker

Cross-Functional Teams Tool Kit by Glenn M. Parker

50 Ways to Teach Your Learner: Activities and Interventions for Building High-Performance Teams by Ed Rose

Getting Together: Icebreakers and Group Energizers by Lorraine L. Ukens

How to Lead Work Teams (now in a second edition) by Fran Rees

Interpersonal Trust Surveys by Guy L. De Furia

Mastering Virtual Teams: Strategies, Tools, and Techniques That Succeed by Deborah L. Duarte and Nancy Tennant Snyder

Organizational Trust Surveys by Guy L. De Furia

Measuring Team Performance: A Step-by-Step Customizable Approach for Managers, Facilitators, and Team Leaders by Steven D. Jones and Don J. Schilling

The Radical Team Handbook: Harnessing the Power of Team Learning for Breakthrough Results by John C. Redding

Remaking Teams: The Revolutionary Research-Based Guide That Puts Theory into Practice by Theresa Kline

Team Guides: A Self-Directed System for Teams by Brad Humphrey and Jeff Stokes

Team Performance Questionnaire by Donna Riechmann

Teams Kit by Learned Enterprises

Teamwork and Teamplay: Games and Activities for Building and Training Teams by Sivasailam Thiagarajan and Glenn Parker

Teamwork from Start to Finish by Fran Rees

25 Activities for Teams by Fran Rees

Working Together: 55 Team Games by Lorraine L. Ukens

Pfeiffer Publications Guide

This guide is designed to familiarize you with the various types of Pfeiffer publications. The formats section describes the various types of products that we publish; the methodologies section describes the many different ways that content might be provided within a product. We also provide a list of the topic areas in which we publish.

FORMATS

In addition to its extensive book-publishing program, Pfeiffer offers content in an array of formats, from fieldbooks for the practitioner to complete, ready-to-use training packages that support group learning.

FIELDBOOK Designed to provide information and guidance to practitioners in the midst of action. Most fieldbooks are companions to another, sometimes earlier, work, from which its ideas are derived; the fieldbook makes practical what was theoretical in the original text. Fieldbooks can certainly be read from cover to cover. More likely, though, you'll find yourself bouncing around following a particular theme, or dipping in as the mood, and the situation, dictate..

HANDBOOK A contributed volume of work on a single topic, comprising an eclectic mix of ideas, case studies, and best practices sourced by practitioners and experts in the field.

An editor or team of editors usually is appointed to seek out contributors and to evaluate content for relevance to the topic. Think of a handbook not as a ready-to-eat meal, but as a cookbook of ingredients that enables you to create the most fitting experience for the occasion.

RESOURCE Materials designed to support group learning. They come in many forms: a complete, ready-to-use exercise (such as a game); a comprehensive resource on one topic (such as conflict management) containing a variety of methods and approaches; or a collection of like-minded activities (such as icebreakers) on multiple subjects and situations.

TRAINING PACKAGE An entire, ready-to-use learning program that focuses on a particular topic or skill. All packages comprise a guide for the facilitator/trainer and a workbook for the participants. Some packages are supported with additional media—such as video—or learning aids, instruments, or other devices to help participants understand concepts or practice and develop skills.

- *Facilitator/trainer's guide* Contains an introduction to the program, advice on how to organize and facilitate the learning event, and step-by-step instructor notes. The guide also contains copies of presentation materials—handouts, presentations, and overhead designs, for example—used in the program.

- *Participant's workbook* Contains exercises and reading materials that support the learning goal and serves as a valuable reference and support guide for participants in the weeks and months that follow the learning event. Typically, each participant will require his or her own workbook.

ELECTRONIC CD-ROMs and web-based products transform static Pfeiffer content into dynamic, interactive experiences. Designed to take advantage of the searchability, automation, and ease-of-use that technology provides, our e-products bring convenience and immediate accessibility to your workspace.

METHODOLOGIES

CASE STUDY A presentation, in narrative form, of an actual event that has occurred inside an organization. Case studies are not prescriptive, nor are they used to prove a point; they are designed to develop critical analysis and decision-making skills. A case study has a specific time frame, specifies a sequence of events, is narrative in structure, and contains a plot structure—an issue (what should be/have been done?). Use case studies when the goal is to enable participants to apply previously learned theories to the circumstances in the case, decide what is pertinent, identify the real issues, decide what should have been done, and develop a plan of action.

ENERGIZER A short activity that develops readiness for the next session or learning event. Energizers are most commonly used after a break or lunch to stimulate or refocus the group. Many involve some form of physical activity, so they are a useful way to counter post-lunch lethargy. Other uses include transitioning from one topic to another, where "mental" distancing is important.

EXPERIENTIAL LEARNING ACTIVITY (ELA) A facilitator-led intervention that moves participants through the learning cycle from experience to application (also known as a Structured Experience). ELAs are carefully thought-out designs in which there is a definite learning purpose and intended outcome. Each step—everything that participants do during the activity—facilitates the accomplishment of the stated goal. Each ELA includes complete instructions for facilitating the intervention and a clear statement of goals, suggested group size and timing, materials required, an explanation of the process, and, where appropriate, possible variations to the activity. (For more detail on Experiential Learning Activities, see the Introduction to the *Reference Guide to Handbooks and Annuals*, 1999 edition, Pfeiffer, San Francisco.)

GAME A group activity that has the purpose of fostering team spirit and togetherness in addition to the achievement of a pre-stated goal. Usually contrived—undertaking a desert expedition, for example—this type of learning method offers an engaging means for participants to demonstrate and practice business and interpersonal skills. Games are effective for team building and personal development mainly because the goal is subordinate to the process—the means through which participants reach decisions, collaborate, communicate, and generate trust and understanding. Games often engage teams in "friendly" competition.

ICEBREAKER A (usually) short activity designed to help participants overcome initial anxiety in a training session and/or to acquaint the participants with one another. An icebreaker can be a fun activity or can be tied to specific topics or training goals. While a useful tool in itself, the icebreaker comes into its own in situations where tension or resistance exists within a group.

INSTRUMENT A device used to assess, appraise, evaluate, describe, classify, and summarize various aspects of human behavior. The term used to describe an instrument depends primarily on its format and purpose. These terms include survey, questionnaire, inventory, diagnostic, survey, and poll. Some uses of instruments include providing instrumental feedback to group members, studying here-and-now processes or functioning within a group, manipulating group composition, and evaluating outcomes of training and other interventions.

Instruments are popular in the training and HR field because, in general, more growth can occur if an individual is provided with a method for focusing specifically on his or her own behavior. Instruments also are used to obtain information that will serve as a basis for change and to assist in workforce planning efforts.

Paper-and-pencil tests still dominate the instrument landscape with a typical package comprising a facilitator's guide, which offers advice on administering the instrument and interpreting the collected data, and an initial set of instruments. Additional instruments are available separately. Pfeiffer, though, is investing heavily in e-instruments. Electronic instrumentation provides effortless distribution and, for larger groups particularly, offers advantages over paper-and-pencil tests in the time it takes to analyze data and provide feedback.

LECTURETTE A short talk that provides an explanation of a principle, model, or process that is pertinent to the participants' current learning needs. A lecturette is intended to establish a common language bond between the trainer and the participants by providing a mutual frame of reference. Use a lecturette as an introduction to a group activity or event, as an interjection during an event, or as a handout.

MODEL A graphic depiction of a system or process and the relationship among its elements. Models provide a frame of reference and something more tangible, and more easily remembered, than a verbal explanation. They also give participants something to "go on," enabling them to track their own progress as they experience the dynamics, processes, and relationships being depicted in the model.

ROLE PLAY A technique in which people assume a role in a situation/scenario: a customer service rep in an angry-customer exchange, for example. The way in which the role is approached is then discussed and feedback is offered. The role play is often repeated using a different approach and/or incorporating changes made based on feedback received. In other words, role playing is a spontaneous interaction involving realistic behavior under artificial (and safe) conditions.

SIMULATION A methodology for understanding the interrelationships among components of a system or process. Simulations differ from games in that they test or use a model that depicts or mirrors some aspect of reality in form, if not necessarily in content. Learning occurs by studying the effects of change on one or more factors of the model. Simulations are commonly used to test hypotheses about what happens in a system—often referred to as "what if?" analysis—or to examine best-case/worst-case scenarios.

THEORY   A presentation of an idea from a conjectural perspective. Theories are useful because they encourage us to examine behavior and phenomena through a different lens.

TOPICS

The twin goals of providing effective and practical solutions for workforce training and organization development and meeting the educational needs of training and human resource professionals shape Pfeiffer's publishing program. Core topics include the following:

Leadership & Management

Communication & Presentation

Coaching & Mentoring

Training & Development

E-Learning

Teams & Collaboration

OD & Strategic Planning

Human Resources

Consulting